CREATING
COLLABORATIVE
ADVANTAGE

CREATING COLLABORATIVE ADVANTAGE

Chris Huxham

SAGE Publications
London • Thousand Oaks • New Delhi

ISBN 0-8039-7498-1 (hbk)
ISBN 0-8039-7499-X (pbk)
© Chris Huxham 1996 Compilation, editorial material and
Chapters 1, 9 and 12
© Arthur Turovh Himmelman 1996 Chapter 2
© Colin Eden 1996 Chapter 3 © Barbara Gray 1997 Chapter 4
© Steve Cropper 1997 Chapter 5 © Dave Sink 1997 Chapter 6
© Catherine Barr and Chris Huxham 1996 Chapter 7
© Sandor P. Schuman 1996 Chapter 8 © Charles B. Finn 1996 Chapter 10
© Arnold de Jong 1996 Chapter 11
First published 1996

SAGE Publications Ltd
1 Oliver's Yard
55 City Road
London EC1Y 1SP

SAGE Publications Inc
2455 Teller Road
Thousand Oaks
California 91320

SAGE Publications India Pvt Ltd
B–42 Panchsheel Enclave
PO Box 4109
New Delhi 110 017

British Library Cataloguing in Publication data
A catalogue record for this book is available from the British Library

Printed on paper from sustainable sources

Typeset by Mayhew Typesetting, Rhayader, Powys
Printed digitally and bound in Great Britain by
Lightning Source UK Ltd., Milton Keynes, Bedfordshire

Contents

Contributors

Catherine Barr gained her first degree from the Department of Management Science at the University of Strathclyde, Glasgow, Scotland. She has recently completed a doctorate in the same department, researching community participation in public decision-making. Her research has focused on participation both in the context of collaboration for community development and of decentralization of local government.

Steve Cropper is a senior lecturer in Health Planning and Management at Keele University, UK. He has a degree and PhD in Town Planning. From 1983 to 1991, he pursued research into problem structuring and group decision support methods largely within public service organizations. Since joining the Centre for Health Planning and Management at Keele University in 1991 his research has focused on the development and evaluation of collaborative working between agencies concerned to promote health, and on the involvement of doctors in management.

Colin Eden is Professor and Head of the Department of Management Science at the University of Strathclyde, Glasgow, Scotland. Following an early career as a construction engineer, he moved to the University of Bath where he developed the use of cognitive mapping as the basis of a group decision support system for organizational problem-solving. Since moving to Strathclyde, Colin's work has focused on strategy development and implementation and he has worked extensively with teams of senior managers in public, private and community sector organizations. His research in group decision support is widely known and accessed across the world. He is co-author of *Thinking in Organizations* (Macmillan, 1979) and *Messing About in Problems* (Pergamon, 1983) and is co-editor of *Tackling Strategic Problems* (Sage, 1990).

Charles B. Finn is a Fellow at the Hubert H. Humphrey Institute of Public Affairs at the University of Minnesota, USA. He is also Director of the Banking and Community Economic Development Project and Administrative Director of the Technology and Group Systems Support Center. His areas of expertise include strategic management of large-scale organizational change, activities of the financial sector that relate to access by low-income and minority populations and analysis of large data sets. He has conducted banking studies throughout the United States and has facilitated strategic management efforts for federal, state and local governments as well as school boards, community and non-profit organizations. He is currently conducting research with communities undertaking collaborative efforts.

Barbara Gray is a Professor of Organizational Behavior and Director of the Center for Research in Conflict and Negotiation at the Pennsylvania State University in the USA. Dr Gray has been studying organizational and international conflict and negotiation processes for 20 years. Her interest in negotiations is reflected in her books, *Collaborating: Finding Common Ground for Multi-Party Problems* (Jossey Bass, 1989) and *International Joint Ventures: Economic and Organizational Perspectives* (Kluwer, 1995), as well as in numerous academic publications on collaboration, dispute resolution and joint ventures. She has worked in industry, education and in academia as a consultant to numerous public and private sector organizations in the areas of conflict management, negotiations and organizational change.

Arthur Turovh Himmelman is a consultant whose practice is focused on the design, facilitation and evaluation of community-based collaboration, a subject about which he wrote, taught and consulted while a senior fellow at the Hubert H. Humphrey Institute of Public Affairs at the University of Minnesota, USA. His monograph, *Communities Working Collaboratively for a Change*, has received extensive acclaim and distribution, including publication in the International City/County Management Association's *Resolving Conflict: Strategies for Local Government*. He has consulted and made presentations nationally for numerous academic, philanthropic and professional organizations including many local governmental and community-based non-profit organizations. Prior to the Humphrey Institute, Himmelman was a senior programme officer at major private and community foundations and also directed community-based, higher educational programmes serving inner-city adults for colleges and universities. Among his volunteer activities, he was board vice-president of a battered women's shelter and a public housing community centre in Minneapolis.

Chris Huxham is Senior Lecturer in the Department of Management Science and Chair of MBA Programmes in the Graduate Business School at the University of Strathclyde, Glasgow, Scotland. Working from a background of research at the Universities of Sussex and Aston in the analysis of conflict and in group decision support, Chris has been researching inter-organizational collaboration for the past six years. In this time she has worked in a variety of collaboration contexts in the public and community sectors. Particular focuses have been with groups concerned with collaboration for economic and social development and for anti-poverty initiatives.

Arnold de Jong graduated from the agricultural university in Wageningen in the Netherlands. He worked for 18 years in a large consulting company. He was alderman of the municipality of Arnhem for four years. In 1982 he launched his own consultancy company specializing in guiding the government in the process of policy-making. He is a freelance teacher in the Dutch schools of public administration.

Sandor P. Schuman has been helping groups work more effectively to solve complex problems and make decisions for more than 20 years. He specializes in participatory problem-solving and decision-making. He is a facilitator who pays careful attention to social as well as analytical processes and makes thoughtful use of information technology. Sandy is president of Executive Decision Services, a private consulting firm, and executive director of the Decision Techtronics Group at the Rockefeller Institute of Government, State University of New York. He has facilitated meetings and decision conferences for a wide variety of public and private organizations. He has developed training courses in facilitation, group decision-making, analytical techniques and information resource management. He helped organize the New York State Forum on Conflict and Consensus, a forum to explore and encourage participatory and collaborative approaches to solving public policy conflicts in New York State and currently serves as Vice-Chair.

David Sink is Professor of Public Administration at the University of Arkansas at Little Rock, USA. Previously he has taught at the University of Alabama at Birmingham and the University of California, Riverside. Professor Sink attempts to integrate his teaching, research and service in a series of efforts focused on community level collaboration, urban politics and management and youth violence. His most recent study deals with the degree of formalization of community-based collaboration and the potential for bringing together opposing elements of the community in a shared-vision collaboration.

Acknowledgements and dedication

Editing a book like this in a world where time is precious is hard on the editor. It must be much harder on the family, friends and colleagues who surround her. I found that the only way of completing the task was to shout loudly about it. Letting all and sundry know I was doing it ensured that I had to be seen to finish it. It was an effective way of getting the job done ... but it must have been very boring to listen to! Max took the brunt of the load but quite a lot also got dumped on other friends and most valued colleagues. To all of you, many thanks.

My thanks also to the authors of the chapters in the book who first responded to the call to come to Ross Priory and latterly coped so admirably with my many finicky editorial demands.

This book is dedicated to the memory of my mum who died just too soon to know of its existence.

C.S.H.

Prologue

Arriving at Ross Priory – the University of Strathclyde's 'place in the country' – one Sunday evening around 10.30 pm in June 1993, I found Arthur Himmelman standing with his back to me on the putting green, entranced by the view up Loch Lomond.

> 'I just wasn't prepared for how beautiful it would be,' he remarked.
> 'Well I did tell you, but ...'

Situated on the south bank of the Loch, Ross Priory is indeed a stunning location. Mountains flank the loch sides and the loch itself is dotted with small islands. Around midsummer in Scotland at 10.30 pm it is still broad daylight. That night the sun was out and the view was breathtaking.

Such was the setting in which the ten authors in this book gathered together, along with Allen Hickling and Siv Vangen, for three days and talked about collaboration. This book represents the agenda of things that we talked about.

In the course of editing the book, I was struck time and time again at the enormous variety within it: variety in definition of collaboration; variety in setting for collaboration; variety in process of collaboration; variety in ideology for collaboration; and so on. I should not be surprised by this; after all I invited this particular set of people to Ross Priory precisely because they came from a diverse range of backgrounds and would bring with them a consequent variety of 'world-taken-for-granteds' about, and perspectives on, collaboration. But the variety that emerged was probably greater than any of us could have imagined. Three days of trying to get inside each others' heads left us confused (I, at any rate, was much more confused than when we started) ... but excited.

Chris Huxham

PART ONE

INTRODUCTION

1

Collaboration and Collaborative Advantage

Chris Huxham

Why collaboration?

For some, the term 'collaboration' carries a negative connotation; this is a hang-over from the Second World War when the term was used to describe those who worked with the enemy. In this book, however, 'collaboration' is taken to imply a very positive form of working in association with others for some form of mutual benefit. The Dutch word *samenwerken*, translated literally as 'working together', captures neatly the intention.

In common parlance, 'collaboration' is often used when individuals work together towards some common aim; in universities, for example, individuals commonly 'collaborate' over a research project. The concern of this book, however, is not with collaboration between individuals but with collaboration between organizations. At a minimum this means that it is concerned with situations in which individuals in one organization work with individuals in another. At a maximum, it implies many complete organizations working in harmony. These situations are known as **inter-organizational** collaborations. The aim of the book is to contribute to a practical understanding of how organizations may collaborate effectively.

Why then is collaboration a subject worthy of a book? As a researcher, it is tempting to answer, 'because it is interesting'! Certainly we hope you will find this book interesting. But there are many important pragmatic reasons for addressing collaboration which would make this book timely even if the topic were boring! Understanding collaboration is important for a number of reasons:

- **Collaboration is happening**:
  right across the world, people are doing it; or rather, people are trying to, often unsuccessfully;

people are frequently being *required* (for example, by government mandate) to do it, also often unsuccessfully.

- **Collaboration is valuable**:
  it can be a good way of achieving things that would be difficult or impossible for an organization to do on its own (the self-interest motivation);
  it is the *only* way to tackle major societal problems (the moral imperative).
- **Collaboration is difficult**:
  it is non-trivial in practice because of a number of inherent hazards.

Collaboration is happening

'Strategic alliance', 'joint venture', 'public–private partnership', 'co-ordinated service delivery', 'community development' are all terms now in common usage, many of which have only slipped into everyday managerial and political vocabulary over the past few years. That these terms are on the lips of managers and politicians is indicative of the quantity of interorganizational arrangements that do exist. The private sector is rife with inter-firm arrangements such as joint marketing agreements, research and development partnerships and supply-chain agreements. In addition, increasing globalization of the marketplace is ensuring that more and more companies are finding partners in other countries; that is, in the national marketplaces in which they wish to compete. Collaboration is no less prominent in the public and community sectors, where organizations are getting together to provide co-ordinated services such as community advice or community education, or to tackle social issues such as community development, drug abuse or even major national conflicts. Cross-sector collaboration, directed, for example, at local economic development, is also common.

Many collaborative arrangements are purely voluntary; the parties get together simply because they see some benefit (usually to themselves, though motivation can be altruistic for 'the greater good') in doing so. However, increasingly collaborations are a response to government edict or incentive. For example, in the UK, the requirement for 'compulsory competitive tendering' for public service delivery has led to a need for public authorities to work with contractor organizations. At a sightly less dictatorial level, there have also been government financial incentives for collaboration, for, for example, public–private partnerships aimed at community development. In the US there have been requirements for public agencies to co-ordinate over the delivery of services such as education for children with special needs. In the Netherlands, government policy is enacted through involvement of organizations that will be affected by it in its design and in countries such as Japan, nationalistic or protectionist considerations ensure that even some private sector collaborations are government mandated.

Collaboration is valuable

Collaboration is not a panacea for tackling all organizational activities. Most of what organizations strive to achieve is, and should be, done alone. Nevertheless, there are situations in which working alone is not sufficient to achieve the desired ends.

A full and detailed investigation of the potential sources of value to be gained from collaboration is the subject of Cropper's discussion of **sustainability** in collaborations in Chapter 5 of this book. Here, we are concerned only to give some indications of the broad kinds of potential output that make collaboration attractive to organizations.

Organizations work together for a variety of reasons. Often the motivation is financial. Joint funding provides one incentive. For example, many city capital improvement projects are jointly funded by a number of agencies and major scientific research is sometimes jointly funded by a number of interested companies in the same industry. Alternatively, the financial draw may be, as Himmelman suggests in Chapter 2, cost-cutting or efficiency.

On the one hand the efficiency argument stems from the practical imperative of avoiding duplication of effort and of ensuring that the efforts of various agencies are co-ordinated into a coherent and directed whole. For example, it is *ceteris paribus* not sensible for two public agencies to provide a housing placement service in the same area. Neither is it sensible for one agency to be promoting the development of housing in an area in which other agencies have given a low priority to development of education or health provision.

On the other hand, the efficiency argument can be seen as political. In the case of public–private partnerships, the political argument is that what is seen as private sector managerial 'good practice' will rub off on what are seen as the more inefficient public agencies. In the case of increasing moves towards the privatized public service delivery which results in 'collaboration' between public authorities and the service deliverers, the argument is that competition to provide the service will, in itself, create efficiency.

While a financial motivation is, in principle, a perfectly reasonable basis for collaboration, it will be argued in the next section that collaboration has serious costs associated with it which could negate the apparent financial gains. There are, however, at least two reasons for collaborating which can be argued to make it worthwhile whatever the costs of collaborating. The first reason is a **self-interest** one, though this is not intended to imply that the self-interest is at the expense of others. In this case, an organization may initiate or participate in a collaboration because it can achieve something through the collaboration that could not be achieved in any other way. Thus, for example, a company might seek to collaborate with another that has local knowledge of a market it wishes to penetrate. Sometimes these 'self-interest' motivations may be more concerned with legitimacy than with the practicality *per se* of the collaborative task. For example, a community organization may wish to set up a forum of local people in order to influence local government policy over a particular issue. It is likely that neither its funding body (quite possibly the local government organization that it wishes to influence) nor its constituents (the local people themselves) would regard this as a legitimate activity for it to be engaged in alone, but both might regard it as quite legitimate for it to be part of a collaboration with this aim.

Many more examples of 'self-interest' reasons for being part of a collaboration could be given. However, some would argue that the really important reason for being concerned with collaboration is a **moral** one. This rests on the belief that the really important problem issues facing society – poverty, conflict, crime and so on – cannot be tackled by any single organization acting alone. These issues have ramifications for so many aspects of society that they are inherently multi-organizational. Collaboration is thus essential if there is to be any hope of alleviating these problems. In addition, some would argue for a further moral imperative; that is, that collaboration aimed at tackling these kinds of issues should also aim to empower those most affected by the problem to be centrally involved in initiatives aimed at addressing them. This point is argued by Himmelman in Chapter 2.

Collaboration is difficult

So, collaboration is happening and, in appropriate circumstances, is valuable. Unfortunately there is a lot of evidence to suggest that it is not always happening successfully and that the potential value is therefore not being realized.

Working with others is never simple! How often do we hear people say 'it would have been quicker to have done this on my own', even when there is only one other person involved? When collaboration is across organizations the complications are magnified. We have conceptualized this phenomenon through the notion of **collaborative inertia** (Huxham and Vangen, 1994; Huxham, 1996). We use this term to describe the situation when the apparent rate of work output from a collaboration is slowed down considerably compared to what a casual observer might expect it to be able to achieve.

There are numerous reasons why collaborations so often reach a state of inertia. Among these are difficulties stemming: from differences in aims, language, procedures, culture and perceived power; from the tension between autonomy and accountability and the lack of authority structure; and from the time needed to manage the logistics.

Differences in aims, language, procedures, culture and perceived power By definition, organizations involved in collaborations will have different aims. It is these differences which provide the leverage that is to be gained from collaborating. But these differing aims also mean that organizations' reasons for being involved in collaborations will differ, and because some of these aims may not relate to the overt purpose of the collaboration, they may not be clearly spelled out. Furthermore, the aims may be in conflict with each other. Finding a way to satisfy *enough* of the aims to allow the collaboration to proceed is often not an easy task.

This difficulty will be exacerbated if, as is often the case, the various parties to the collaboration come from different professional groups (for example, when the police and social workers or research scientists and marketers collaborate). In this case, not only will their aims often be in conflict, but they will work with entirely different professional languages. Communication can then become difficult. Differences in organizational culture and procedures can aggravate the situation further because seemingly straightforward tasks can be carried out quite differently in different organizations. Difficulties arise because individuals make unwarranted assumptions about the way things are carried out in partner organizations, or because of the time needed to make arrangements for even trivial matters to the satisfaction of all concerned. Perceived power imbalances (which often occur, for example, when a large public agency collaborates with a small voluntary organization) serve to make some parties feel vulnerable and exacerbate the potential for misunderstandings further.

The focus of the above arguments has been largely on the *inherent* communication difficulties which *will* underlie all collaborative situations. It has also been suggested that there can be real and not easily reconcilable differences in aims. For these reasons, collaborations, at best, tend to need to spend unusual amounts of time in reaching understandings and agreements compared to other situations, and at worst become embroiled in misunderstanding and conflict.

The tension between autonomy and accountability and the lack of authority structure The arguments above would tend to suggest that collaboration will work best where organizations have similar (or at least compatible) aims, involve similar professional groups and involve organizations with similar culture, procedures and perceived power. However, even in an 'ideal' situation of this type, there is still potential for a slowing down of activity arising out of the tension between autonomy and accountability.

In a nutshell, this argument rests on the presumption that the individuals from the various organizations who are directly involved in collaborative activities need a fair degree of autonomy in order to make progress. The problem is that the activities of the collaboration will affect the 'parent' organizations, so the individuals also need to be accountable to the various organizations or other constituencies which they represent. Unless those individuals are all fully empowered by their organizations to make judgements about what they may commit to, there will need to be continual checking-back to the 'parents' before action can happen. Much lapsed time can pass in this process, during the course of which impetus and energy levels for the proposed action can wither.

The autonomy–accountability dilemma does not only apply to the collaboration. In committing to be a part of the collaboration an organization is also, often unwittingly, committing to have its own autonomy checked around the areas of its activities which relate to the collaboration. Suddenly, it becomes anti-social to respond to environmental stimuli in these areas without first checking that partners are happy with this. It can even be a problem for an organization to act alone when the activity is intended to contribute to the collaborative effort rather than to its own, 'personal' gain.

Related to the autonomy–accountability issue is the issue of authority hierarchy. Even in situations where one organization is significantly more powerful than others, there can be no formal authority hierarchies between the parties. This means that working relationships between individuals from different organizations can only be formed on a goodwill basis. For example, if a member of one organization is assigned to support the work of someone in another organization, normal subordinate–superordinate relationships cannot apply. Furthermore there will often be a conflict of priorities on the part of the 'subordinate' between work for the collaboration and direct work for their organization.

The lack of authority structure thus has two implications for the time involved in collaborating. On the one hand, time needs to be invested in creating goodwill between individuals. On the other hand, the lapsed time to achieve things can be greater than expected if collaboration activities take low priority. Such problems are not unique to collaborative situations, but they are inherent in them.

The time needed to manage the logistics Finally, the sheer logistics of collaboration also tend to make it consuming of both lapsed and actual time (as well as of other resources). Core group members are likely to be based in locations which are physically remote from one another. It is not generally possible for them to meet in the corridor or arrange spontaneous meetings to deal with matters as they arise. Everything has to be planned and co-ordinated. This takes organizing time and often travel time too.

A key theme running through each of the preceding sections is that collaboration is inherently more time-consuming – and hence resource-consuming and costly – than non-collaborative activities. The time required is of two sorts: actual time invested in achieving mutual understanding, gaining goodwill, negotiating bases for action and co-ordination (all of which are related to creating trust) – and lapsed time to cope with accountability issues and other organizational priorities. While none of these is an insurmountable block, they do tend to be demotivating, particularly if, as is usually the case, the need for this kind of time has not been recognized and hence not budgeted for. Under these circumstances it is not surprising that those involved tend to feel a great sense of frustration. Progress seems painfully slow and duty to the collaboration preys on the mind but is never prioritized high enough to generate the energy required to overcome the inertia.

Given the importance of collaboration and the difficulties inherent in it, it is obviously important to understand as much as possible about its nature and to develop processes which can help make it work successfully. The development of such understanding and the development of such processes are the twin themes of this book.

Before introducing these themes, however, it is important to set the scene by exploring rather more deeply what the authors in this book mean by 'collaboration', and by introducing the notion of 'collaborative advantage'.

What is collaboration?

At the start of this introductory chapter, a rough definition of collaboration was given:

> 'collaboration' is taken to imply a very positive form of working in association with others for some form of mutual benefit. . . . the concern . . . is . . . with collaboration between organizations.

While this definition does not contradict any of the conceptions of collaboration used by authors in this book, it belies the complexity of their different perspectives. As you will discover as you read on, there is a great deal of variety – and hence confusion – in understandings of the meaning of it. It is worth trying to untangle some of this confusion, both in order to be able to interpret what each of the authors is saying relative to the others and because the various interpretations all have merit and are hence worthy of exploration if for no other reason than to test the reader's assumptions.

Confusion in interpreting 'collaboration' arises from two directions. On the one hand, there is a mass of related terminology used to describe inter-organizational structures which are the same or similar to collaboration. On the other hand, there are multiple interpretations of the term 'collaboration' itself.

Alternative terminology

Many terms are used to describe positive forms of inter-organizational relationship. For example, as well as 'collaboration', the terms 'co-operation', 'co-ordination', 'coalition', 'network', 'alliance', 'partnership' and 'bridge' are all in fairly common usage. These may be compared with 'conflict', 'competition', 'co-option' and 'collusion', which are typically used to describe inter-organizational relationships with more negative connotations. Some authors deliberately try to use the variety of terms as ways of distinguishing between different forms of inter-organizational relationship. Himmelman's spectrum of inter-organizational forms in Chapter 2 is typical of this approach. While such distinctions have value in principle, there seems to be little consensus in the field about how the terms are used either in theory or practice, so they do not provide a consistent framework. Indeed as we are about to see, a vast variety of meanings are attributed to 'collaboration' alone.

In this book the term 'collaboration' is used by all authors to describe whatever conception of inter-organizational relationship they are concerned with – except where there is a deliberate intention to do otherwise for the purpose of distinguishing between one structure or intent and another. However, it should be noted that much of what is referred to in this book as 'collaboration' may sometimes be referred to elsewhere by a variety of different labels.

Alternative meaning

Of much greater significance than the variety of labels is the variety of meaning associated with collaboration. At a broad level, the variety can be seen as having three dimensions. The first dimension focuses on collaboration as an 'organizational form'. Thus Cropper argues in Chapter 5 that:

> ... collaboration is a distinct mode of organizing. . . . an intense form of mutual attachment, operating at the levels of interest, intent, affect and behaviour: actors are bound together by the mutually supportive pursuit of individual and collective benefit . . .

and Finn, in Chapter 10, that:

> When groups and organizations begin to embrace collaborative processes . . . they are in essence inventing a new type of organization. . . . [a] type of transformational organization . . .

The second dimension of meaning is concerned with 'structural form'. Thus, Cropper (Chapter 5) again:

> Between the extremes of independence and fusion, the spectrum of structural form within which collaboration falls is nevertheless wide. It ranges from wide networks through loose alliances and tight federations to the creation of novel organizational entities, sometimes separate from the partner organizations, sometimes vested in one partner.

In the context of this book, the third dimension of meaning, the 'rationale' for collaborating, is much more significant than either of the above two.

Dimensions of rationale for collaboration

The various perspectives implicit (and sometimes explicit) in the chapters which follow suggest a highly interrelated set of contrasts which may be thought of as a framework of dimensions upon which alternative rationales for collaboration can be distinguished. The interrelated nature of the dimensions makes them difficult to discuss within the linear confines of a book; the discussion has thus been divided by subheadings into five areas – empowerment and participation; power relationships; addressing conflict;

substantive change; and ambitiousness – which cut across the dimensions. The dimensions are represented in Figure 1.1, which also indicates some of the more significant relationships between them.

Empowerment and participation   A first dimension of rationale is:

    (a) **ideological** ———— **instrumental**

This relates closely to the arguments put forward earlier about self-interest and moral value for collaboration. The term 'ideology' is used here in its visionary sense, to imply the pursuit of a moral ideal.

Most conceptions of collaboration would appear to be nearer the instrumental end of this spectrum, the purpose being to achieve some practical end through working with others. Himmelman's perspective (Chapter 2), however, which focuses strongly on the notion of **collaborative empowerment** is centred much closer to the ideological end of the spectrum. Thus, though Himmelman conceives of collaborations as having a practical purpose – to contribute to alleviation of various forms of social deprivation – his emphasis on empowering those directly affected by the deprivation – 'the weak' – suggests that he views this as at least as important a goal as the instrumental end of alleviating the deprivation itself. It is interesting to compare Himmelman's perspective with that of the community collaborations described by Barr and Huxham in Chapter 7, which suggest that involvement of 'the community' is important, but with the emphasis on the practical leverage (that is, on the instrumental value) to be gained from doing so.

The focus on community empowerment and involvement leads both to the second dimension of rationale which focuses on participation, and the third and fourth dimensions, which focus on power.

One observation made by Barr and Huxham is that the so-called community collaborations which they studied were hardly *inter-organizational* collaborations at all. These groups appear to envisage collaboration as a form of participation by 'the community' (however that may be defined) in a 'joint' endeavour. The notion that participation should be enacted through organizations working together appears to be less (if at all) significant to them. The second dimension of rationale is thus:

    (b) **participation** ———— **organizations working together**

The view of collaboration as a form of participative management is also implicit in Himmelman's 'empowerment' perspective, though he stresses that community based *organizations* should be at the centre of this. Himmelman is writing from a United States (US) perspective, where inclusion of minority groups in federally funded social projects is a high-profile issue. In the US, the term 'collaboration' is often used to mean exactly that.

'Collaboration' and 'participation' are also often linked in the European context, though in this case the intention is to involve any group affected

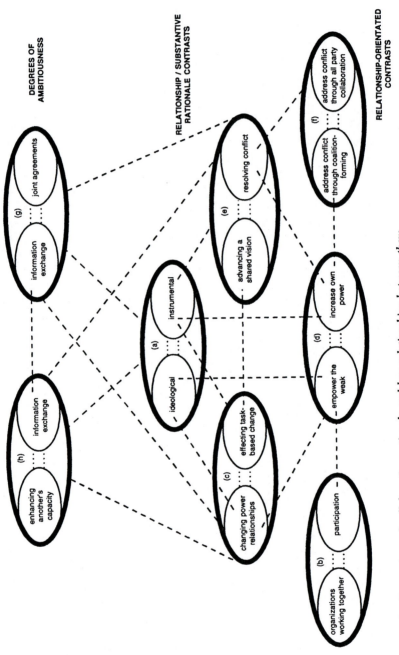

Figure 1.1 *Dimensions of collaboration rationale and key relationships between them*

by a policy in its development rather than just minority groups. The Scandinavian countries and the Netherlands in particular have a long history of this kind of involvement. In Chapter 11 of this book, de Jong describes interactive processes for involving key organizations in the implementation of Dutch government policy. The extent to which these situations may be full organizational collaborations or simply elaborate processes of consultation varies from situation to situation and from organization to organization. Inevitably some of the individuals involved in the participative process will be there on the basis of their expertise and will only be representing others in the broadest of senses.

Power relationships The third dimension of rationale (highlighted by Cropper, 1993) also follows from the notion of empowerment, but, as mentioned above, in a rather different way:

(c) **changing power relationships** ———— **effecting task-based change**

At face value this could be regarded as a more specific version of the ideological–instrumental dimension, with 'changing power relationships' as the particular form of 'ideology' and 'effecting task-based change' as the particular form of instrumentalism. However, there are alternative interpretations of the 'power relationships' end of this latter spectrum which make the relationship more complex.

As has already been emphasized, one way of changing power relationships through collaboration is to use the collaboration as a vehicle for empowering the weak. An alternative perspective on power relationships is that collaboration can be used to increase an organization's own power to achieve its aims. This is the implied perspective in Eden's discussion of the formation of coalitions of those who have low power but high interest relative to a strategic issue (Chapter 3). The coalition then becomes powerful relative to other players in the arena. This suggests a fourth dimension of rationale:

(d) **empower the weak** ———— **increase own power**

The 'increase own power' perspective is driven by considerations which are closer to the instrumental end of the ideological–instrumental dimension, though empowering the weak may be one of the spin-offs.

Addressing conflict Closely related to coalition-building is the notion of collaboration for conflict resolution. In Chapter 4, Gray classifies motivating factors for collaboration along the following dimension:

(e) **resolving conflict** ———— **advancing a shared vision**

Implied in Gray's writing is that conflicts may be resolved if all parties to the conflict can find a collaborative way of moving forward. This is in contrast to the coalition approach which suggests that a subset of the conflicting parties may form a collaboration (coalition) to make themselves more powerful than the others. This strategy would, if successful, thus lead to conflict resolution through changing power relationships. This leads to a sixth dimension of rationale:

(f)   *address conflict through*:
coalition-forming ———— **all-party collaboration**

Substantive change The arguments above have been, in the main, around notions of collaboration which focus on power, empowerment, participation and conflict resolution. In other words, they have focused on *relationships* between organizations. Dimensions (b), (d) and (f) have been entirely concerned with different conceptions of the relationships. However, dimensions (a), (c) and (e) have sought to distinguish between this relationship focus and a focus on a substantive product from the collaboration. Before introducing the final two dimensions of rationale, it is appropriate to review the substantive end of the contrasts in (a), (c) and (e).

Most common conceptions of collaboration tend to focus, at least in the first instance, on the achievement of some substantive end. Thus collaboration may be seen as **instrumental** in **effecting task-based change** or in **advancing a shared vision**. In these cases the motivation could be, as was suggested earlier, financial, self-interested achievement of something that cannot be achieved alone or the moral imperative of tackling major societal problems.

Many of the examples referred to in this book are of this general type. For example: in Chapter 4, Gray discusses cases of a sewing council formed to develop a training programme to attract job applicants and of a youth employment initiative; the ideas in Chapter 5 derive from Cropper's experience with a collaborative anti-smoking campaign; Sink (Chapter 6) is concerned with delivery of public services; Barr and Huxham (Chapter 7) focus on poverty action groups; my own ideas in Chapter 9 derive from collaboration over economic development strategy; Finn (Chapter 10) describes work concerned with a strategy for medical services delivery; and de Jong (Chapter 11) describes development of policies for the environment, for the use of the Amsterdam–Rhine canal, for cultural development and for a day nursery.

Whether there is intended to be a distinction between Cropper's 'task-based change' and Gray's 'shared vision' is open to question. Certainly the latter implies a more strategic or grand aim than the former, and the former implies a greater sense of 'getting hands dirty' through detailed tasks than the latter. This range of possibilities is reflected in the variety of the examples just listed. However, the main intention of both concepts is a focus on the substantive purpose for collaboration rather than a statement about the level at which that purpose is directed. It is thus likely that the authors are using different terminology for what they envisage as essentially similar notions.

Ambitiousness The final dimensions can cut across all others and relate to the ambitiousness of the aims of the collaboration. Gray (Chapter 4) contrasts the 'expected outcomes' of collaboration as:

(g) exchange of information ———— joint agreements

and suggests that this is an orthogonal dimension to her 'resolving conflict *vs* shared vision' dimension (that is, (e) above). Thus she argues that resolving conflict may be tackled either through information exchange (a 'dialogue') or with the aim of reaching a joint agreement (a 'negotiated settlement'). Similarly, advancing a shared vision may be carried out either through information exchange ('appreciative planning') or by reaching a joint agreement (a 'collective strategy'). Similar arguments could be made for empowerment, for coalition-forming, for participation and so on.

Clearly exchange of information is a much less ambitious aim than is a joint agreement. The former will be much easier to achieve, but usually less powerful in addressing the collaborative purpose. Which end of this spectrum is aimed for will generally depend not only on the nature and importance of the collaborative purpose, but also on the degree of comfort that the particular organizations have in working with each other. Often it may be better to start a relationship with modest aims.

This point is made by Himmelman (Chapter 2), who also focuses on a range of ambitiousness of objectives through his 'continuum of definitions and strategies'. At one extreme he defines networking as 'the exchange of information for mutual benefit'. At the other extreme, he defines collaboration as 'exchange of information, altering activities, sharing resources and enhancing the capacity of another for mutual benefit and to achieve a common purpose'. Co-ordination and co-operation are defined to fall in between these two extremes. Thus the eighth and final dimension of rationale to be discussed here is:

(h) information exchange ———— enhancing another's capacity

Clearly, and not surprisingly given Himmelman's emphasis on empowerment, the more ambitious side of this latter dimension is relationship-orientated in its language. This is in contrast to the more ambitious side of dimension (g) which is couched in language suggestive of substantive ends. Both, however, can be interpreted in terms of substantive or relationship-orientated goals.

Using the dimensions The above dimensions of rationale undoubtedly do not provide a complete picture of all possible conceptions of collaboration, because they derive solely from the perspectives implicitly or explicitly referred to in this book. An examination of other work would presumably reveal additional contrasts. However, it seems not unreasonable to suppose that the eight dimensions listed here are likely to be indicative of the broad areas of variation.

It was suggested at the start of this section that the eight dimensions could form a framework for distinguishing between one conception of collaboration and another. In practice, however, this would not be a clear-cut process. In the first place, as Figure 1.1 indicates, there is a great deal of overlap and linkage between the dimensions so they cannot be used to specify the 'co-ordinates' of any particular collaboration in a neat fashion.

More significantly, it would be difficult actually to place any individual's perspective on collaboration – or any actual collaboration – on any of the scales. For example, though discussion of Himmelman's notion of empowerment above has indicated that he might be located towards the ideological end of dimension (a), he also stresses that collaboration aims to achieve a common purpose. This suggests that he also has an instrumental focus. Following similar arguments, it would not be surprising if a great many conceptions would be placed towards the centre of many of the dimensions. Thus rather than conceiving of the dimensions as a precise recipe for categorizing collaboration, they should be regarded as a framework for consideration of different possible perspectives.

Perhaps the most important conclusion to draw from this is that there *is* variation in the way that people conceive of collaboration. It is tempting to argue that some of the above conceptions are simply not what is meant by collaboration. Yet each has been derived from a situation in which people are thinking of it as collaboration. While it is reasonable to define certain conceptions as outside of a particular area of interest, it is rare to find authors placing their own perspective against that of others. Clearly it is important to be able to do so in order to make judgements about how commentary about collaborative practice may be transferable from one situation to another.

What is collaborative advantage?

This chapter has focused so far on justifying the importance of collaboration as a topic and on exploring various interpretations of its meaning. The title of this book, however, refers not simply to collaboration, but to **collaborative advantage**.

Collaborative advantage is concerned with the creation of synergy between collaborating organizations. The concept arose during the work by the current author concerned with collaboration between large public agencies over city economic and social development which also provides the basis for Chapter 9 of this book. The definition produced at that time was:

> Collaborative advantage will be achieved when something unusually creative is produced – perhaps an objective is met – that no organization could have produced on its own and when each organization, through the collaboration, is able to achieve its own objectives better than it could alone. In some cases, it should also be possible to achieve some higher-level . . . objectives for society as a whole rather than just for the participating organizations. (Huxham, 1993: 603)

The key point about this definition is that it focuses on outputs of collaboration that could not have been achieved except through collaborating. It thus has relevance for both the 'self-interest' and 'moral imperative' arguments for the value of collaboration made earlier in this chapter. The additional emphasis on the need for each individual organization to achieve its own objectives better than it could alone, is not only an ideal, but also stems from a recognition that it is a necessary requirement of successful collaboration. Thus, if collaboration is voluntary, organizations generally need to justify their involvement in it in terms of its contribution to their own aims or remit; if organizations are mandated to be part of a collaboration, getting something out of it for themselves is important in motivating them to inject sufficient energy into it to make it work.

Not all collaborations need aim for collaborative advantage; for example, joint funding of a project would not, in itself lead to collaborative advantage as defined above. However, given the high investment in resources required to avoid collaborative inertia, it will often be difficult to justify collaborating except when real advantage can be gained from it. Collaborative advantage defines a high value and ambitious form of collaboration and so affords a useful focus for discussion.

The above definition derives from an instrumental, task-based change, shared vision perspective on collaboration, but it is not incompatible with any of the relationship-orientated perspectives. It is not, for example, inconsistent with notions of empowerment, participation or conflict resolution, though it does stress the requirement for *all* parties to benefit from the collaboration, rather than just the weaker ones. It is important to stress that the above definition is *not* intended to imply that the advantage to be gained from collaboration is an advantage over another party, though in the 'coalition-forming' variety of collaboration this might be an additional outcome.

One of the main values of the notion of collaborative advantage is in raising the profile of collaboration and in legitimizing it as an activity worthy of resource investment. The term alone can, for some managers, be a powerful driver of the collaborative process. It is, of course, deliberately intended to contrast with the more familiar, 'competitive advantage'.

Because the term has some intrinsic meaning, it has been picked up by others and sometimes used in different ways. For example, Kanter (1994) defines a company's collaborative advantage as its propensity to be a good partner. Taking a completely different viewpoint, Hickling (1994) has argued that collaborative advantage should be used to describe the kinds of 'invisible products' of collaboration – such as shared knowledge and mutual understanding – which de Jong discusses in Chapter 11. This is perhaps also what Finn (Chapter 10) is suggesting when he argues that as a facilitator of a collaborative group:

> . . . I lacked the capacity the group developed by the exercise of 'collaborative advantage'.

The authors in this book appear to give a variety of different interpretations of the term. Cropper (Chapter 5) and Eden (Chapter 3) work with definitions close to the original, though Cropper defines it only as 'greater "whole system effectiveness"', and hence ignores the focus of greater individual effectiveness, while Eden's focus on individual effectiveness is limited to that of what he refers to as the 'primary organization'; that is, to the organization which he, as facilitator, regards as primary client. Gray (Chapter 4), on the other hand, appears to take a contradictory view by equating collaborative advantage to 'collaborating to compete'. From yet another perspective, Sink (Chapter 6) argues that

> Collaborative advantage may be a process of transforming power relations . . . so that less powerful elements of society have a voice in policy-making

and Himmelman describes it as 'elements of collaborative process'.

The attractiveness of the term, 'collaborative advantage', means that a plethora of interpretations of it is inevitable. While the original definition *is* powerful in focusing attention on how to gain real advantage from collaborating, variety in interpretation may be helpful in fuelling a debate about the nature of the advantage and, consequently, in refining the definition. In addition, individually 'owned' interpretations are likely to enhance its value in awareness-raising about collaborative processes.

How does this book address collaboration and collaborative advantage?

It has been argued that collaboration is an important activity in which organizations are becoming increasingly involved, but often struggle with. This book aims to contribute to a practical understanding of collaboration and of how real advantage may be achieved from it. This aim is addressed from three directions – experience, theory and process.

Each of the subsequent chapters in this book is based on **experience** of work with active collaborative groups. Most of the authors have very considerable experience in this area. Many of the chapters describe in some detail cases of collaboration in which the author has been involved. In many cases, the authors have played some facilitative role, and have thus taken an active part in assisting the process of the collaboration. Even where specific case descriptions are not given, the issues raised arise out of experience of this sort.

Though some of the authors in the book do also work with business organizations, the book is largely concerned with **collaboration as a means of tackling social issues**. As has already been noted, key themes are community development, community empowerment, co-ordinated service provision, environmental issues, conflict resolution, health and social policy development. The book thus aims to contribute to addressing the moral imperative for collaboration: that it is the only way in which serious social problems can be tackled. Nevertheless, many of the insights about collaboration in this book have relevance beyond this immediate setting; they are generic to many forms and focuses for collaboration. The book therefore has relevance to all interested in collaboration.

In addition to the focus on experience, each of the chapters also develops a **theoretical** perspective on collaboration. In some cases, the theory is primarily descriptive theory about the nature of collaboration in practice. In other cases the theory is concerned with processes to assist those involved in collaborations.

A concern with collaborative **process** is the third focus of each of the chapters. Even where the theoretical perspective is primarily descriptive, there are implications for the design of collaborative processes. A particularly strong theme in the book is the design of **facilitator-led** processes for aiding collaborative groups. A number of alternative ways in which a facilitator may intervene to work with groups in which the individuals come from different organizations are discussed. Facilitating such groups effectively is far from straightforward, as the variety of considerations raised in the book demonstrates. Given the propensity for collaborations to reach a state of inertia, the effective intervention of a facilitator can nevertheless make the difference between a lively, active collaboration and one that struggles to find the motivation to maintain its own survival. The conditions under which the use of a facilitator is appropriate as well as the degree to which the facilitator should direct the group process is the subject of Schuman's chapter (Chapter 8).

The combination of experience, theory and process, together with the focus both on facilitating collaborative groups and on the wider aspects of inter-organizational collaborations as a whole, is the distinctive contribution of this book. All of these aspects are considered in all of the chapters, but the degree to which this is explicitly done for each aspect varies across the chapters. This variation is a reflection of the deliberately diverse backgrounds of the authors, some of whom come at this topic from a background in facilitating (often *intra*-organizational) groups, some of whom come from a background of researching collaboration and some of whom have experiences somewhere in between!

How is the book organized?

The main body of the book is organized into three sections. The first of these (Part Two) picks up the theme of rationales for collaboration with three chapters giving quite different perspectives. Virtually all sides of the eight dimensions of rationale are present in the different conceptions of collaboration implied in these chapters. The second group of chapters (Part Three) develops some theoretical perspectives on collaboration in practice, focusing on potential value, inherent hazards and the relevance of community involvement in collaboration. The final section of the main body of the book (Part Four) focuses on facilitated processes for working with collaborative groups. The ground is laid for the section with Schuman's discussion of the moral stance taken by a facilitator when deciding how to direct the group process. This theme is picked up in my own chapter which follows Schuman's, and this and the following two chapters describe, with theoretical explanation, some alternative approaches to facilitation of collaborative groups.

The placing of chapters into particular sections should not be regarded as especially significant. Because the chapters all consider experience, theory and process, it would have been possible to have put many of them in more than one section. For example, Eden's chapter (Chapter 3) describes a facilitated group process in some detail and would thus fit as well into Part Four as Part Two. Likewise, Gray's chapter (Chapter 4) discusses success factors in collaboration and would thus fit well into Part Three. Similar arguments could be made for any of the others.

The overwhelming conclusion from this book is that while collaboration is undoubtedly difficult, it is possible to devise processes to aid effective practice. The book concludes in Part Five with a brief chapter summarizing some of the main insights of the book.

References

Cropper, S. (1993) 'Ross Priory reflections'. Note following the International Workshop at Strathclyde University on Making Collaboration Happen. University of Keele.

Hickling, A. (1994) Personal communication following the International Workshop at Strathclyde University on Making Collaboration Happen.

Huxham, C. (1993) 'Pursuing collaborative advantage', *Journal of the Operational Research Society*, 44 (6): 599–611.

Huxham, C. (1996) 'Advantage or inertia? making collaboration work', in R. Paton; G. Clark; G. Jones; J. Lewis and P. Quintas (eds), *The New Management Reader*. London: Routledge. pp. 238–54.

Huxham, C. and Vangen, S. (1994) 'Naivety and maturity, inertia and fatigue: are working relationships between public organizations doomed to fail?' Working Paper 94/17, Department of Management Science, University of Strathclyde.

Kanter, R. Moss (1994) 'Collaborative advantage: the art of alliances', *Harvard Business Review*, July–August, 96–108.

PART TWO

RATIONALES AND CONTEXTS FOR COLLABORATION

2

On the Theory and Practice of Transformational Collaboration: From Social Service to Social Justice

Arthur Turovh Himmelman

The purpose of this chapter is to introduce concepts and practices of community and systems change collaboration that can produce improved public and social service outcomes while also transforming power relations in collaborative change efforts. The chapter argues that, in order for a transformation in power relations to occur, collaborative change practice must move beyond its current focus on integrating social services and improving their cost-effectiveness. As a bridge from social service to social justice, collaboration must challenge the existing practices of power, wealth and control that substantially contribute to growing class, race, gender and other inequities in many societies. As would be expected, resistance to the use of collaboration for this purpose is common among powerful public, private and non-profit institutions in which 'organizational cultures' can subvert change and reform by their insistence on needless rules and regulations, their toleration of high levels of incompetence, and by their general lack of decency, passion, vision and creativity.

The chapter suggests that, if transformational collaborative strategies are to be considered among the prerequisites for new societies, they must reflect the values and practices of possible new societies. Many agree that such

This chapter is drawn, in part, from the author's monograph, *Communities Working Collaboratively for a Change* (Himmelman, 1992).

values and practices include those providing for mutual recognition and for the establishment of respect, trust and power which is defined and shared by all those joined in common efforts. Such values and practices are often:

- the basis for a shared vision among those revitalizing communities;
- maintained by recognizing that people seeking assistance should fully share power and make vital contributions to community problem-solving; and
- characterized by shared responsibility for common goals, a willingness to be held accountable, and commitments to democratic practices.

Unfortunately, power is often associated with violence, either as a method of control by elites, or as acts of rage by those who violently demand 'respect' or act out feelings of despair, self-hate and powerlessness, most often against their own families and neighbours. Although most movements to transform power relations have been characterized by violence used to maintain or remove dominant elites, the logic of collaborative (working together) change obviously requires that violence is not an acceptable part of the process. In general, the greater the use of violence to bring about change, the more likely that violence will be used to limit further change. While this is true to a greater or lesser extent in specific cases, such a relationship seems clear. The use of violence also greatly restricts the possibilities for creating a new basis for personal and community relationships and experimentation with necessary new institution building. New societies created within existing societies are far more able to survive non-violent births. Therefore, those using collaborative strategies should attempt to recruit holders and gatekeepers of power into processes that move them, with as little violence as possible, from domination and control to democratically shared power.

With good reason, much of the hope for new societies is based on building them collaboratively from the 'ground up' within and among communities, neighbourhoods, villages, workers' organizations, constituencies (for example, African-Americans), or other self-defined associations. However, it is also important to recognize the limitations of such solutions to many societal problems. While localized efforts in the United States (US) are now gaining well deserved attention, they must be coupled with substantial policy changes and new funding for human needs at all levels of government, particularly at the federal or central governmental level, if such initiatives are to succeed. There is a clear danger that too much will be expected from smaller, localized efforts when most major societal problems result from national and international economic and political policies, particularly those contributing to the loss of employment with which people can support families. Indeed, this problem is becoming more acute as job growth has occurred because wages and benefits, adjusted for inflation, have continued to decline. Many families must work several jobs to maintain even a moderate standard of living. Therefore, because of this and other larger realities – which underscore both the scale and kinds of resources communities need, and the importance of redesigning their delivery and redirecting their focus – it is critical that community-based collaborative change include the active support of all levels of government.

It is important to keep in mind that collaborative principles and practices described here are taken primarily from the experience of the US. Therefore, considerable modification may be necessary before they could be applied to the circumstances of other countries. For example, in the US the size and scope of the non-profit (non-governmental) sector is far more extensive in relationship to the public sector than in other countries, and its history and role in relationship to government reflects this unusual characteristic when contrasted with other regions of the world (Hall, 1987). This is important to keep in perspective because a central feature of collaborative change in the US is its emphasis on government/non-profit partnerships (these collaborative efforts often include the private/business sector as well, although to a lesser degree). Further distinguishing collaboration in the US from other countries is the large philanthropic support from private US foundations and corporations for collaborative initiatives among public, private and non-profit organizations.

It may be helpful to determine this chapter's relevance to particular circumstances through dialogues about whether non-profit or non-governmental organizations should seek to extend their power, authority and responsibility through collaborative initiatives. The conclusions from these dialogues will vary greatly and are far from simple to predict. For example, some believe that greater non-profit or non-governmental sector responsibility may not be a prudent course on large social concerns, if they believe health care should be guaranteed by and provided by government. Therefore, there is a need to examine, determine and assess public, private and non-profit roles and responsibilities within particular traditions and values as a part of the collaborative process. If collaborative strategies are used to challenge fundamentally such traditions and values, they will have to produce a transformation of power relations based on broad-based, visionary, well organized and highly effective processes of mutual engagement.

Organization of the chapter

The chapter is divided into six sections: (1) offering an overview discussion of collaboration in relation to: (a) power; (b) the cost-effective service 'ideology' of doing more with less; and (c) collaborative change as a bridge from social service to social justice; (2) examining collaboration in relation to other change strategies along a continuum of developmental complexity; (3) providing a framework for understanding basic concepts of power and decision-making in collaborative processes; (4) suggesting nine constructs that can form the basis for a theory and practice of transformational collaboration; (5) describing a variety of roles that can be played by partners in collaborative processes; and (6) outlining a planning guide, based on a series of questions that can be answered by participants in collaborative processes, to provide an example of how the concepts described in this chapter can be made user-friendly in their application (this is suggested as a central responsibility for those making contributions to theories of collaborative change).

Collaboration overview

Collaboration and power

The word 'power' comes from the Latin *posse*, meaning 'to be able', and is defined as the ability to do, act, or produce and, additionally, as the ability to control others (Webster, 1970). In common usage, power is associated with control and domination. The word 'elite' is also derived from a Latin root, *eligere*, meaning 'to pick or choose', and is defined as the group or part of a group selected or regarded as the finest, best, most distinguished, most powerful etc. (Webster, 1970). In this chapter, the word 'elite' is used generically (instead of the term 'power elite') to describe members of an upper class leadership group which protects and maintains upper class privileges by dominating a society's cultural, social, political and economic institutions and organizations (Domhoff, 1983; Mills, 1956). In any society, the elites are mainly, but never exclusively, members of its upper class and not all members of an upper class function as a part of an elite protecting its class power (Domhoff, 1983). In this chapter, the word 'gatekeeper' is used to describe elites who are not members of an upper class, but who play a significant role in maintaining upper class power.

When used in relation to collaboration, power is not defined here in terms of dominance, but as the 'capacity to produce intended results'. This definition of power is related to feminist theories that describe power in terms of capacity, competence and energy in contrast to traditional (masculine) views of power that define it as the ability to dominate or control (Hartsock, 1985). A definition of collaboration also can be taken from a Latin root, *collaboratus*, meaning 'to work together'. However, in this chapter collaboration is defined as the most complex process along a developmental continuum that includes networking, co-ordination, co-operation and collaboration (Himmelman, 1992). Specifically, organizational collaboration is defined as a 'process in which organizations exchange information, alter activities, share resources and enhance each other's capacity for mutual benefit and a common purpose by sharing risks, responsibilities and rewards' (Himmelman, 1992). In offering this definition of collaboration (or any other) to an international audience, it is important to acknowledge that the word took on a very negative connotation in Europe during the Second World War, implying working with the enemy as a traitor to one's country. Because of this most unfortunate usage, it is important to emphasize that the word collaboration must be clearly and carefully defined. In general, it is recommended that 'partner', rather than 'collaborator', is a better way to describe participants in a collaborative process.

The theory and practice of collaboration is receiving increasing attention from scholars and practitioners which is resulting in excellent literature on collaborative processes (IEL, 1993; NCSI, 1993; Potapchuk and Polk, 1992). Studies analysing and distilling elements of collaborative processes, described by some researchers as 'collaborative advantage', are becoming more refined and providing greater assistance in business, community and systems change efforts (Blank and Lombardi, 1992; Gray, 1989; Huxham, 1993; Kagan et al, 1993; Kanter, 1994; Potapchuk and Polk, 1993; Rosenthal and Mizrahi, 1994; Wolff, 1994). While such contributions are very significant, the concepts and practices advocated in much of this developing literature still require further refinement to be useful in efforts to transform the power of economic and political elites and their gatekeepers. Particularly challenging is the task of directing more research and debate to how collaboration can transform the power and dominance of elite and gatekeeper institutions that fund collaborative change.

In the US, transforming power relations is increasingly difficult for many reasons, but perhaps primarily because power continues to concentrate among elites as a result of growing wage and wealth disparities between the rich and poor (Barlett and Steele, 1992, 1994; Domhoff, 1983; Phillips, 1992, 1994). In large part, this trend in power relations is emerging from the internationalization of the economy which has increased the wealth and power of elites by:

1   providing elites with control of highly sophisticated communications, technological, and transportation systems as an infrastructure for the rapid movement of information, capital, and goods;
2   creating a vast global reservoir of underemployed people willing to work for very low wages, increasingly as 'temporary workers' without benefits, whose labour can be accessed more easily because of reduced national trade barriers and less effective unions; and
3   establishing the dominance of capital accumulated from financing the production of goods and services, over capital accumulated as the result of the sale of goods and services, as the basis of wealth creation and control (Goldsmith and Blakely, 1992; Sweezy, 1994).

As their involvement in the global economy grows, most elites (not all) find local communities, particularly inner cities, of importance only to the degree that they provide opportunities for wealth creation equal to the international marketplace (significant distinctions between national and local elites on this issue are well discussed by Katz, 1993). This can be very difficult for local communities because the international marketplace includes opportunities for highly profitable investments as well as for trading in goods and services. When elites do not view local communities as vital to their economic interests, it is increasingly common for elites to call for reduced spending on human needs that cannot be met by marketplace competition. For example, most low-income communities are of little interest to elites because 'investing' in the human and infrastructure needs within them, such as publicly financed schools, will not produce profits comparable to those in international finance or trade.

Collaboration and the call for cost-effectiveness

In the US and in Western Europe, there appears to be general agreement, with some important exceptions, among elites, and their governmental, trade union and philanthropic gatekeepers (such as elected officials or foundation executives), that communities and workers must learn to do more with less (with notable exceptions like more prisons and police). In many cases, these communities are without sufficient jobs to support families, decent housing, good schools, accessible, quality health care, or safe environments. Nevertheless, elites and their gatekeepers agree that such communities and workers must be convinced that they should not expect increased public or private funding and also be prepared to give up benefits won in the past. Taking their direction from elites, public (federal, state and local government) and private (foundation and corporation) gatekeepers now promote collaboration as the strategy of choice for helping communities and workers adjust to doing more with less. In Sweden, for example, some argue that the Social Democrats (Socialdemokratiska Arbetarpartiet) engage in 'class collaboration' with the wealthy to hold back wage increases and impose cutbacks in public services and workers' benefits (Cohen, 1994). In such cases, which are now quite common for governments, collaboration is used as a primary gatekeeper strategy to ease the pain associated with decreasing benefits and resources for human and infrastructure needs, particularly where there are high concentrations of lower-income people.

Doing more with less requires that communities, organizations and workers must lower their expectations about new funding for services and benefits; that is, they must look for no increases, while working harder to become more cost-effective and productive. In this context, collaboration is described by depoliticized, technical qualities; that is, by its practical usefulness as a cost-effectiveness strategy. Businesses, governments and philanthropic funders are reinforcing this message by increasingly requiring new kinds of 'teamwork' in the workplace and collaboration among service providers. The continuing promotion of doing more with less has become an 'ideology'; an idea on which a system of thinking and acting is based. It is closely related to the call for collaboration as a response to what are described as new, leaner 'economic necessities', many of which result from political decisions and private sector policies reducing resources for human development and community revitalization.

In the US, few organizations engaging in collaboration seem willing to question seriously the power relations through which the doing more with less ideology is being sent. In part, this is because the potential of collaboration for transforming power relations is overwhelmed by funding requirements to engage in 'innovative', very time-consuming and highly complex service change strategies. While these efforts produce small-scale demonstrations of very positive service changes in institutions and communities, they generally leave the status quo in power relations untouched. This is to be expected because transforming power relations is viewed by most public and private funders of collaboration as outside the boundaries of depoliticized change; that is, change that does not raise fundamental questions about or take direct action on issues of power inequities. Indeed, government and philanthropy strongly imply that those receiving service contracts or charity need to abandon political advocacy that could challenge, embarrass or fundamentally alter the status quo.

A bridge from social service to social justice

It is important to acknowledge that many public and social services are essential and are provided in very helpful ways. It is also clear that some services need improvement and can be made available collaboratively and more cost-effectively without damaging quality. Nevertheless, it is essential to look beyond service improvements for the primary purposes of collaborative change efforts. No matter how much services are integrated, organizations are reinvented, or institutions are re-engineered, a focus on services will never be sufficient to address fundamental societal issues: class, race and gender oppression and discrimination. Those using collaborative strategies to resolve these issues must recruit holders and gatekeepers of power into processes that move them, with as little violence as possible, from domination and control to sharing power. In the US, the usefulness of electoral political processes (as a strategy integrated with community-based collaboration) for this purpose is related to the possibilities of fundamental campaign finance and lobbying/special interest reforms (Greider, 1992). For many, the results (or lack thereof) of the US congressional health care reform process in 1994 underscore the need for major campaign finance and lobbying/special interest reforms.

Transformed power relations find elites sharing power with those whom they had historically excluded from governance, democratic institutions and opportunities for self-determination. In some societies, perhaps at this time most clearly in South Africa, there are historic opportunities to transform power relations by bringing representatives of institutions dominated by elites to tables set by representatives of community-based organizations and progressive social movements. At such tables, these representatives can establish a common vision, mutual respect and basis for trusting each other. Once achieving meaningful shared power, partners can then commit to enhancing each other's capacity for mutual benefit and a common purpose by sharing risks, responsibilities, resources and rewards. In this process of 'collaborative empowerment' power relations can be transformed.

In creating the basis for transforming power relations, it is essential to acknowledge fully centres of power that exist in societies other than those dominated by elites or their gatekeepers. Indeed, it is upon these centres – communities, neighbourhoods, villages, workers' organizations and other self-defined associations and constituencies – that collaborative change seeking to transform power relations with elites is being and can be built. The power existing in these centres is based upon indigenous human and physical assets as well as capacities for organized change and problem-solving that can be identified and consciously supported (Barnett, 1993; Dhuly, 1981; Kretzmann and McKnight, 1993; Lappe and DuBois, 1994; Mayer, 1994).

Although building upon assets and capacities in communities is vital for transforming power relations, change strategies must also acknowledge that these same communities also confront serious problems. These include high levels of poverty; very limited employment opportunities, particularly those with wages that can support families; violent crime and drug and physical abuse; and very inadequate housing, schools and health care (Curtis, 1993). It is both foolish and dangerous to say that problem-focused community change is wrong; the problems are real and require the same attention as community capacities. In doing so, a balance can be achieved that acknowledges community problems and links their solutions to community (as well as larger societal) assets and capacities. A part of the struggle to gain a better balance in community change efforts requires that funding sources be convinced to spend as much, if not more, on community organizing and revitalization as they do on human and social service agencies. Such a balance would also require a willingness among those seeking change to address self-imposed powerlessness (surplus power-lessness) based in self-defeating behaviour (Lerner, 1986) as a central requirement for engaging outside institutional power. This can assist community-based organizations to establish ground rules and expectations for mutual accountability.

The use of collaborative strategies to make such changes requires, in addition to strengthening community-based power, the transformation of institutionalized power. This chapter argues that this transformation can happen in collaborative processes among community-based organizations and elite-dominated institutions if such processes are specifically designed to do so. As is the case in successful programme change efforts (Schorr, 1988), transformational collaboration must be highly creative, strategically planned, schoolfellow implemented and continually assessed for lessons learned.

Collaboration defined: a continuum of definitions and strategies

If collaboration is to be a strategically chosen process for transforming power relations, it can be useful to view it in relationship to three other common change strategies – networking, co-ordination and co-operation – that build upon each other along a continuum of complexity and commitment (Himmelman, 1992). *It is important to emphasize that each of these four strategies can be appropriate for particular circumstances depending on the degree to which three limitations to working together – time, trust and turf – can be overcome and a common vision, commitments to share power and responsible and accountable actions are agreed upon.*

Networking is defined as exchanging information for mutual benefit

Networking is the most informal of the inter-organizational linkages and, as a result, can be used most easily. It often reflects an initial level of trust and commitment among organizations and is a very reasonable choice for such circumstances. Networking is best done when connections or linkages between organizations are made person-to-person rather than organization-to-organization. When networking or making a referral, it is clearly more helpful to be able to have a contact person through whom you can get the information required and, as necessary, have a continuing dialogue of mutual benefit.

Example of networking Two organizations meet to share information about their missions, goals, major community programmes, and their respective service areas.

Co-ordination is defined as exchanging information and altering activities for mutual benefit and to achieve a common purpose

Co-ordination requires more organizational involvement than networking and, given the degree to which organizational 'systems' are poorly co-ordinated, it is a very important change strategy. This is particularly true from the point of view of those who find unco-ordinated systems very unfriendly, yet regard services as essential for their well-being. It is clear that our major educational and human service systems were not designed to work the way they do intentionally; it would have taken a genius far beyond known human capacity to make such a mess of conflicting rules, regulations, activities and relationships on purpose. These systems have grown to be the way they are because countless public and private 'refinements' have been piled one on top of another over many years without any overall plan. Needless to say, greater user-friendly co-ordination is much in demand.

Example of co-ordinating Two agencies share information about pro-gramme activities and then decide to change their programme content and schedules in order better to serve their common client or customer service areas.

*Co-operation is defined as exchanging information, altering activities
and sharing resources for mutual benefit and to achieve a common
purpose*

Co-operation requires even greater organizational commitments and, in
some cases, may involve legal arrangements. Shared resources can encompass a variety of human, financial and technical contributions, including
knowledge, staffing, physical property, access to people, money and others.
It is important to emphasize that shared resources be broadly defined and
that those bringing financial resources not be given greater power or
deference in co-operative efforts. For example, a person who shares the
resource of their personal credibility as a basis for gaining access to a
community brings a very valuable resource; often this is far more valuable
than money.

Example of co-operating Two agencies share information about programme activities, decide to change their programme content and schedules
in order to better serve their common client or customer service areas, and
share physical space for programmes and vans for transportation needs.

*Collaboration is defined as exchanging information, altering
activities, sharing resources and enhancing the capacity of another
for mutual benefit and to achieve a common purpose*

Enhancing the capacity of another organization requires sharing risks,
responsibilities, resources and rewards, all of which can increase the potential of collaboration beyond other ways of working together. In this context,
collaboration is a relationship in which each person or organization wants
to help their partners become better at what they do. Some theories of adult
development suggest that considering the other's enhancement in a relationship requires greater maturity and, as such, is more evolved than co-
operation which considers involvement with another primarily for self-
enhancement (Kegan, 1982). In these developmental definitions, collaboration includes networking, co-ordinating and co-operating.

Example of collaborating Two agencies share information about programme activities, decide to change their programme content and schedules
in order better serve their common client or customer service areas, share
physical space for programmes and vans for transportation needs, and offer
a series of staff training workshops to each other in areas in which each
organization has special expertise related to their common purposes.

Collaboration in practice: decision-making, control and ownership

Both research and informal insights from experience suggest that the power
to make decisions and the ownership of any social change process are

among its most important characteristics. There are few more fundamental indicators of whether community initiatives will have long-lasting benefits. Decision-making power and ownership are also a reflection of a community's capacity for self-determination and can be enhanced or limited depending upon how collaboration is designed, implemented and evaluated. In this chapter, ownership relations in collaboration are described in two basic forms: 'collaborative betterment' and 'collaborative empowerment' (Himmelman, 1992). Each form has particular effects on community ownership, self-determination and the long-term sustainability of the collaborative's efforts. Studies on how to 'map' movement along the betterment–empowerment continuum can offer significant insights on ownership in collaborative processes (Sink, 1992).

Collaborative betterment: definition and key principles

Collaborative betterment begins outside the community within public, private or non-profit institutions and is brought into the community. Community involvement is invited into a process designed and controlled by larger institutions. This collaborative strategy can produce policy changes and improvements in programme delivery and services, but tends not to produce long-term ownership in communities or to increase significantly communities' control over their own destinies.

Most collaboratives can be classified as betterment processes. In this way, their processes are similar to those used by large institutions to deliver most human and educational services and community programmes. The collaborative betterment model includes a number of key principles.

- Large and influential institutions initiate problem identification and analysis, primarily within institutional language, frameworks, assumptions and value systems.
- Governance and administration are controlled by institutions, although limited community representation is encouraged in advisory roles. Frequently, groups within the collaborative are intentionally separated to give decision-making roles to those considered in the community's 'leadership' and implementation roles to those providing or receiving services.
- Staff are responsible to institutions and, although they seek advice from target communities, staff are not directly accountable to them.
- Action plans are usually designed with some direct community involvement but normally emphasize the ideas of institutionally related professionals and experts.
- Implementation processes include more community representation and require significant community acceptance, but control of decision-making and resource allocation is not transferred to the community during the implementation phase.
- Although advice from the community is considered, the decision to terminate the collaborative is made by the institutions that initiated it.

Collaborative empowerment: definition and key principles

In this chapter, empowerment is defined as 'the capacity to set priorities and control resources that are essential for increasing community self-determination'. Collaborative empowerment begins within the community and is brought to public, private or non-profit institutions. An empowerment strategy includes two basic activities: (a) organizing a community in support of a collaborative purpose determined by the community; and (b) facilitating a process for integrating outside institutions in support of this community purpose. The empowerment approach can produce policy changes and improvements in programme delivery and services. It is also more likely to produce long-term ownership of the collaborative's purpose, processes and products in communities and to enhance communities' capacity for self-determination.

Key principles of the collaborative empowerment model are as follows:

- The process is initiated by community-based organizations and is assisted by community organizing; early discussions include dialogues about beliefs, motivations and what people want to accomplish as the basis for a community change vision.
- Challenges to be addressed by the community are identified by including both data-based trend analysis and narrative examples from community residents. The latter are given equal credibility in considering options for setting priorities.
- Community priorities are focused in the mission statement of the collaborative. Community-based organizations select representatives who invite, strategically, partners from public, private and non-profit institutions outside the community based on the mission statement created by the community.
- Negotiations with outside agencies and institutions produce agreements to proceed on a collaborative basis based on the mission established by the community, and within a governance and administrative process in which power is equally shared by the community and outside organizations.
- The governance and administrative structure supports a policy council that can serve as the policy advocacy focus, an executive committee to help maintain operational processes, action groups for implementing action plans, and staff agreeable and accountable to the community to assist the collaborative.
- Substantial attention is given to balancing administrative and management continuity with an openness to easily accessible community participation. Emphasis is placed on the recruitment and capacity-building of members; ongoing community organizing is a central characteristic.
- Contributions are sought based on broad definitions of capacities, assets and resources. Non-financial contributions, such as providing access to communities based on personal credibility, and financial contributions

are equally valued. Goals are implemented through action plans supported by community residents as well as by representatives from the public, private and non-profit institutions from outside the community.
- Commitments to ongoing assessment and evaluation in user-friendly formats provide community-based organizations with opportunities for monitoring the progress of the collaborative, both in its processes and products (outcomes).
- Community control of resources needed to continue priority efforts beyond the termination of the collaborative is agreed upon and implemented.

In practice, betterment and empowerment processes exist along a continuum on which they can be seen as approaching or moving away from the characteristics ascribed to them here. Therefore, the processes described above are best used not as mutually exclusive descriptions, but as guides to the consequences of particular methods of collaboration

Transforming betterment to empowerment collaboration

When attempting to transform a betterment collaborative into an empowerment collaborative, it is important to discuss the relationship of collaboration to social change and social justice. As has been discussed previously, empowering communities and neighbourhoods, with the assistance of larger public, private and non-profit institutions, is not simply a matter of using particular organizational or management techniques. This kind of transformation must encourage and respect a diversity of values and beliefs and strongly promote shared power to achieve common purposes. When there is a conscious decision to move from betterment to empowerment, both large institutions and community organizations find themselves challenged to change beliefs and practices.

The transformation of betterment processes into empowerment processes is often quite complicated even if those involved have the best intentions. In large part, this is because institutions transforming a betterment process usually cannot easily secure the confidence and trust of those whom they initially excluded. In addition to overcoming mistrust, the institutions seeking to move toward sharing power and decision-making with community-based organizations also need to redesign their collaborative plans with the active and meaningful participation of community-based organizations. An initial framework for mapping the continuum from betterment to empowerment has been developed to help assess the degree to which power is being transformed in a collaboration process (Sink, 1992).

Transformational collaboration: some constructs for discussion

Those interested in developing a theory and practice of a transformational collaboration will perhaps agree that such a project must be based on constructs that both frame and provide a content basis for debate and discussion. The nine constructs outlined briefly below are offered to stimulate further dialogue about how a theory and practice of transformational collaboration might be developed.

Paradigm change

Paradigm changes fundamentally redefine the conceptual structures through which we know and act upon our knowledge, from things very personal to those considered cosmic (Kuhn, 1970). It is possible that collaboration is central to a significant spiritual, cultural and social paradigm shift that is currently under way (Montuori and Conti, 1993). Perhaps the most obvious paradigm shift involving collaboration is taking place among those for whom information super-highways and global telecommunications systems provide almost unimaginable opportunities. However, as with every new elite technology, cyberspace raises questions about who gets access to it, for what costs and for what purposes. While many would like to see collaborative values and practices influence a paradigm change that would broadly affect basic personal, community and societal beliefs and actions, this will depend on multiple factors, a great many of which are yet to be understood.

Power relations, class disparities and the renewal of democracy

The transformation of existing power relations is closely related to reducing growing disparities between rich and poor as discussed above. Such a transformation through collaborative strategies may be very helpful in a revitalization of democratic institutions and an expansion of democratic communities. Interesting work is being done on the relationship of democracy and community and the importance of community organizing in changing power relations (Brookings Institution, 1994; Etzioni, 1993; McDougall, 1994; Putnam, 1994). In considering democratic renewal, the relationship of the collaborative process to electoral politics needs far more analysis because applying collaborative strategies in competitive electoral arenas poses different challenges than those faced in expanding democratic practices in community problem-solving efforts.

Racism (white privilege) and cultural diversity/inclusiveness

Closely related to the transformation of power relations is the larger context in which race and cultural diversity are fully considered as a central part of collaborative change. These issues should be discussed, debated and better understood and addressed as a result of collaborative change processes. Some excellent examples of how such discussions and practices can take place in collaborative change are now available (Chang et al., 1994) as well as very insightful essays on the nature of the challenges of race and diversity (West, 1993).

Gender differences

Gender differences also need to be acknowledged, understood and fully integrated in well-conducted collaborative processes. Fortunately, a literature has emerged that provides insightful analysis of gender differences in defining and using power, communications, leadership, problem-solving and group dynamics. This literature ranges from highly sophisticated (Eisenstein and Jardine, 1990) to mass consumption (Gray, 1992).

Collaborative change processes led by women, generally, move more quickly to shared power, are characterized by higher levels of creative problem-solving and value human more than financial resources. Collaboratives led by men, generally, are more limited to positional power and authority, focus more on staying within the rules and regulations of existing power structures, and emphasize financial rather than human resources.

Public, private and non-profit sector roles and responsibilities

Multi-sector collaboration implies participation from the public (governmental), private (business and labour) and non-profit sectors (non-governmental, tax-exempt organizations, including foundations and religious organizations). It is very useful to provide time for discussion and debate about the best roles and responsibilities in community change for organizations from these sectors because their histories may, or may not, suggest their most useful futures (Hall, 1987; Knowlton and Zeckhauser, 1986).

Intra-organizational and multi-organizational dynamics and processes

There is a growing awareness that organizations engaging in planned change must become 'learning organizations' (Senge, 1990). However, the depth and quality of intra-organizational change necessary is far from well understood or practised by most organizations working in partnerships. A stronger focus is needed on how large bureaucratic institutions can be fundamentally reformed in collaborative efforts with community-based organizations and, in particular, on how to support 'inside-out' change agents in such bureaucratic institutions. Of particular significance are the resistances within bureaucracies to collaborative change challenging long-standing rules, regulations and the attitudes and behaviours associated with the 'cultures' of bureaucracies. Among the central issues in multi-organizational change is how well such efforts prepare people to access and effectively use changing technologies. As expected, multi-organizational dynamics are the focus of most theorists and practitioners of collaboration and, as noted above, there is a growing, excellent literature available on this topic. This literature includes insightful guides on how to best understand and practise general collaborative processes and on lessons learned from more specific and focused collaboratives (Blank and Melaville, 1993; Bruner, 1991; Loquanti, 1992; Shields, 1994).

Facilitative leadership and group processes and problem-solving

These issues are also central to a theory and practice of transformational collaboration. New work in this area provides excellent insights on the concept of facilitative, collaborative leadership appropriate for the post-industrial world of the next century (Chrislip and Larson, 1994; Rost, 1991). Equally valuable is the literature on group problem-solving (Johnson and Johnson, 1987), which is a central feature of collaborative processes, and practical, 'how-to-do-it' skill-related materials, for example, conducting effective meetings (Doyle and Straus, 1976), and resolving conflict (Herrman, 1994).

Adult development

In this chapter, the definition of collaboration draws upon adult development literature to suggest that a willingness to enhance another must exist for collaboration to take place. In practice, immature, controlling, ego-centred individuals often make a collaborative process very problematic. Establishing ground rules is one method of addressing these concerns (Gray, 1989). Adult development issues suggest that it is important to know to what degree individuals are capable of the mature behaviour associated with collaborative relationships (Kegan, 1982), and, based on this assessment, if they wish to learn how to move beyond ego-centred or destructive interpersonal communications patterns, many of which may be limiting them to immature behaviour (Hendrix, 1988; Lerner, 1986). Some of these issues can be addressed with good conflict resolution training for members in a collaborative without focusing on particular individuals. In some cases, however, it may be necessary to ask very difficult individuals to leave the collaborative if their behaviour threatens to do serious damage to the relationships among other members.

Arts, culture and celebration

It is difficult to imagine the transformation of a community or society without the significant participation of artists, the sharing of cultural traditions and experiments, and the celebration that can be drawn from these central qualities of the human condition. Unfortunately, many community change collaboratives do not substantially integrate arts, culture and celebration into their efforts. Collaboratives are well advised to think carefully about how arts, culture and celebration can become an important characteristic of their ongoing activities. The music, the poem, the story, the painting, the photograph and the play are among the many ways that human beings find connections and integration within themselves and with each other. All such human expression is essential for transforming ourselves, our communities and the world in which all of us share an increasingly common destiny.

Collaborative roles: a range of organizational options

The following are some common collaborative roles. They are not mutually exclusive; one role often leads to or is integrated into another. All the roles can be played to some extent by any organization engaging in collaborative efforts.

Convener Organizations often play the role of community convener on significant issues that may, or may not, result in further community action. The convening role usually includes a highly visible public discussion of community issues. These discussions are often related to data-gathering or studies which provide information intended to highlight a common understanding of the issues at hand. Such discussions are important prerequisites for collaborative community problem-solving.

Catalyst Organizations may use the convening role to stimulate discussion with a longer-term strategy in mind. When an organization is catalytic, it makes an early and clear commitment to participate in longer-term community problem-solving that begins with an initial discussion of issues. In this way, it uses its influence and resource base to make the collaborative initiative 'real' in the minds of various other potential partners who may be waiting for leadership before making commitments to an action agenda.

Conduit Organizations may serve as conduits for funding that is essential for collaborative action. For example, many federal grants require a particular organization to be the 'lead agency' in providing grants for local collaborative initiatives. A similar situation occurs when foundations make grants with the condition that an agency be a lead partner. This stipulation can be very problematic, however, if the conduit role appears to be, or is in fact, a way for an organization to dominate a collaborative process because of its fiscal role. This can result in conflicts related to power on the surface and to trust as a deeper undercurrent.

Advocate Some partners view their primary role as advocacy, either for individuals or groups that are the primary focus of the collaborative's activities and/or for policy and systems change proposals that emerge from the collaborative. Partners that play this role may be viewed as problematic by other partners in a collaborative and, therefore, it is helpful to develop frameworks and internal processes within which advocacy efforts can emerge with support from as many partners as possible. In general, it can be argued that any collaborative seeking systems change would have to have commitments from its partners to play an advocacy role. Without such advocacy, collaboratives would be limited to data gathering, public education and programme or service innovation change strategies.

Community organizer   Partners may include community organizing among their contributions to collaboratives. In this role, partners have a primary interest in paying attention to who is at the decision-making table and, in particular, how those who are traditionally excluded from decision-making are included as full partners. A community organizing role often includes the ongoing recruitment, welcoming and sustaining of participation by community-based, neighbourhood-based and constituency-based organizations and individuals.

Funder   Some organizations may wish to encourage a variety of collaborative activities by being a funder, either alone or with other funding sources. This is an increasingly common practice but, again, one with complexities. Many recipients of such funding find that funders – public and private – fail to understand that a collaborative is more than a proposal to which many organizations attach letters of endorsement. What must be made clear is that it takes time for organizations to create a well-designed, mutually respectful and trusting collaborative; unfortunately, funders often do not fully appreciate the time required for these characteristics to emerge, and as a consquence, expect substantial results before the collaborative has fully formed.

Technical assistance provider   Many organizations have substantial human and technical resources which can be made available in creating and sustaining collaborative efforts. These resources include, among others, data retrieval, new research and information-gathering, planning expertise, meeting space, legal opinions, other specific expertise on a wide variety of subjects, access to information and assistance in preparing funding applications, and lobbying assistance. Organizations do not have to be a highly visible or formal partner in collaborative efforts to provide many kinds of technical assistance.

Capacity-builder – building on assets   Capacity-building is usually part of a longer-term strategy to increase the ability of community and neighbourhood-based organizations to initiate and effectively follow through on problem-solving processes that, to a large extent, community- and neighbourhood-based organizations determine for themselves. Capacity-building is a primary goal of a local government that chooses to encourage empowerment, rather than betterment, strategies. Capacity-building can take many forms but usually includes:

1   acknowledging community assets and the important contributions all partners can make;
2   inquiring about and, whenever possible, providing specific requested skill-development opportunities for those interested;
3   being honest and open about motivations and being realistic about what can and cannot be provided in what amount of time;

4   facilitating user-friendly access to resources that normally may be restricted to those only with power, status, or money;

5   sharing risks when others may find themselves in situations perceived to be dangerous or threatening to their well-being.

In a collaborative empowerment strategy, larger public and private institutions are not afraid of increasing the power of communities and neighbourhoods in relation to power based in city hall or corporate power structures. To the contrary: a capacity-building strategy proclaims that the primary task of the power structure is to increase power-sharing and community ownership rather than to retain power as a method of control.

Partner   This would appear to be the most obvious role in a collaborative but, as has been noted, the way that this role is played greatly affects the quality of the collaborative process and the likely outcomes of its activities. When large institutions play a partner role as part of a betterment strategy, they may find the collaborative has made progress on key community issues. However, given the limitations of a betterment collaboration for fully sharing the ownership of activities and outcomes with smaller organizations, institutional partners may also find this role contributing to only short-term successes. The sustainability of the betterment effort among those most affected by an initiative is usually very difficult. Indeed, a collaborative with relatively little power-sharing can elicit strong opposition or meet apathetic responses or both.

As has been noted, empowering partners share risks, responsibilities, resources and rewards in collaborative efforts. They establish mutually respectful, trusting relationships, take the time to understand each other's motivations and hoped-for accomplishments, and state problems in a manner that provides opportunities for others to share in their solutions.

Facilitator   In this role, an organization attempts to help make collaborative, community problem-solving efforts among non-profit, government, business, labour, religious, academic and other organizations possible and effective. This can be difficult when an organization is a key partner because the facilitator role may be perceived as another way of adding greater decision-making authority to the organization's partner role. When it works well, however, facilitation is valued as a source of fairness, encouragement and as a resource to all those who might need it in the collaborative process.

A user-friendly guide to the collaborative process

The following guide is offered in order to demonstrate how the concepts and ideas described in this chapter can be useful in actual practice. The guide, which can be considered as an introduction to designing a collaborative, draws both from these concepts and ideas and on extensive participant–observer research of many collaborative change processes. The guide is best used by small groups which answer its questions based on either possible or existing collaborative initiatives. The guide can be useful to complete on an occasional basis to see how its questions are answered over time, as a measure of progress.

Design step 1 (1a) Should your organization participate in a collaborative initiative? (1b) What costs and benefits are involved in this decision? (1c) How well prepared is your organization to be a quality partner in a collaborative; for example, has it allocated the time and other resources necessary to participate fully?

Design step 2 What is your vision? Before beginning your discussion, please interview each other for five minutes, in teams of two, by asking your partner the following questions and then reversing the interview: (2a) What motivates you to be involved in your collaborative initiative? (2b) What do you most want to accomplish through your involvement? After the interviews, take some time so that those who wish to can tell the group the name of the person they interviewed, and what they learned about that person's motivations and about their hoped-for accomplishments. After these presentations, please discuss the vision you have as a group for your collaborative and describe it in writing.

Design step 3 (3a) Who is currently involved in your collaborative? (3b) Are those who will be most affected by your collaborative involved at this time? (3c) Who else should be involved? (3d) How will you involve them? (3e) How could community organizing become a central method of ensuring the participation of those traditionally excluded from decision-making?

Design step 4 (4a) What expectations should you have for each other? (4b) What are some basic ground rules you have, or wish to have, for participating partners?

Design step 5 A mission statement can be defined as a simple, clear statement of purpose that is also a call to action. What is the mission statement of your collaborative?

Design step 6 (6a) What are the goals and objectives of your collaborative? (6b) If you have not formulated them, please discuss possible goals and objectives and write them below (a goal is a long-term guide to and measure of progress on achieving a mission; an objective is a short-term (often annual) activity to implement a goal and from which progress toward achieving a goal can be measured).

Design step 7 (7a) Who will get the work done? (7b) How can you link specific individuals and organizations to the specific objectives you have identified above to ensure that the objectives will be carried out in a timely manner?

Design step 8 (8a) What do you know about other collaborative efforts that have worked on a similar mission and goals? (8b) What are some key lessons your collaborative can learn from these efforts?

Design step 9 What can each partner contribute to the collaborative? In making this inventory, please remember that it can include a wide variety of financial and non-financial contributions. For example, a partner who brings credibility with and access to community residents adds something as valuable as any financial contribution.

Design step 10 (10a) How does the collaborative identify and encourage new members to participate? (10b) How well are new members informed about the roles, responsibilities and rewards of participation? (10c) How well do new members reflect the diversity of the communities that the collaborative serves?

Design step 11 (11a) What are some incentives and rewards that can be used to recognize and sustain (11b) partners' contributions to the collaborative and (11c) changes they make in their own organization's policies and practices that are consistent with the collaborative's vision, mission and goals?

Design step 12 (12a) How is your collaborative governed – who makes decisions and what authority do they have to make them? (12b) How will governing responsibilities be rotated over time? (12c) How will governance reflect and respect the collaborative's diversity?

Design step 13 (13a) How effective is your leadership? (13b) Who is providing leadership for your collaborative? (13c) How adequate is the leadership team? (13d) What might be done to improve it or better support it? (13e) How is new leadership identified and rotated into key positions? (13f) What expectations do you have for the collaborative's leadership?

Design step 14 (14a) How is your collaborative administered and managed? (14b) Are the arrangements adequate? (14c) If not, what could you do to improve the administration and management of your collaborative?

Design step 15 (15a) How are staff provided for your collaborative? (15b) How are the staff accountable to the collaborative? (15c) If staff are being donated by a partner or partners, what, if any, challenges does this arrangement present?

Design step 16   (16a) What barriers or conflicts make progress difficult? (16b) How can such barriers and conflicts be resolved or overcome?

Design step 17   (17a) How does the collaborative offer training for its members in areas such as group process, conflict resolution and cultural diversity and inclusiveness? (17b) How can this training be most helpful in addressing and resolving important issues?

Design step 18   (18a) How will people find out about your activities? (18b) How will you publicize your activities and provide effective community education and information about the work of the collaborative? (18c) How well can you inform and engage people, organizations and communities that represent diverse cultural and ethnic interests or for whom English is not their first language? (18d) Do you communicate well and regularly with grass-roots groups and organizations?

Design step 19   (19a) How much money do you need and how will you secure it in a timely manner? (19b) What kinds of funding sources will be necessary if you are to be successful? (19c) Is there a written financial plan and a clear strategy with identified responsibilities for implementing it? (19d) Has the collaborative made certain that the organization through which funding flows does not have greater decision-making authority in the collaborative simply because of this fiscal management role?

Design step 20   (20a) How will you monitor progress and evaluate the overall success of your collaborative? (20b) How can you monitor and evaluate both the products/results and the processes of your collaborative? (20c) How can your evaluations be used by the collaborative to make changes in the collaborative's processes based on the findings of such evaluations?

Closing comment

The seriousness of the challenges facing societies seeking peacefully to transform power relations and create far more humane and equitable communities cannot be underestimated. It is fair to say, given the irrational needs of dominant power structures to limit and control progressive social change, that it is unlikely that such transformations can occur in the foreseeable future. Nevertheless, acting on hope in spite of what is known, rather than because of what is known, is part of accepting responsibility in societies that breed widespread despair. Either we find ways to struggle for social justice together or, isolated, we will become, as the great poet Langston Hughes said, 'like a dream deferred . . . like a raisin in the sun'.

References

Barlett, Donald L. and Steele, James B. (1992) *America: What Went Wrong?* Kansas City: Andrews and McMeel.

Barlett, Donald L. and Steele, James B. (1994) *America: Who Really Pays the Taxes?* New York: Simon & Schuster.

Barnett, Kevin (1993) 'Collaboration for community empowerment: re-defining the role of academic institutions, developing new partnerships to improve community quality of life'. Berkeley, CA: Center for Community Health, School of Public Health, University of California.

Blank, Martin J. and Lombardi, J. (1992) 'Toward improved services for children and families: forging new relationships through collaboration'. Washington, DC: Institute for Educational Leadership.

Blank, Martin J. and Melaville, Atelia (1993) 'Together we can: a guide for crafting a profamily system of education and human services'. Washington, DC: US Department of Education/Office of Educational Research and Improvement.

Brookings Institution (1994) 'The rebirth of urban democracy'. Washington, DC: Brookings Institution.

Bruner, Charles (1991) 'Thinking collaboratively: ten questions and answers to help policy-makers improve children's services'. Washington, DC: Education and Human Services Consortium.

Chang, Hedy, Salazar, Denise and Leong, Cecilia (1994) 'Drawing strength from diversity: effective services for children, youth, and families'. San Francisco: California Tomorrow.

Chrislip, David D. and Larson, Carl E. (1994) *Collaborative Leadership: How Citizens and Civic Leaders Can Make a Difference.* San Francisco: Jossey Bass.

Cohen, Peter (1994) 'Sweden: the model that never was', *Monthly Review*, July–August: 41–9.

Curtis, Lynn A. (1993) 'Investing in children and youth, reconstructing our cities: doing what works to reverse the betrayal of American democracy'. Washington, DC: The Milton S. Eisenhower Foundation.

Dhuly, Milan J. (1981) *Changing the System: Political Advocacy for Disadvantaged Groups.* London: Sage.

Domhoff, G. William (1983) *Who Rules America Now?* New York: Simon & Schuster.

Doyle, Michael and Straus, David (1976) *How To Make Meetings Work.* New York: Jove Books.

Eisenstein, Hester and Jardine, Alice (eds) (1990) *The Future of Difference.* New Brunswick: Rutgers University Press.

Etzioni, Amitai (1993) *The Spirit of Community.* New York: Crown Publishers.

Goldsmith, William W. and Blakely, Edward J. (1992) *Separate Societies: Poverty and Inequality in US Cities.* Philadelphia: Temple University Press.

Gray, Barbara (1989) *Collaborating: Finding Common Ground for Multiparty Problems.* San Francisco: Jossey Bass.

Gray, John (1992) *Men Are From Mars – Women Are From Venus.* New York: Harper Collins.

Greider, William (1992) *Who Will Tell the People? The Betrayal of American Democracy.* New York: Simon & Schuster.

Hartsock, Nancy C.M. (1985) *Money, Sex, and Power: Toward A Feminist Historical Materialism.* Boston, MA: Northeastern University Press.

Hall, Peter Dobkin (1987) 'An overview of the nonprofit sector', in Walter W. Powell (ed.), *The Nonprofit Sector: a Research Handbook.* New Haven, CT: Yale University Press. pp. 3–26.

Hendrix, Harville (1988) *Getting the Love You Want.* New York: Harper Perennial.

Herrman, Margaret (ed.) (1994) 'Resolving conflict: strategies for local government'. Washington, DC: International City/County Management Association.

42   *Creating collaborative advantage*

Himmelman, Arthur Turovh (1992) *Communities Working Collaboratively for a Change.* Minneapolis, MN: The Himmelman Consulting Group.

Huxham, Chris (1993) 'Pursuing collaborative advantage', *Journal of the Operational Research Society*, 44 (6): 599–611.

IEL (1993) Bibliography in 'Developing collaborative leaders'. Washington, DC: Institute for Educational Leadership.

Johnson, David W. and Johnson, Frank P. (1987) *Joining Together: Group Theory and Group Skills*, 3rd edn. Englewood Cliffs, NJ: Prentice Hall.

Kagan, Sharon L., Rivera, Ann Marie, Brighman, Nancy and Rosenblum, Sheila (1993) 'Collaboration: cornerstone of an early childhood system'. New Haven, CT: Yale University Press.

Kanter, Rosabeth Moss (1994) 'Collaborative advantage: the art of alliances', *Harvard Business Review*, July–August, 96–108.

Katz, Wallace (1993) 'The new local–global cosmopolitanism, or prolegomena to a politics of post-industrialism', *Aesthetik und Kommunikation*, April, 16–24.

Kegan, Robert (1982) *The Evolving Self.* London: Harvard University Press.

Knowlton, Winthrop and Zeckhauser, Richard (1986) *American Society: Public and Private Responsibilities.* Cambridge, MA: Ballinger.

Kretzmann, John and McKnight, John (1993) *Building Communities from the Inside Out.* Evanston, IL: Northwestern University Press.

Kuhn, Thomas (1970) *The Structure of Scientific Revolutions.* Chicago: Chicago University Press.

Lappe, Frances Moore and DuBois, Paul Martin (1994) *The Quickening of America.* San Francisco: Jossey Bass.

Lerner, Michael (1986) 'Surplus powerlessness'. Oakland, CA: The Institute for Labor and Mental Health.

Loquanti, R. (1992) 'Using community-wide collaboration to foster resiliency in kids: a conceptual framework'. Oak Brook, IL: Midwest Regional Center for Drug-Free Schools and Communities.

Mayer, Steven E. (1994) 'Building community capacity: the potential for community foundations'. Minneapolis: Rainbow Research Inc.

McDougall, Harold (1994) *Black Baltimore: a New Theory of Community.* Philadelphia: Temple University Press.

Mills, C. Wright (1956) *The Power Elite.* Oxford: Oxford University Press.

Montuori, Alfonso and Conti, Isabella (1993) *From Power to Partnership.* San Francisco: Harper.

NCSI (1993) 'Service integration: an annotated bibliography'. New York: National Center for Service Integration, c/o Columbia University.

Phillips, Kevin (1992) *The Politics of Rich and Poor.* New York: Harper Perennial.

Phillips, Kevin (1994) *Arrogant Capital: Washington, Wall Street and the Frustration of American Politics.* Boston, MA: Little Brown.

Potapchuk, William R. and Polk, Caroline G. (1992) 'Building the collaborative community: a select bibliography for community leaders'. Washington, DC: Program for Community Problem Solving.

Potapchuk, William R. and Polk, Caroline G. (1993) 'Building the collaborative community'. Washington, DC: National Institute for Dispute Resolution.

Putnam, Robert (1994) *Making Democracy Work.* Princeton, NJ: Princeton University Press.

Rosenthal, Beth and Mizrahi, T. (1994) 'Strategic partnerships: how to create and maintain interorganizational collaborations and coalitions'. New York: Education Center for Community Organizing. (Also numerous training materials and bibliography.)

Rost, Joseph (1991) *Leadership in the Twenty-First Century.* New York: Praeger.

Schorr, Lisbeth B. (1988) *Within Our Reach: Breaking the Cycle of Disadvantage.* New York: Anchor Press Doubleday.

Senge, Peter M. (1990) *The Fifth Discipline: the Art and Practice of the Learning Organization.* New York: Doubleday.

Shields, Katrina (1994) *In the Tiger's Mouth: an Empowerment Guide to Social Action.* Philadelphia: New Society Publishers.

Sink, David (1992) 'Empowering the community to prevent youth violence: a case study of Little Rock, Arkansas'. Working Paper, University of Alabama.

Sweezy, Paul. (1994) 'The triumph of financial capital', *New York: Monthly Review Press,* June, 1–11.

Webster (1970) *Webster's New World Dictionary of the American Language*: 2nd College Edition. New York: The World Publishing Company.

West, Cornell. (1993) *Race Matters.* Boston: Beacon Press.

Wolff, Thomas. (1994) 'Coalition building: one path toward empowered communities'. AHEC Health and Human Service Coalitions, Amherst, MA. (Also numerous other publications and training materials.)

3

The Stakeholder/Collaborator Strategy Workshop

Colin Eden

Background

About four years ago a colleague (Fran Ackermann) and I were invited to help the Northern Ireland Prison Service develop a new strategy. The prison service is a part of the Northern Ireland Office and was seen as a critical part of any attempts to develop a strategy for Northern Ireland. The prison service was unlike any other in the world – it housed mostly political prisoners who were often members of para-military groups. Many of the prisoners were senior officers of these groups and consequently many terrorist strategies were presumed to have emanated from the prisons of Northern Ireland. The number of what are known as 'ordinary decent criminals' (ODCs) housed in the prisons was very small (indeed the reported crime rate in the province is very low). This context meant that the ability of the Prison Service properly to manage security issues, segregation issues and effective prison regimes was taken to be crucial to maintaining order and encouraging peace in the province. The well-known disturbances from prisoners in the 'H-blocks' of the Maze prison (what used to be called 'Long Kesh') stick in the memory of all sides in the Northern Ireland conflict.

The strategy development process used an adaptation of the SODA strategic problem-solving process (Eden, 1989, 1993). The process was designed to respond to a commitment from the Chief Executive for high levels of real participation from all levels of staff in the Service in the process of developing the strategy. The process involved workshops with the senior management team of prison governors and senior civil servants and a series of internal strategy development workshops involving just under 200 staff. As a designed part of all these workshops (each involving about 20 staff) one of the tasks was that of deliberately exploring the relationship between the Service and important stakeholders in its future. Each workshop was split into two work groups of ten staff and membership of the groups was interchanged throughout the day. Each group extended and analysed the work of the alternate group.

Using a mix of nominal group techniques (Delbecq et al., 1975), computer based facilitation (Eden and Ackermann, 1992), and carefully designed problem structuring tools ('Cognitive Mapping' – see Eden, 1988), each staff member was assured of extensive participation and comment. During the workshop, each group of participants was asked to identify the stakeholders that might affect the strategic future of the service and of the province as it is affected by the service. Subsequently they focused on a small number of them that were assumed to be key. The consequential 'role think' exercises (Huxham and Eden, 1990) and formal analysis of stake-holders' relations one to another as potential coalitions or collaboratives are the focus of this chapter.

In particular this chapter describes the approach taken to conceptualizing and so identifying stakeholders and their potential for collaborating with the Service in such a way as to promote **collaborative advantage** (Huxham with Macdonald, 1992).

A framework for thinking about stakeholders

An important task in developing a robust strategy for an organization is that of 'stakeholder analysis' (Freeman, 1984). Freeman claims that the term originates from the work of the Stanford Research Institute and meant 'stockholder' – those groups without whose support the organization would cease to exist. The SRI approach sought to develop 'measures of satisfaction' for these stakeholders within the context of environmental scanning. Others rejected this notion in favour of stakeholders being seen as constraints. The difference between the two approaches is that one sees them as interfering and the other as being responsible for their welfare (paternalistic at best!). However, these approaches were oriented to seeing stakeholders at the generic level in order to produce better forecasts. There was no concern with changing stakeholder behaviour, rather just fore-casting it.

This was in contrast to seeing stakeholders as potential *actors* – people or small groups with the power to respond and change the future. These ideas did not see stakeholder interactions as dynamic and interactive. Neither did they emphasize a conflict perspective of 'win/lose'. In particu-lar, specific interest groups who see a role for negotiation had no place. Thus the notion that negotiations take place with someone rather than a reified entity was not encompassed.

Nevertheless, 'Systems/Operational Research' people (particularly Ackoff, 1970) argued for a systems view of strategy. Ackoff specifically argued that many societal problems could be solved by the redesign of fundamental institutions *with the support and interaction of the stakeholders in the system*. The notion of 'stakeholders in the system' differed from the approach in the strategy literature. In essence it argued for more co-operative activity and assumed common value systems (in particular between, for example, the 'poor' and 'capitalists'). This view was particularly represented by Ackoff's book *Redesigning the Future* (1974), which encompassed some radical proposals for participative organizations.

This brief history of stakeholder analysis provides a backdrop to the process of analysis for the purpose of exploring potential coalitions and collaboratives. While not advocating the approach taken by Ackoff we shall be recognizing the potential for managing stakeholders in a proactive but highly focused manner.

In undertaking stakeholder analysis it is usual to focus our attention upon a vast array of actors who have an interest (stake) in the strategic future of the organization, whether or not they have power in relation to the organization. Indeed stakeholder analysts often make a plea for the specific inclusion of disadvantaged and powerless groups, the analysis being driven by a value-laden, rather than utilitarian, view of the role of the stakeholder analysis (see, for example, Ackoff, 1974) comparable to that advocated by Himmelman in the preceding chapter. When collaboratives are being formed these issues are of particular significance to resolving the issues relating to 'who is expected to come to the table' and 'who is to be invited to the table', which are discussed by Finn in Chapter 10.

By contrast, our own concern with stakeholder analysis has a more utilitarian aim; that of identifying stakeholders who will, or can be per- suaded to, *support* actively the strategic intent of the organization. We are concerned with those who will seek to *sabotage* the successful management of our strategic intent as well as provide support. In particular the analysis considers the possibility of enacting a particular strategic intent which would have the consequence of encouraging the formation of *coalitions* amongst those stakeholders who have little power into a collaborative grouping with significant power. In this sense stakeholder analysis is focused on identifying strategic and tactical options that arise for the organization itself by anticipating the dynamics of stakeholder attitudes and actions. In the work discussed here, with the Northern Ireland Office, we were concerned specifically with exploring the ways in which apparently powerless groups might build a coalition with the media and others so that they could increase their power to sabotage the strategic intent of the Northern Ireland Prison Service.

Thinking about stakeholders

To help conceptualize the relationship between different types of stake- holder, and so think productively about stakeholders, we have found that it is helpful to categorize according to the following two dimensions:

- Their **interest** in the strategic activity of the specific strategy-making organization.
- Their **power** to influence the achievement of the strategic intent.

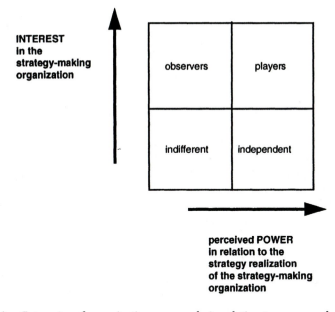

INTEREST
in the
strategy-making
organization

observers	players
indifferent	independent

perceived POWER
in relation to the
strategy realization
of the strategy-making
organization

Figure 3.1   *Categories of organizations or people in relation to power and interest*

Thus Figure 3.1 characterizes the mode of behaviour of other organizations or people in relation to the interest and power:

● Those in an **indifferent** mode are characterized, on the one hand, by a minimal interest in the strategic future of the organization and, on the other hand, by a lack (or perceived lack) of power to influence that future.

● An opposite to the indifferent mode, those in a **playing** mode have a clear interest in the strategic behaviour of the organization and are capable of taking action to hinder or help the organization promote their objectives. Indeed they will often have goals compatible with or in direct conflict with those of the organization. Some of their **power** derives from their concentrated interest in the organization rather than from any 'objective' power.

● Those in an **observing** mode have a clear interest in the strategy-making organization but lack (or see themselves as lacking) the power required to influence the outcome of that strategy. As we see later, those in observing mode will seek the power to become players. Sometimes it becomes a part of the deliberate strategic management of stakeholders to help some observers gain power by, for example, contriving to facilitate the formation of a coalition or collaborative.

● Those in an **independent** mode have no interest in the strategy-making organization but do have the power to influence the success of the strategy-making.

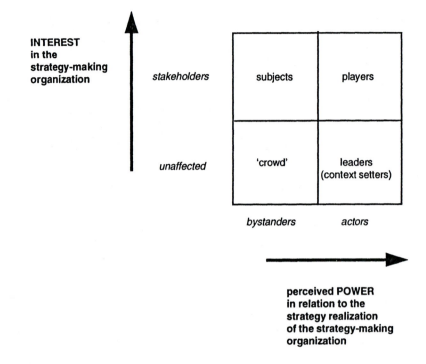

Figure 3.2   *Categories of organizations or people in relation to stakeholder analysis and collaborative formation*

Clearly there are two important ways of constructing the graph: (a) on the basis of an evaluation made by the strategy-making organization of the potential power of others to influence; and (b) on the basis of an estimate of the potential power the organization, person or group being evaluated believes they have.

This conceptualization of stakeholders can usefully be expanded to describe the nature of the rows and columns in the matrix. In Figure 3.2, interested observers, or the **subjects** of strategy, and **players** are **stakeholders**. **Actors**, who have the power to act in a way which has an impact on the future of the strategy-making organization, are both **players** and independents or **leaders/context setters**. Without other considerations, an organization must, at least, pay attention to all **actors**. Those actors who are also stakeholders are those who will respond to the strategies declared – to this extent they can be manipulated by the organization and also may, on their part, seek to manipulate the organization.

Leaders are to be treated as a part of the environment – they can significantly influence the organization but do not do so with intent, similarly they will not see, hear, care about, or respond to strategies implemented by the organization. **Leaders** are 'independent' actors who can fundamentally affect the context within which the strategy must work and yet have no stake in the organization, but they are largely uncontrollable by the strategy-making organization and so need to be treated as a part of possible futures. In the Northern Ireland situation, the US population supporting the provisional IRA with funds had no interest in the prison service and yet could significantly affect the work of the service. In exploring collaboration and seeking to attain collaborative advantage it is the players and subjects who are of interest. For the most part the unaffected bystanders – **crowd** – are unimportant for stakeholder analysis, unless they can be encouraged to become interested and powerful.

For private sector organizations the actor–stakeholders (**players**) will be the primary focus of attention. However, in the public sector there are likely to be public service values which focus attention on stakeholders who are both subjects and players. Indeed it is one of the important roles of strategy-making in the public sector that the identification of subjects as important and valued stakeholders will imply the construction and implementation of strategies to empower subjects so that they become players.

The creation, and implementation of, strategies to help form coalitions of subjects and so give them power to support the organization is an important part of stakeholder management. Vice-versa, the disempowerment of players who are destructive to the goals of the organization is also important. Our experience in strategy-making for the Northern Ireland Office provided an example of the first of these almost occurring unintentionally. As we considered a possible strategy we became aware that the wives and families of para-military prisoners would respond to the strategy by developing a coalition with the media. We had judged wives of prisoners to be subjects with a very high level of interest in the strategy of the Prison Service but little power or influence to affect its strategic future. By jerking them to life through imagined implementation of a particular strategy we were enabling them to gain enough power to become players. And yet, they are a possible member of what could become another powerful collaborative who might gain power, move from the top left of Figure 3.2 to the top right, and support the goals of the Prison Service.

The reason for categorizing organizations and people in these ways is that:

1   It helps to narrow a very large number of possible organizations and people down to those of significance in strategy-making. Without such a tool, strategy analysts, and management teams, are likely to generate a list of potential stakeholders and actors which is too long to be helpful.
2   It clarifies those who have the power to ruin or support the intent of the strategy-making organization (actors: players and leaders), and those who have a stake in the organization (stakeholders: subjects and players).
3   It suggests categories which inform a traditional stakeholder analysis

(players), and those which need to be encompassed in an environmental analysis (leaders) because their behaviour may be forecast but
not influenced.
4   It suggests a framework for understanding the changing nature over
time of those in each of the categories; thus suggesting, in its own right,
a developing scenario.
5   It indicates the way in which the strategy-making organization may
consider strategic action to shift subjects to become players (and vice-
versa), and shift leaders to become players, for example through
encouraging the formation of coalitions and collaboratives, and
encouraging their destruction or re-focusing.

Thus, for example, we expect 'players' to act deliberately to sabotage or
support the strategies the organization seeks to play out, whereas we expect
the success or failure of the strategies to be significantly influenced by the
behaviour of 'leaders'. Thus a possible act by the strategy-making organization might be to move, for example, the media from being a 'leader' to
'player' when they can be convinced that those defined as 'subjects' (who
have a stake in the organization) are media consumers. If the media is
defined as a leader, in this way, then they have been taken to have the
power significantly, but unintentionally, to influence the strategic success of
the organization.

Of interest in this chapter is the extent to which strategy-makers may
also deliberately attempt to gain **collaborative advantage** by encouraging
subjects to form themselves into a coalition, and so gain enough power to
be defined as collaborating players. Sometimes an appropriate strategic
action can be to find ways of reducing the power of a coalition, who are the
'players', so that they are broken into a number of 'subjects' – so
successfully managing a 'divide and rule' policy.

Following the categorization of stakeholders in the above manner, the
influence network expected to exist between key stakeholders is usually
modelled. This process involves converting the matrix of Figure 3.2 into
a network of arrows where each arrow represents the likelihood of a
coalition. Thus an arrow from, for example, subject X to player Y implies
that X has the ability to influence the thinking and actions of Y. The
overall picture will suggest which stakeholders are key to the dynamic
response of stakeholders to particular strategies.

In addition we usually encourage the testing of potential strategies by
conducting 'role think' (Huxham and Eden, 1990) exercises. During these
exercises members of the management team are encouraged to step into the
roles of a number of players, in turn. They attempt to think about what the
proposed strategy looks like from the point of view of the player and to
determine how they will respond. The role think will consider responses in
the light of the influence network. Thus a player might respond by seeking
to build a coalition of subjects and other players to sabotage the proposed
strategy.

Stakeholders as collaborators? The stakeholder workshop

All of the above analyses had been conducted by members of the management team in the Prison Service. A conversation with the Chief Executive about these analyses led to the suggestion that a strategy workshop *with* some of these stakeholders (both players and subjects) could achieve a number of useful outcomes. In particular, involving those who had been identified by the network analysis as **potential collaborators** would provide them with a chance to participate in the development of the strategy, to express a view about their own and others' reaction to some strategic options, and for them to begin to see themselves as potential collaborators. In addition, it would provide an opportunity for stakeholders with extensive experience of working with the Service to evaluate the potential problems the Service might face in enacting strategic change. Thus involving key stakeholders, as potential collaborators, in a replay of the workshops conducted internally was seen as one way of beginning to implement one of the emerging strategies related to better stakeholder management.

Clearly many important stakeholders could not be invited to join such a workshop (for example, those designated as terrorists!), but others who potentially could act as individuals to represent their organization in support or against the strategy could be invited. In every case, those invited were seen as having the opportunity to identify with strategies for the Service which could also help them. In particular, the 'role think' episodes had shown that collaboration between these stakeholders could create outcomes that each would want, but which none could achieve on their own.

The stakeholders invited were an interesting 'mixed bunch': representatives of both churches (Catholic and Protestant) who had regular interactions with the prisons; the Chief Probation Officer; two senior staff from the Northern Ireland Association for the Care and Rehabilitation of Offenders; the Chief Medical Officer and Chief Nursing Officer; the Northern Ireland Chairman of the Prison Officers Association (their trade union); someone to represent the prisoners' relatives (from the Quakers organization); the secretary of the Prison Governors' Association (their trade union); two representatives from the Board of Visitors (an organization with responsibility to 'inspect' prisons); and a senior civil servant from the Northern Ireland Office 'treasury'. The Permanent Secretary for the Northern Ireland Office had hoped to attend but other business meant he could not.

The workshop was seen as exceedingly important to our strategy development process. It could generate important different perspectives and create the potential for strategic collaboration. The 'role think' episodes which had been a regular part of the internal workshops had suggested that these stakeholders could gain significant power to sabotage as a result of gaining an insight into the strategies of the Service.

Several senior civil servants, as well as Fran Ackermann and I, had been wary of the idea – was there a security risk in having all these people in the same place at the same time? Would any of them selectively leak to the media (identified as a possibility in the 'role think')? Would the hidden agendas of the stakeholders, and their own conception of a 'meta-strategy' (Huxham with MacDonald, 1992; Vangen et al., 1994) for the potential collaborative, generate unmanageable conflict? Some of the individuals did not get on together – would their history nullify any of the objectives the workshop was designed to meet? The culture of each of the organizations was significantly different – would it be possible for them to work together for one day only, or would it need two days to warm them up? Even if they agreed to attend would they actually turn up? Would some of them (such as the Probation Service) see the event as a clever 'trick' for the Prison Service to become dominant?

However, the Chief Executive became increasingly committed to the idea. A hotel was booked and Fran and I (as facilitators) were asked to tailor the design of previous workshops to meet the agreed objectives.

Issues in designing a 'collaborator' workshop

Early discussion about the design had suggested that it would be appropriate to replicate the principles of the other workshops so that the stakeholder participants could see themselves as significant as internal staff. There was a need to recognize that new perspectives were required. In the internal workshops staff had been prompted in their initial thinking about the strategic issues facing the organization. These 'triggers' to the debate had been the particular issues surfaced by the senior management team in which they had thought staff contributions could be helpful. Staff had been invited to respond to the 'triggers' if they so wished but were also given clear instructions that these were only to prompt discussion if participants felt they were important also. In this way the management team had some power to set the agenda, but not overwhelmingly so. Staff responded to triggers by building up a 'picture-on-the-wall' (Ackermann, 1992; Schnelle, 1979) of their own views. This picture was made up of elliptical cards which were written on by participants and organized in relation to one another so as to create a structure of issues, where each ellipse related to others and each cluster of ellipses related to other clusters.

For the 'stakeholder workshop' the process was similar. The process sought to provide all participants with plenty of chances to influence proceedings without the normal necessary social skills demanded of such workshops. Given the mix of skills, verbal and social, it was important to give all participants a chance to air their own views. Once again we used a set of 'triggers' to start the initial 'picture on the wall'; these were selected to encourage views divergent from those that were currently framing the developing strategy.

The purpose of selecting particular triggers was to encourage deliberately alternative views of the strategic issues facing the organization. We were keen to open the mindset of the organization to conflicting views. In addition the normal role think exercise we had used in staff workshops was seen as potentially a source of new perspectives on the stakeholders. This would exploit the views of participants as *real stakeholders*.

These considerations of developing alternative perspectives resulted in an interesting, and worthwhile, debate between Fran and myself, and our internal facilitator team (or 'partners' – Bryson and Roering, 1988). Fran and I had always envisaged many alternative and contrary ways of understanding the role of the Northern Ireland Prison Service from the perspective of other stakeholders, and yet each of these seemed implausible to others integrally involved with the Service. The 'world-taken-for-granted' of members of staff in an organization is always, by definition, obvious to those who use it, but can be at significant variance to the values and beliefs of important players and potential players ('subjects'). The internal facilitators, and senior managers, were not peculiar in their resistance to seeing alternatives, the driving force of the implicit and now emergent value system of the Service was in evidence during all the strategy workshop debates. However, eventually, ten 'triggers' to start the workshop were selected – each of which was designed to be unconstraining in the way in which it would trigger the thinking of participants. They were: integration and segregation; falling prison population; morale of prison officers; vulnerability of prison officers; role of prison officers; industrial relations; regimes; dealing with paramilitaries; female officers; and public image.

Designing the 'role think' part of the workshop raised a number of issues. When workshop participants are asked to predict the response of themselves to the behaviour or intention of their own stakeholders, they often idealize their own intentions (providing a tension between 'espoused theories' and 'theories in action' – Argyris and Schon, 1974). Presenting your own organization in an unrealistic manner results partly from a wish to present the organization as you would like it to be rather than as it is.

To protect the outcome of the workshop from this possibility the role think was organized so that we could benefit from each organization – as stakeholder – being present, but also from each organization having years of experience of others in the room which had built important prejudices about that other organization. The whole group was split into work groups of four stakeholders. Each member of the work group of four persons was asked to role think another member in the same group by anticipating and explaining the response of that other person's organization to a carefully selected set of potential strategies of the Service. The potential strategies were selected from the material generated in the workshop by responses to the triggers, in exactly the same manner as for the internal workshops, except that a small number of the critical potential strategies that had emerged from internal workshops were introduced so that the robustness of these strategies could be evaluated using the views of stakeholders.

This contrived role think was expected to meet two objectives: the declared aim of providing new data about the possible responses of stakeholders, and in addition the hidden aim of encouraging the workshop participants to understand the possibilities for collaboration around common strategic aims of particular interest to the Northern Ireland Prison Service.

Another variation from the typical workshop pattern involved accessing the direct experience of the Service of each participant in order to evaluate their views of the capabilities of the Service to manage strategic change. The question was asked towards the end of the day so that it could be related to the practicalities of changing in relation to the strategies they had developed.

In other internal workshops we had paid attention to the development of the 'influence network' of stakeholders. In this workshop this was presumed to be more significant because it could provide information about *informal* as well as formal links between 'stakeholders' (ignoring the 'unaffected'). To help this process we used large sheets of acetate and 'Post-Its'. A 'Post-It' labelled with a stakeholder could then be moved easily and repositioned on the acetate, arrows showing the direction of influence between any two stakeholders could be written on to the acetate and yet also deleted or modified with ease. In this way the 'influence map' was constructed and recorded, with easy conversation able to take place around the acetate pinned to the wall. After the workshop the maps were analysed using special purpose software (Graphics COPE[1]) so that the central stakeholders could be identified and the dynamics of the growth of coalitions simulated.

Although the Chief Executive had always shown confidence in the ability of his own organization to manage strategic change, Fran and I were less confident. Our lack of confidence derived as much from our experience of other organizations as from our developing view of the Service. We were particularly anxious to get some clues about likely blocks and how these might be removed. In the event the participants were positive about the capability of the Service to manage major strategic change – some of the participants claimed that they could be more important blocks than the staff of the Service!

The workshop

The workshop itself was easier than the facilitators had expected. Participants who started the day acting as individuals strongly representing the stance of their own organization quickly moved to working as a part of the group. Although this behaviour suggested a positive attitude to the workshop itself and to the Chief Executive's attempt to involve them, it also worked against Fran's and my own wish to collect multiple perspectives rather than perspectives generated through collaborative social behaviour.

The participants of this workshop were all people who had different and important experiences of working within the community. The scenarios developed elsewhere within the project had been based upon a government view of the Province. This workshop was an opportunity to 'tap into' direct experience rather than statistical and analytical data. None of the previous workshops had attended to exploring alternative scenarios, but the participants this time were qualified to validate the more formal approach. In particular their views about the growth of 'ordinary decent crime' in the community could go well beyond official statistics.

The potential for 'collaborative advantage'

One purpose of the workshop had been to promote the potential for support rather sabotage of the Prison Service strategy – whatever that was to be. Thus a significant outcome of the workshop was the influence it had on the strategies being formulated and tested. Nevertheless we had hoped that it would provide the basis for identifying new strategies that were in the interests of multiple stakeholders and yet could not be achieved by any of them. This is what happened. The conceptual framework discussed in the first half of the chapter informed the way in which the facilitators designed and managed the workshop. However, the workshop as a vehicle for allowing a primary organization (the Northern Ireland Prison Service) to involve stakeholders in 'naturally' developing a view of the potential for collaboration seems to be of great significance in understanding the potential for collaborative advantage amongst public and community groups. It both reinforces the strategic intent of the primary organization *and* allows new strategies to emerge that can only be achieved through collaboration.

Collaboration which achieves something of significance depends on many factors; however in the approach discussed in this chapter, the process of bringing together a selection of 'subjects' and increasing their power and influence so that they become positively disposed 'players' depends significantly on understanding the goal system of each collaborator. It is the process of analysing the possible congruence of aspects of the goals of each individual collaborator at the level of the organization and the level of the individual representing that organization which can reveal the potential for a realization of meta-goals – those goals which none of the organizations could attain on its own (Vangen et al., 1994). Only when meta-goals can be identified is it possible to conceive of potential collaborative advantage for the members of the collaborative. The trick for the 'sponsor' of the collaborative is to anticipate the potential for a meta-strategy and to manipulate a sharing of perspectives in such a way as to enable the collaborators to see meta-goals that will coincide with the strategic intent of the sponsor. In this chapter we have suggested a method for formal analysis that is likely to increase the probability of this occurring.

Acknowledgements

The work reported here was undertaken with Dr Fran Ackermann of the University of Strathclyde. It has also been informed by extensive collaboration with Professor John Bryson and Charles Finn at the University of Minnesota, and with Professor Kees van der Heijden of the University of Strathclyde.

Note

1 Graphics COPE is software designed to represent and analyse 'cause maps' (see Eden et al., 1992). It runs within Microsoft Windows and is available in Europe from the University of Strathclyde, and in North America from Realizations Inc.

References

Ackermann, F. (1992) 'Strategic direction through burning issues – using SODA as a strategic decision support system', *OR Insight*, 5: 24–8.

Ackoff, R. (1970) *A Concept of Corporate Planning*. New York: Wiley.

Ackoff, R. (1974) *Redesigning the Future: a Systems Approach to Societal Problems*. New York: Wiley.

Argyris, C. and Schon, D.A. (1974) *Theories in Practice*. San Francisco: Jossey Bass.

Bryson, J. and Roering, W. (1988) 'The initiation of strategic planning by governments'. Discussion Paper No. 88, May. Strategic Management Research Center, University of Minnesota.

Delbecq, A.L., Van de Ven, A.H. and Gustafson, D.H. (1975) *Group Techniques for Program Planning*. Glenview, IL: Scott Foresman.

Eden, C. (1988) 'Cognitive mapping: a review', *European Journal of Operational Research*, 36: 1–13.

Eden, C. (1989) 'Strategic options development and analysis – SODA', in J. Rosenhead (ed.), *Rational Analysis in a Problematic World*. Chichester: Wiley. pp. 21–42.

Eden, C. (1993) 'Strategy development and implementation – cognitive mapping for group support', in J. Hendry and G. Johnson with J. Newton (eds), *Strategic Thinking: Leadership and the Management of Change*. Chichester: Wiley. pp. 115–36.

Eden, C. and Ackermann, F. (1992) 'Strategy development and implementation: the role of a group decision support system', in B. Bostrom, S. Kinney and R. Watson (eds), *Computer Augmented Teamwork*. New York: Van Nostrand & Reinhold. pp. 325–43.

Eden, C., Ackermann F. and Cropper S. (1992) 'The analysis of cause maps', *Journal of Management Studies*, 29: 309–24.

Freeman, R.E. (1984) *Strategic Management: a Stakeholder Approach*. Marshfield, MA: Pitman Publishing.

Huxham, C. and Eden, C. (1990) 'Gaming, competitor analysis and strategic management', in C. Eden and J. Radford (eds), *Tackling Strategic Problems: the Role of Group Decision Support*. London: Sage. pp. 120–8.

Huxham, C. with Macdonald, D. (1992) 'Introducing collaborative advantage: achieving inter-organizational effectiveness through meta-strategy', *Management Decision*, 30: 50–6.

Schnelle, E. (1979) *The Metaplan-Method: Communication Tools for Planning and Learning Groups*. Hamburg: Quickborn.

Vangen, S., Huxham, C. and Eden, C. (1994) 'Understanding collaboration from the perspective of a goal system'. Paper presented to the International Workshop on Multi-Organisational Partnerships: Working Together Across Organisational Boundaries. EIASM, Brussels, September.

4

Cross-Sectoral Partners: Collaborative Alliances among Business, Government and Communities

Barbara Gray

Problems in which the interests of business, government and communities intersect are now everyday occurrences. In some cases, the parties' interests converge because they share a common vision about the future (for example, the Newark Collaboration, a consortium of private and public interests designed to revitalize the City of Newark, New Jersey, see Gray, 1989). In other cases, interests collide. Disputes over local development, siting of new landfills and hazardous waste facilities, construction of new highways, toxic dumps, energy use, natural resource management are now commonplace. For example, local citizens often oppose government or industrial proposals for disposal of wastes and other undesirable land uses (LULUs) (Edelstein, 1988; Elliott, 1984; Freudenberg and Pastor, 1992; Kasperson et al., 1992) and have been successful in blocking or stalling many (Walsh et al., 1993). These kinds of collisions among business, government and stakeholders often prove to be particularly adversarial, intractable and unresponsive to conventional methods of problem resolution (Gray, 1989).

This chapter examines the development of collaborative alliances in which business, government and other stakeholders team up to generate constructive solutions to problems that they confront. Whether the stakeholders have come together to advance a shared vision or to resolve conflicts, innovative techniques for generating production solutions are available (Carpenter and Kennedy, 1988; Gray, 1989; Susskind and Cruikshank, 1987). Stakeholders in these cases are increasingly turning to alternative dispute resolution (ADR) approaches that include facilitation, mediation, mini-trials and regulatory negotiation to craft joint solutions (Bureau of National Affairs, 1985). In these approaches stakeholders create temporary collaborative alliances (often with the assistance of a third party) to develop common visions or to search for mutually acceptable solutions to their controversy. Increasingly such alliances have been used to solve environmental disputes (Bingham, 1984; Carpenter and Kennedy, 1988; Crowfoot and Wondolleck, 1990; Gray, 1989; Lynn, 1987; Pasquero, 1991), to create public private partnerships (Brooks et al., 1984; Gray and Wood,

1991; Waddock, 1986) and to deal with cross-sectoral disputes in international arenas (Golich and Young, 1993; Gray, 1995a; Heenan and Perlmutter, 1979).

Despite their increased use, however, collaborative alliances are not a panacea. Sheer initiative does not ensure success. This chapter examines four factors that influence the nature of success enjoyed by a collaborative: the larger context in which the collaboration is occurring; the design or structural form that collaboration adopts; the process of collaborative formation; and the mode of convening of the collaborative. Four recent cases of collaborative alliances involving business, government and other stakeholders are presented to illustrate how these success factors affect the outcomes of the collaboration.

Theoretical overview of the success factors

Collaborative alliances have been identified as a logical and necessary response to turbulent conditions (Astley and Fombrun, 1983; Emery and Trist, 1965; Trist, 1977; Wamsley and Zald, 1983). Under turbulent conditions organizations become highly interdependent with others in unexpected but consequential ways. Turbulence occurs when organizations, acting independently in diverse directions, create unanticipated consequences for themselves and others (Emery and Trist, 1965, 1972; Trist, 1977, 1983; Wildavsky, 1979). Turbulence cannot be managed individually because disruptions and their causes cannot be adequately anticipated or averted by unilateral action. In the face of turbulence, the ability of any single organization to plan accurately for its future is limited by the unpredictable consequences of actions taken by seemingly unrelated organizations:

> Especially when further limited by a finite resource base drawn on by all, the corporation can no longer act simply as an individual entity but must accept a certain surrender of sovereignty much as the nation-state. (Perlmutter and Trist, 1986: 9)

Collaboration offers an antidote to turbulence by building a collective capacity to respond to turbulent conditions. Through collaborative efforts, the stakeholders gain appreciation of their interdependence, pool their insights into the problem, increase variety in their repertoire of responses to the problem (Trist, 1983) and achieve increased reciprocity, efficiency and stability among themselves (Oliver, 1991). In most cases, creative solutions are needed that exceed the limited perspectives of each individual stakeholder.

Contextual incentives for collaboration

The trend to form alliances among business organizations to 'collaborate to compete' (Mitroff, 1987; Peters, 1988) or gain 'collaborative advantage'

(Huxham with Macdonald, 1992) has been well documented in the management literature as a response to turbulence. In order to keep up with rapid-fire technological changes and compete in global markets, firms have been forced to take on partners of all stripes (Peters, 1988; Gray, 1989). But firms have also been forced to undertake cross-sectoral alliances to stay competitive, to manage externalities and to shape the future of the global environment (Gray and Wood, 1991). As Huxham and Macdonald (1992) have noted, the pitfalls of not collaborating include repetition, omission, divergence and counterproduction and often add up to an inability to compete with the market leaders.

Several contextual incentives have been identified that have stimulated the formation of alliances (Gray, 1989). Table 4.1 lists seven factors that have propelled businesses, governments, non-profit agencies, and interest groups to try collaboration and shows the kinds of collaborative responses that have emerged and their intended impacts. The incentives include:

- Rapid economic and technological change
- A declining growth rate and increasing competitive pressures
- Global interdependence
- Blurred boundaries among business, government and labour
- Shrinking federal revenues for social programmes
- Dissatisfaction with the judicial process for solving complex problems
- Differing perceptions of environmental risk

As the definition of turbulence implies, many of these factors are interconnected. Indeed, some in the list may be partial causes or consequences of others. The objective of mentioning them here is to call attention to their collective impact on the formation of collaborative alliances.

Designs for collaboration

A framework for classifying collaborations has been suggested by Gray (1989). The framework is conceptualized along two dimensions: the factors that motivate the parties to collaborate and the type of outcome expected. Typically stakeholders are motivated either by a shared vision or by a desire to resolve a conflict. The outcomes of a collaboration may be simply an exchange of information or the generation of some kind of agreement among the parties. Figure 4.1 provides a framework for classifying four types of collaboration according to these two dimensions. **Appreciative planning** involves information exchange in the interest of advancing a shared vision. **Dialogues** create a forum for exploring solutions to a multi-party conflict. **Collective strategies** involve reaching agreement about how to implement a shared vision. **Negotiated settlements** represent solutions to conflicts among the stakeholders. Since the outcomes of each design are different, the criteria for judging the success of each design also will vary. However, the process by which the stakeholders engage in collaboration is similar across all four designs.

Table 4.1   *The impact of incentives to collaborate*

Incentive	Collaborative response	Intended impact
Economic and technological change	Inter-firm joint ventures	Stimulate innovation Minimize risk
	Business–university consortia	Exchange expertise Expand market access Reduce competition
	Public–private partnerships	Cope with economic decline Stimulate socioeconomic revitalization
Declining growth rate and increasing economic development	Labour–management committees	Improve productivity Increase worker output into planning
	Interfunctional collaboration	Facilitate introduction of new-technology/new-product designs
Global interdependence	Multilateral collaboration (nations/NGOs/multi-nationals)	Facilitate world preservation Facilitate global management of resources/technology Prevent violence
Blurred boundaries	Labour–management committees	Create broader collective bargaining agenda Increase worker input into planning
	Policy dialogues (business/government/communities/interested groups)	Resolve policy disputes Develop broad consensus on new policies
	Intergovernmental collaboration	Resolve policy disputes Speed decisions
Shrinking federal revenues	Public–private partnerships	Cope with economic decline Stimulate socioeconomic revitalization
Dissatisfaction with courts	Policy dialogues Regulatory negotiation Mediated site-specific disputes	Overcome impasse Settle conflicts Improve solutions
Differing perceptions of environmental risk	Regulatory negotiation Policy dialogues Mediated site-specific disputes	Settle conflicts over regulations Explore areas of agreement Improve understanding and reach agreement on acceptable risk

Source: adapted from Gray, 1989

EXPECTED OUTCOME

	exchange of information	joint agreements
advancing a shared vision	**APPRECIATIVE PLANNING** • search conference • community gatherings	**COLLECTIVE STRATEGIES** • public–private partnerships • joint ventures • R and D consortia • labour–management co-operatives
resolving conflict	**DIALOGUES** • policy dialogues • public meetings	**NEGOTIATED SETTLEMENTS** • regulatory negotiations • site-specific disputes • mini-trials

MOTIVATING FACTORS

Figure 4.1 *Designs for collaboration*

The process of collaborative formation

There appear to be some common issues that crop up repeatedly during the process of collaborating. These conform to a general sequence of phases regardless of the nature of the problem under consideration. The phases include:

1 a problem-setting phase in which convening the appropriate stake-holders and getting a commitment to collaborate are critical;
2 a direction-setting phase in which the stakeholders explore the problem in depth and reach agreement about alternatives;
3 an implementation phase in which steps to ensure follow-through on the agreement are taken if the collaboration is a collective strategy or negotiated settlement (Gray, 1989).

Clearly, the length, the significance and the difficulty of a particular phase may vary considerably depending on whether the collaboration is over a site-specific environmental dispute, a public–private partnership, or an inter-firm research and development initiative. In cases where the stake-holders are convening to advance a shared vision, gaining a commitment to collaborate may take considerably less time than it would in a fractious environmental dispute.

Tables 4.2, 4.3 and 4.4 provide overviews of the key issues that need to be resolved in each phase of the collaborative process. Not all collaborations, however, proceed through these phases in sequence. As Inskip (1993) notes,

Table 4.2   *Phase 1: problem-setting*

Goal: stakeholders agree to talk about the issues		
Issue	Question	Description
Common definition of the problem	'What is the problem?'	Need argument that a community issue causes problems important enough to collaborate. The problem must be common to several stakeholders
Commitment to collaborate	'What's in it for me?'	Stakeholders feel that collaborating will solve their own problems. Need to be dissatisfied with current conditions. Shared values are key
Identification of stake-holders	'Who should participate?'	An inclusive process that includes multiple stakeholders so the problems can be understood
Legitimacy of stakeholders	'Who has the right and capability to participate?'	Not only expertise but also power relationships important
Leader's characteristics	'Do I trust and respect the leader – the organization and the person?'	Collaborative leadership is key to success. Stakeholders need to perceive the leader as unbiased
Identification of resources	'How can we fund the planning process?'	Funds from government or foundations may be needed for less well-off organizations

Source: Inskip, 1993; adapted from Gray, 1989

the phases are not necessarily separate and distinct in practice. Overlapping and recycling back to earlier issues that were not addressed may be necessary (Burns, 1981; Inskip, 1993), particularly if leadership is conflicted and/or third party facilitation is absent. For example, Inskip (1993) found that problem-setting issues continually crept up during the direction-setting phase. Failure to address adequately a critical issue can severely hamper the success of the collaborative efforts (Gray, 1995). Therefore, awareness of the critical process issues, and conscious efforts to address them throughout the collaborative efforts, can mean the difference between success and failure (Gray, 1989; Wondolleck, 1985).

The mode of convening of the collaborative

One critical issue that deserves careful consideration at the inception of collaboration is: how are the stakeholders convened? The term **convener**

Table 4.3 *Phase 2: direction-setting*

	Goal: negotiating	
Issue	Question	Description
Establishing ground rules	'What is acceptable and unacceptable behaviour?'	Gives stakeholders a sense of fair process and equity of power
Agenda-setting	'What are the substantive issues we need to examine and decide?'	Stakeholders' different motivations for joining mean that establishing a common agenda may be difficult
Organizing subgroups	'Do we need to break into smaller groups to carry out our work?'	Large plenary committees need to be broken into smaller working groups
Joint information search	'Do we really understand the other side of this negotiation?'	Parties have different sets of information and/or not enough information to make a judgement. Joint search can help find common basis for agreement
Exploring options	'What are all the possible options to solving our problems?'	Multiple interests mean that multiple options need to be considered before closure. Stakeholders' own interests are important
Reaching agreement and closing the deal	'Are we committed to going ahead on one option or a package of options?'	Stakeholders can agree on recommendations for a formal organization or a joint voluntary course of action

Source: Inskip, 1993; adapted from Gray, 1989

refers to one or more stakeholders who create a forum for deliberations among the stakeholders and entice others to participate. The convening function has been found to differ substantially from one collaboration to the next (Wood and Gray, 1991). Conveners use a variety of tactics to exert influence over stakeholders and to control the process of collaborating. Four modes of influence have been identified according to the type of influence exerted (for example, formal or informal) and the source of intervention into the problem domain (either by invitation or by the convener's own initiation) (Wood and Gray, 1991) (Figure 4.2).

Legitimation Conveners using the legitimation mode possess formal authority and respond to an invitation from other stakeholders to organize the problem domain. Their ability to do so derives from their formal clout

Table 4.4   *Phase 3: implementation*

	Goal: systematic management of inter-organizational relations	
Issue	Question	Description
Dealing with constituencies	'How do we persuade our constituencies that this was the best deal we could negotiate?'	Stakeholders need time to make sure that their constituents understand the trade-offs and support the agreement
Building external support	'How do we ensure that organizations that will implement are onside?'	A concern that senior officials in government or business have not been briefed fully
Structuring	'Do we need a formal organization to fulfil our agreement?'	Voluntary efforts can work. A formal organization may be needed to co-ordinate long-term collaboration
Monitoring the agreement and ensuring compliance	'How do we figure out assets, legal obligations and compliance with contracts?'	Time for lawyers and possible more legal/financial negotiations

Source: Inskip, 1993; adapted from Gray, 1989

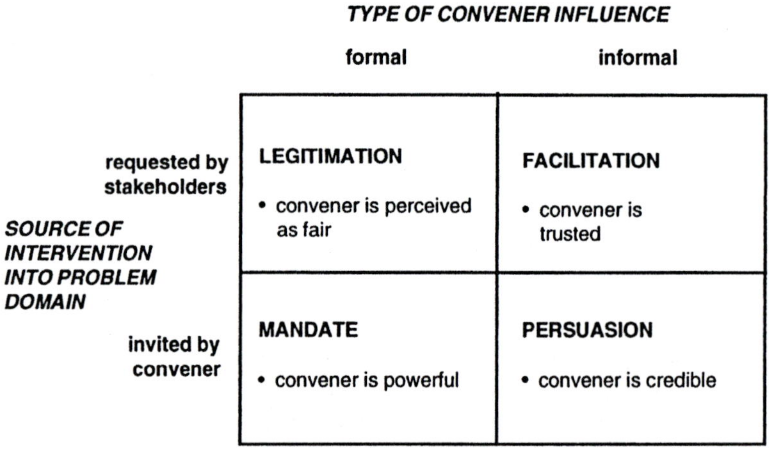

TYPE OF CONVENER INFLUENCE

	formal	**informal**
requested by stakeholders	**LEGITIMATION** • convener is perceived as fair	**FACILITATION** • convener is trusted
invited by convener	**MANDATE** • convener is powerful	**PERSUASION** • convener is credible

SOURCE OF INTERVENTION INTO PROBLEM DOMAIN

Figure 4.2   *Dominant mode and central attribute of conveners*

within the domain and the belief that they will be fair in that role. This results in others attributing legitimacy to them.

Facilitation   In this mode conveners rely on their credibility, influence and/or knowledge as a source of informal authority. Facilitators are invited to intervene because the other parties trust they can be helpful:

The central attribute of the convener is trustworthiness, because the convener has no formal authority to establish the collaboration, enforce the rules, or ensure outcomes and must depend on the trust of the participants to be effective. (Wood and Gray, 1991: 152)

Mandate Stakeholders who convene by mandate elect to exercise the formal power they possess within the domain to assemble other stakeholders. Mandated collaborations may be required by statute, judicial or executive order and may carry sanctions such as loss of federal funding for failure to comply. The Canadian government's efforts to establish national, provincial and local round tables for addressing sustainable development issues in Canada represents mandated collaboration (Pasquero, 1991). Judicial mandate produced a collaborative agreement among Exxon Corporation and the governments of New York and New Jersey over clean-up responsibilities for an off-shore oil spill.

Persuasion Conveners who exercise persuasion must rely on informal authority and their own initiative. They must present a credible argument to other stakeholders that involvement in the collaborative will be worthwhile because they have no formal clout with which to induce participation.

Judging success

As noted earlier, not all collaborative efforts meet with success. Some stakeholders refuse to participate; others are unwilling to sign a final agreement; others who are excluded from the process may undermine implementation of any agreements reached (Gray, 1989, 1995; Walker and Daniels, 1993). A critical question is, 'What constitutes success?' As noted earlier, the criteria for success vary according to the design that the collaboration takes. Figure 4.3 summarizes the relevant success criteria for each collaborative design.

Appreciative planning and dialogues are, by nature, temporary collectivities. Therefore, success criteria such as survival and duration, are irrelevant measures for them. However, several basic outcomes related to information exchange are important measures of success. Did the stakeholders exchange information about their visions and expectations about the issue or problem? Did they gain a better understanding of how others see the problem, especially if others see it differently? Do the stakeholders achieve a more complete picture of the problem after conferring with one another? For appreciative planning, appropriate outcomes to expect include the stakeholders' understanding each other's intentions and gleaning a broader comprehension of the problem than they had at the beginning.

Because dialogues seek to resolve conflict, they also need to deal with issues of trust and respect. In order for the parties to appreciate fully the problem, they will need to recognize and accept that each stakeholder has different perspectives on the problem that must be considered in resolving

EXPECTED OUTCOME

	exchange of information	joint agreements
advancing a **shared vision**	**APPRECIATIVE PLANNING** • exchange of information about visions and understanding • understanding of others' visions and expectations • fuller comprehension of problem by stakeholders • agreement on problem definition	**COLLECTIVE STRATEGIES** • agreement reached • agreement implemented • survival of alliance • partners' goals achieved • problem alleviated
resolving **conflict**	**DIALOGUES** • development of trust • recognition of legitimacy of others' interests • generation of integrative ideas • ongoing interaction • recommendations for action	**NEGOTIATED SETTLEMENTS** • integrative agreement reached • agreement implemented • reduction in negative reactions from constituents • extent of compliance with the agreement

MOTIVATING FACTORS (label at left, between the two rows)

Figure 4.3   *Criteria of success*

the conflict. Trust ensues when members' interests are heard and acknowledged as legitimate by others. Two additional criteria that indicate that a dialogue was successful are the generation of integrative ideas for resolution and ongoing interaction among the players once the dialogue is concluded. Dialogues may or may not produce agreements, but if they do, they only serve as recommendations to another body (such as a legislature) which has decision-making authority.

For collective strategies, duration (or 'sustainability' – see Cropper's discussion of this in Chapter 5) of the agreement is necessary to alleviate the problem. Success in relieving or reducing a social ill may require extended effort, however, so it is useful to have two short-term measures of success as well: that is, whether an agreement was reached and whether initial steps were taken to implement it.

Negotiated settlements, like collective strategies, have a fairly stringent set of success criteria. As in dialogues, the development of trust and respect for the legitimacy of others' interests are prerequisites to reaching an integrative agreement. Implementation of the agreement is also important; otherwise the problem will resurface. Longer-term consequences include a reduction in negative reactions to the problem from constituents of the collaborators and the extent of compliance with the terms of the agreement.

Four cases of collaboration

We now turn our attention to four cases of collaboration. Each case is analysed according to three organizing issues (context, convening and design and process) and the success criteria appropriate to its design.

Hazardous Waste Study Tours (HWST)

In 1989, a group of 21 US stakeholders interested in hazardous waste management facilities undertook an unusual collective venture. They agreed to participate in a tour of three hazardous waste facilities in Europe to learn about both the technical as well as the social and political issues associated with the siting of these facilities. Several factors made the tour unique. First was the assortment of participants, which included representatives from business, environmental groups, government (regulators and legislative aids), academia and the media. Second was the group's focus on both the technical and the social and political aspects of facility siting. Third was the explicit attempt by the conveners to promote dialogue among the participants about controversial issues associated with the use of hazardous incineration technology.

Contextual factors This case clearly illustrates two of the incentives for collaboration identified earlier: the blurring of business, government and community boundaries and differing assessments of environmental risks. The chemical industry has proposed incineration as an environmentally sound alternative to land disposal of waste. Environmentalists have claimed that expanded incineration capacity will create disincentives for investing in more efficient production processes which generate less waste (Flynn, 1989). Intense public opposition to the siting of incineration facilities in the US has transformed a 'business decision' into a public policy one (Buchholz et al., 1992). Questions of what risks should be borne by whom and who has the right to decide these questions quickly became salient. Typically, decisions about the allocation of these risks are relegated to the regulatory arena and the courts, where acrimonious debate over the right way to proceed traditionally results in some sides eventually concluding they have lost (Gellhorn, 1984). The study tour offered an alternative to the usual interaction among the parties.

Conveners Initiative for the tour first came from the manager of public policy at CIBA–Geigy Corporation who shared the convening role with the director of an academic research centre concerned with the management of hazardous substances. CIBA–Geigy manufactures waste incinerators so they clearly had a stake in the lessons learned from the tour.

Design and process   The European HWST is an example of a dialogue. During the one-week tour participants inspected industrial waste incineration plants in Denmark, Sweden, Switzerland and West Germany. They met with hazardous waste facility managers, local and regional regulatory officials and environmental activists.

Since the HWST represents a dialogue, reaching and implementing an agreement was not an intended outcome. Although the project planners originally hoped to develop a consensus about hazardous waste issues, this expectation was revised after sharing initial plans with environmentalists well in advance of the tour (Flynn, 1990). An important part of the process was the seriousness of the substantive work that was undertaken, including the distribution of a 300 page reference book on European hazardous waste management. Conveners were also mindful of the need to diversify the funding base for the project. Clearly, if CIBA–Geigy was the sole sponsor, the environmentalists could not participate without loss of credibility with their constituents. Fortunately, the bulk of the funding was secured from the German Marshall Fund, a non-profit agency whose aim is to foster interest in German economic and cultural heritage in the US.

A critical feature of the process was the dialogue sessions guided by two facilitators who accompanied the stakeholders on the trip. After each visit, time was allocated for participants to share reactions to both the technical and the public policy aspects of each site.

A year after the original tour, the same group reconvened for a tour of US hazardous waste incineration facilities. Thirteen of the 21 original participants participated in the second tour (representing the basic stakeholder groups) as did the two facilitators. In the dialogue sessions that were held after site visits, discussion centred on three general areas: the design and management of technologies used in reducing and treating industrial waste; public policy issues raised in meetings with industry, government and citizen groups' representatives; and comparison of industrial waste issues in North America and Europe.

Analysis of success   A study on the project by an independent researcher who accompanied the tour (Chess et al., 1990), reported that:

- 95 per cent found the tour 'useful' or 'very useful';
- 85 per cent changed or broadened their definition and scope of hazardous waste issues (this particularly reflected an increased interest in social and policy issues);
- 76 per cent increased their understanding of the perspectives of other stakeholders in the US controversy.

This is consistent with two of the success criteria for dialogues shown in Figure 4.3. Among them are the development of trust and recognition of the legitimacy of others' views. The researchers concluded:

> the data suggest that overall most participants felt that the tour raised their level of understanding of relevant issues. (Chess et al., 1990: 15)

While the participants did gain a better understanding of each other's views, they did not substantially change their own beliefs about the issues.

The process of the trip, specifically the value associated with travelling together (Gray and Hay, 1986), went a long way to overcoming hostilities and building trust among adversaries. According to Flynn: 'Site visits break down barriers and encourage participants to interact' (1990: 11). The fact that a second tour was organized suggests that the success criterion of ongoing interaction was beginning to be met. While the overall impact of the second tour was positive, one incident marred the rapport that had been built over both trips. After the conclusion of the second trip, a journalist in the group wrote a series of newspaper articles about the adversarial mindset of industry and environmentalists in his jurisdiction (which the tour had visited). In one article, he quoted a fellow tour member from industry who had privately criticized the adversarial posture of the industry they had observed. This was perceived by the industry participant and others on the tour as a violation of the confidentiality agreement to which they had agreed at the outset as part of the ground rules.

Despite this incident, the second tour was generally regarded as beneficial to those involved. While consensus on the issues was not an objective, an informal consensus was reached among the group that hazardous waste incineration is a political, not a technical issue. According to Flynn, 'industry just can't assume that technological efficiency will outweigh any political considerations' (1991). They also concluded that Europe was not ahead of the US technically and that a political comparison is difficult because of different political party structures. Thus, the HWST satisfies the criteria for generation of integrative ideas. Also, true to its intentions, it did not, however, generate any recommendations for action.

Finally, the importance of a support base within the convening firm was critical. Flynn's dual reporting relationship as manager of public affairs, provided support from both the vice president for public affairs and the head of environmental engineering. Additionally, he kept the company's top four production managers apprised of the project's developments throughout in order to maintain realistic expectations.

Andersonville Sewing Council

The Andersonville Sewing Council[1] is a consortium of six garment manu-facturers who, in conjunction with an industrial development corporation, a local vo-technical school and one of the state's advanced technology centres (ATCs), developed a joint training programme to increase qualified job applicants for their industry (see Sharfman et al., 1991, for a detailed account of this case).

Contextual factors The broad contextual incentives that spurred the need for collaboration in Andersonville were economic depression and declining productivity in the region. However, forging this collaborative arrangement took some time since the garment industry as a whole had long sustained an image as sweatshops with exploitive working conditions. Early efforts by several of the garment manufacturers to enlist the support of regional development authorities (such as the Private Industry Council, PIC) to help the companies overcome labour shortages and high turnover met with strong resistance because of the industry's negative image.

Conveners The convener of the Sewing Council was the owner of the garment firm who employed the most workers in the area. He rallied the other manufacturers to seek public funding for the training programme.

Design and process Despite the PIC's rejection, the garment manufacturers continued to look for support for a training programme and eventually discovered the Advanced Technology Center. The ATC typically funded tripartite collaborations among government, private industry and educational institutions to improve productivity, create jobs, diversify the state's economy and promote the use of advanced technology. Working with the vo-technical school and the local development authority (who actually received the grant), the garment manufacturers designed a programme (that the ATC then funded) to train trainers for the sewing industry. Participating garment manufacturers each contributed matching funds to the training effort. The Sewing Council's efforts represent a collective strategy. Altogether, the funding supported five classes in which 36 people enrolled, and 23 were ultimately placed in employment. Although the grant was a one-time event, members of the Sewing Council continued to meet and consider other ways to continue their collaboration after it ran out.

Analysis of success The Sewing Council satisfies the first two success criteria for collective strategies including the construction and implementation of an agreement among the stakeholders. Additional, more demanding criteria include satisfaction of the partners' goals and alleviation of the initial problem. Typically, this requires that the alliance continue for some duration so that its impact can be felt. The third criterion was partially satisfied, but the problem was not permanently alleviated. The firms clearly would have liked a continuing mechanism for training and screening workers. With respect to duration, members did continue to meet after the training programme was completed. Among the indirect effects of the project were improved communication and increased trust among the Council members, who, in the past, had interacted little and suspected each other of 'stealing workers' (Sharfman et al., 1991). The primary reasons for their lack of long-term success (as well as for their initial difficulties) were institutional ones, including the industry's image and restrictions in federal funding procedures. Subsequently, the industry was hit badly by the recent recession, and several of the firms were sold or closed and others were forced to lay off workers. Thus, as a collaborative, the Sewing Council was not powerful enough to avoid the negative effects of turbulence in its wider environment. It could not provide an enduring or sustainable solution to the problem (see Cropper, Chapter 5).

New York City Partnership Youth Employment Initiative (YEI)

This case describes the efforts of the New York City Partnership to deal with severe problems of youth unemployment in New York City. The New York City Partnership (NYCP) was itself a collaboration among businesses, civic and educational organizations in the city. It was created in 1979 with an economic development mission of preparing residents for service industry jobs, retaining back-office jobs in the city, and general improvement of the city's business climate. Among the NYCP's successful efforts was the creation of the Summer Jobs Program designed to locate summer jobs for unemployed youth. The Youth Employment Initiative (YEI) was a subsequent effort of the Partnership to develop a more systemic programme to counteract unemployment and provide entry level workers for business.

Contextual factors The primary incentives for the formation of the YEI were economic and technological change and shrinking federal revenues. New York City was facing a demand for more skilled workers in the service sector, but was faced with a large population of unskilled, disadvantaged youth whose futures were placed in jeopardy by cutbacks in federal social programmes resulting from Reaganomics. Public–private partnerships sprang up to fill the void in the social arena (Brooks et al., 1984).

Conveners The YEI began when a few members of a task force on youth employment recommended that the NYCP establish an apprenticeship programme patterned after successful ones in West Germany. Champions of the recommendation worked with NYCP staff to convene a group of stakeholders (including representatives of the United Federation for Teachers, the New York City Department of Employment, the NYC Public Schools, the State Department of Employment, the AFL-CIO and several major corporations) to investigate the German experience and to design its US counterpart. The NYCP was envisioned as a broker for the diverse interests represented in this endeavour.

Design and process The YEI is considered a collective strategy since it was motivated by the stakeholders' desire to advance a shared vision and to implement an agreement. With funding from the German Marshall Fund, in November 1984 the stakeholder group undertook an unprecedented tour visiting apprenticeship programmes in three European countries –

Germany, England and Sweden. Three outcomes of the trip were identified (Gray, 1995b): it provided a rich common focus for considering programme elements; it reinforced the notion that collaboration was essential to tackle youth employment problems; and considerable bonding occurred among the group members. In the words of two participants (a Chief Executive of a major corporation and the Chancellor of Schools):

> . . . solutions to the problems of youth unemployment can only be successfully developed if business, government and labor cooperate. The problem is too great for any one entity or sector to handle alone.

> We gelled together. This was something that brought us together socially and politically. It was an intense period of time. We became more comfortable and overcame the usual cautions that would prevail across these institutional boundaries. (Gray, 1995b: 82)

After their return from Europe the YEI group spent another nine months intensively designing a workable US version of a youth employment programme linking business to the schools. While several trip members were unable to meet, they were replaced by others from their agency. One additional stakeholder from the Urban Coalition joined. A final report was prepared by September 1985 for presentation to the NYCP's committees. Ultimately, however, the YEI died; that is, its recommendations were never implemented by the NYCP. Curiously, however, within two years, a virtually identical programme called New York Working was launched by the School and Business Alliance. After its acceptance, the programme was housed within NYCP to be implemented under NYCP's new president.

Analysis of success   The YEI was clearly successful in reaching an agreement. Several factors appear to account for the failure of the YEI to implement its collaborative agreement (Gray, 1995b). First, two original stakeholders left their positions at the agencies they headed during the project, and the key staff person at NYCP resigned in March 1986. The latter's departure was described by some as the 'death blow'. A second reason concerns whether implementation of the programme would or could have been forthcoming from the group of highly placed administrators who participated in its design. It is not clear that the group conceived itself as implementers, and most neglected to enlist subordinates in the follow-up planning. Instead, the NYCP was vaguely envisioned as the implementer. A third interpretation was that the leadership of NYCP was not behind the project from its inception. Internal rivalry between NYCP's Vice-President and President over differing visions for the Partnership's involvement in education and unemployment were never resolved. Additionally, the President had formerly been the Chancellor of Schools, and animosity between him and the two subsequent Chancellors was no secret. As a result, the administrative structure of the NYCP did not lend itself to managing the collaborative programming among the disparate public and private organizations involved (DeLone and Associates, 1985), there was an absence of CEO champion for the project, and no impetus was forthcoming from the Chancellor's office. Finally, there was no constituency waiting for the NYCP to follow through with its plans. Since community groups had largely been overlooked in the planning, they did not have a stake in lobbying to keep the effort alive. These kinds of trade-offs influence sustainability of the collaborative. All of these represent process failures since the contextual incentives for collaboration remained strong throughout. The fact that a second collaborative initiative eventually took place can be understood in terms of Friend and Hickling's (1987) model of the recursiveness of collaborative processes – that is, the process may require several iterations before it succeeds.

Collaboration on Residential Lending (CORL)

Contextual factors Urban Heights[1] was an upper-middle-class residential suburb adjacent to a major US city. When the city began to become racially integrated in the 1960s, efforts to avert 'white flight' and to prevent discriminatory real estate practices such as 'racial steering' were actively undertaken by the city government and a community congress. In 1974, a citizens' group affiliated with the congress undertook a study of lending practices in the community to discover if subtle disinvestment of the community by major lending institutions (a practice called redlining) was under way. The citizens' research suggested that some lending institutions had begun to disinvest, but little heed was paid to the report by the lenders. Still, national attention to the issue of redlining was growing, and conflict between citizens and lenders in other communities was escalating.

Conveners Against this background of simmering conflict and in response to pressure from the citizens' group, Urban Heights' city manager convened a new municipal advisory committee called the Committee on Residential Lending (CORL). He invited representatives of two major banks, two savings and loan associations, one mortgage banker, two appraisers, three realtors, four citizens, and one member each from the city council and the school board. Without pointing any fingers, the mayor asked the committee to come up with a plan to ensure continued investment in the community.

Design and process CORL met regularly over the next two years, and its efforts represent a negotiated settlement. Initially, various stakeholders were asked to present their views on the factors contributing to the lending patterns uncovered by the citizens. Each group presented details that were important in mortgage-lending decisions from their perspective. After the initial opening presentations the city manager, who chaired the meetings, solicited suggestions for the agenda and broke the group into three sub-committees:

> Between CORL's second and eighth months of operation, conflict between the groups continued to dominate much of the exchange, but gradually a structure and informal norms governing the members' interactions evolved. . . . Gradually the discussion was reoriented from blame and defensiveness to recognition of mutual responsibility and capability to prevent disinvestment. (Gray, 1989: 107)

As members aired their different viewpoints in these informal settings, they developed a more sophisticated and differentiated understanding of the alleged causes and consequences of disinvestment. Eventually, members began to reveal their real interests, that of preserving the racially integrated character of the community while maintaining housing values. This conclusion led to the formulation of several proposals for action that were adopted by the whole group. Implementation of the agreements was primarily turned over to the city staff. The need for an ongoing group to review progress and to consider other investment issues in the community prompted the city manager to continue CORL as a temporary referent organization (Trist, 1983) for some time.

Analysis of success　As a negotiated settlement, CORL's success should be judged on the criteria appropriate to negotiated settlement including: whether an integrative agreement was reached and implemented, whether there was a reduction in negative reactions from constituents and compliance with the agreement that was adopted. With respect to the first criterion, CORL was definitely successful. During its first eight months several objectives were agreed upon including: (a) revitalizing the city's commercial areas; (b) reducing the mortgage foreclosures; and (c) promoting interior home inspection. CORL was also successful in prompting other organizations to implement several of its agreements. In particular, the city government initiated a commercial revitalization programme and a foreclosure rehabilitation programme for which the lenders raised funds (Gricar and Brown, 1981). The group was unsuccessful in getting federal agencies to tighten up mortgage lending criteria to prevent foreclosures, however.

The aspect of interior home inspection became a hotly contested issue within the Urban Heights city council, but after two years was eventually adopted. Therefore, with respect to the third success criterion, CORL experienced little resistance to its first two objectives but negative reactions from some constituents on the third. After extensive negotiations among constituents in the political arena, CORL was eventually successful in securing adoption of its third objective.

Ensuring compliance with the agreements became the responsibility of the city government, which was committed to doing so. Additional testimony of CORL's success was its continuation for three and a half more years (at the request of the city) to address other housing issues in the community.

Cross-case analysis

The four cases described above illustrate three of the four designs for collaboration. The Hazardous Waste Study Tours represent dialogues, the Andersonville Sewing Council and the Youth Employment Initiative are collective strategies and the Committee on Residential Lending is a negotiated settlement. Not all of these were fully successful collaborations, however, for the reasons pointed out above.

While the YEI was successful on one of the short-term measures (for example, agreement was reached) it failed at implementation. Essentially, no plans were set in place for implementation responsibility, the NYCP's structure did not facilitate ratification and implementation, and competing political agendas within NYCP blocked efforts to build a support base. Thus, a series of process failures thwarted implementation of the YEI's agreement.

The Hazardous Waste Study Tours were largely successful although the development of trust was marred by breaches of confidentiality, also a process issue. Sustainability was an issue for both YEI and the Sewing Council but for different reasons.

Process failures plagued the YEI while contextual pressures inhibited the continuation of the Sewing Council. Reaching agreement and implementing it were not problems for the Sewing Council. However, the ASC was unable to satisfy the duration criteria. The type of convening mode also played a role in the Sewing Council's outcome.

The cases illustrate three of the four different types of convening mode (Figure 4.4). Legitimation was the kind of intervention made by the Urban Heights city manager. His involvement in convening the collaboration was sought by the citizen group. His formal authority as the executive of the city enabled him to attract lenders and realtors to the table. Therefore, he had substantial clout to create an attractive forum and back-up resources to support CORL's efforts.

The Youth Employment Initiative illustrates the facilitation mode of convening since members of one of NYCP's committees asked NYCP staff to co-ordinate the European trip that marked the beginning of that project. Subsequently, the Vice-President continued in the convening role by virtue of her knowledge of both the substantive area and her ability to plan and run meetings. In this case, however, the informality of her role and the lack of support for it within her own organization, contributed to the failure of the collaboration.

The other two cases are exemplars of the persuasion mode of convening: the Andersonville Sewing Council and the Hazardous Waste Study Tours project. In each case the convener had no formal authority, but used his persuasive abilities and knowledge of the problem domain to rally other stakeholders. In the case of convening via persuasion, the convener must have high credibility in order to convince others that the collaborative initiative has some value for them and that they should join him or her in

TYPE OF CONVENER INFLUENCE

	formal	informal
requested by stakeholders *SOURCE OF INTERVENTION INTO PROBLEM DOMAIN*	**LEGITIMATION** • Committee on Residential Learning (CORL)	**FACILITATION** • Youth Employment Initiative (YEI)
invited by convener	**MANDATE**	**PERSUASION** • Hazardous Waste Study Tours (HWST) • Anderson Sewing Council (ASC)

Figure 4.4 *Dominant mode and central attribute of conveners: the cases categorized*

it. The Sewing Council may have been more successful over the long haul if they had persuaded a legitimate authority, such as city or county government or the Private Industry Council, to serve as convener. To do so, may have broadened or changed the nature of the collaborative activities, but might have included the training programme among a wider array of activities that benefited both garment manufacturers and the community at large.

The persuasion mode of convening appears to have been successful for the HWST. Since reaching and implementing an agreement were not its intended objectives and duration was not an issue, less stringent and tangible measures such as the development of trust among the participants, the expansion of perspectives, continuing contacts among the participants after the collaboration, and respect for the others' views appear to be reasonable outcomes to expect from this type of collaboration. The evidence to date suggests that the Hazardous Waste Study Tours were at least moderately successful using these criteria. Attention to the process was also a strong factor in this case.

The Committee on Residential Lending is in the best position to be evaluated on both short- and long-term criteria since it is the oldest of the cases. It clearly meets the short-term criteria of reaching agreements and of implementing them. It also demonstrates some longevity since the committee continued to meet after the problem for which it was initially created had been addressed. Of the four collaborations, it appears to have had the most substantial impact.

Conclusion

Countless examples of cross-sectoral collaborative initiatives have been instigated and successfully concluded all across the US and in the international arena. Despite our growing experience with them, they still remain vulnerable to political vagaries, economic shifts, institutionalized norms and ecological barriers. Despite this, the trend favouring such alliances continues upward. As the nature of public–private sector relationships continues to change (Smith, 1983), it behoves public and private sector managers alike to develop the requisite skills for diagnosing when cross-sectoral alliances are appropriate and advantageous mechanisms for addressing problems. Initiatives for launching successful collaborations can originate from any of the relevant stakeholders. Clearly, for business organizations participation in these forums, in which joint authority for managing the global resources of the future is being exercised, is a critical feature of managing the business-to-society relationship.

Notes

1 The names of the cities in which the Anderson Sewing Council and Collaboration on Residential Learning cases occurred have been disguised in order to respect the confidentiality of the participants.

References

Astley, G.H. and Fombrun, C. (1983) 'Collective strategy: social ecology of organizational environments', *Academy of Management Review*, 8 (4): 576–87.

Bingham, G. (1984) *Resolving Environmental Disputes: a Decade of Experience*. Washington, DC: Conservation Foundation.

Brooks, H., Liebman, L. and Schelling, C. (eds) (1984) *Public–Private Partnerships: New Opportunities for Meeting Social Needs*. Cambridge, MA: Ballinger.

Buchholz, R.A., Marcus, A.A. and Post, J.E. (1992) *Managing Environmental Issues*. Englewood Cliffs, NJ: Prentice Hall.

Bureau of National Affairs (1985) *Resolving Disputes Without Litigation*. Washington, DC: BNA.

Burns, T.F. (1981) 'Planning networks and network agents: an approach to adaptive community planning'. Doctoral dissertation, University of Pennsylvania, Philadelphia, PA.

Carpenter, S. and Kennedy, W.J.D. (1988) *Managing Public Disputes: a Practical Guide to Handling Conflict and Reaching Agreements*. San Francisco: Jossey Bass.

Chess, K., Salomone, K.L., Greenberg, M.R., Sandman, P.M. and Saville, A. (1990) 'Impact of a European Hazardous Waste Study Tour on participants' viewpoints'. Environmental Communication Research Program, Rutgers University, May.

Crowfoot, J.E. and Wondolleck, J.M. (1990) *Environmental Disputes*. Washington, DC: Island Press.

DeLone, R.H. and Associates (1985) 'Tomorrow's Work Force: Issues and Opportunities for Human Capital Investment in New York City'. Report prepared for the New York City Partnership, Youth Policy Group, Summer.

Edelstein, M. (1988) *Contaminated Communities: the Social and Psychological Impacts of Residential Toxic Exposure.* Boulder, CO: Westview.

Elliott, M.E.P. (1984) 'Improving community acceptance of hazardous waste facilities through alternative systems for mitigating and managing risk', *Hazardous Waste*, 1 (3): 397–410.

Emery, F.E. and Trist, E.L. (1965) 'The causal texture of organizational environments', *Human Relations*, 18: 21–32.

Emery, F.E. and Trist, E.L. (1972) *Towards a Social Ecology.* New York: Plenum.

Flynn, J.M. (1989) *A Report on: The European Hazardous Waste Study Tour.* CIBA–Geigy Corporation, 31 August.

Flynn, J.M. (1990) *A Report on: The United States Hazardous Waste Study Tour.* CIBA–Geigy Corporation, 14 June.

Flynn, J.M. (1991) Personal communication, 19 September.

Freudenberg, W.R. and Pastor, S.K. (1992) 'Nimby's and LULU's: stalking the syndromes', *Journal of Social Issues*, 48 (4): 39–61.

Friend, J. and Hickling, A. (1987) *Planning under Pressure.* Oxford: Pergamon.

Gellhorn, E. (1984) 'Too much law, too many lawyers, not enough justice', *Wall Street Journal*, 8 June, p. 28.

Golich, V.L. and Young, T.F. (1993) 'Resolution of the United States–Canadian conflict over acid rain controls', *Journal of Environment and Development*, 2 (1): 63–110.

Gray, B. (1995a) 'The development of global environmental regimes: organizing in the absence of authority'. Paper presented at the conference on 'The Organizational Dimensions of Global Change: No Limits to Cooperation', Case Western Reserve University, 3–6 May 1995.

Gray, B. (1995b) 'Obstacles to success in educational collaboration', in M. Wang and L.C. Rigsby (eds), *School/Community Connections: Exploring Issues for Research and Practice.* San Francisco: Jossey Bass. pp. 71–99.

Gray, B. (1989) *Collaborating: Finding Common Ground for Multiparty Problems.* San Francisco: Jossey Bass.

Gray, B. and Hay, T.M. (1986) 'Political limits to interorganizational consensus and change', *Journal of Applied Behavioral Science*, 22 (2): 95–112.

Gray, B. and Wood, D.J. (1991) 'Collaborative alliances: moving from practice to theory', *Journal of Applied Behavioral Science*, 27 (1): 3–22.

Gricar, B. and Brown, L.D. (1981) 'Conflict, power and organisation in a changing community', *Human Relations*, 34 (10): 877–93.

Heenan, D.A. and Perlmutter, H.V. (1979) *Multinational Organizational Development.* Reading, MA: Addison-Wesley.

Huxham, C. with MacDonald, D. (1992) 'Introducing collaborative advantage', *Management Decision*, 30 (3): 50–6.

Inskip, R. (1993) 'A study of facilitating interorganizational collaboration'. Paper prepared for the CAIS/ASCI Conference, Antigonish, Nova Scotia, 12–14 July.

Kasperson, R.E., Golding, D. and Tuler, S. (1992) 'Social distrust as a factor in siting hazardous facilities and communicating risks', *Journal of Social Issues*, 48: 161–87.

Lynn, F.M. (1987) 'Citizen involvement in hazardous waste sites: two North Carolina success stories', *Environmental Impact Assessment Review*, 7: 347–61.

Mitroff, I. (1987) *Business Not as Usual: Rethinking our Individual, Corporate and Industrial Strategies for Global Competition.* San Francisco: Jossey Bass.

Oliver, C. (1991) 'Strategic responses to institutional processes', *Academy of Management Review*, 16: 145–79.

Pasquero, J. (1991) 'Supraorganizational collaboration', *Journal of Applied Behavioral Science*, 27 (1): 38–64.

Perlmutter, H.V. and Trist, E. (1986) 'Paradigms for societal transition', *Human Relations*, 39 (1): 1–27.

Peters, T. (1988) 'Restoring American competitiveness: looking for new models of organizations', *The Academy of Management Executive*, 2 (2): 103–9.

Sharfman, M.K., Gray, B. and Yan, A. (1991) 'The context of interorganizational collaboration in the garment industry', *Journal of Applied Behavioral Science*, 27 (2): 181–208.

Smith, B.L.R. (1983) 'Changing public–private sector relations', *The Annals*, 446: 149–64.

Susskind, L. and Cruikshank, J. (1987) *Breaking the Impasse: Consensual Approaches to Resolving Public Disputes*. New York: Basic Books.

Trist, E.L. (1977) 'A concept of organizational ecology', *Australian Journal of Management*, 2: 162–75.

Trist, E.L. (1983) 'Referent organizations and the development of interorganizational domains', *Human Relations*, 36 (3): 247–68.

Waddock, Sandra. (1986) 'Public–private partnership in Boston: an urban case study'. Working Paper, Boston College, School of Management.

Walker, G.B. and Daniels, S.E. (1993) 'Clinton and the Northwest Forest Conference: a case of conflict mis-management'. Paper presented at the Speech Communication Association Conference, Miami, FL, 21 November.

Walsh, E., Warland, R., and Smith, D.C. (1993) 'Backyard NIMBY's and incinerator siting: implications for social movement theory', *Social Problems*, 40 (1): 25–38.

Wamsley, G. and Zald, M. (1983) 'The environments of public managers: managing turbulence', in W. Eddy (ed.), *Handbook of Organization Management*. New York: Marcel Dekker. pp. 62–79.

Wildavsky, A. (1979) *Speaking Trust to Power: the Art and Craft of Policy Analysis*. Boston, MA: Little Brown.

Wondolleck, J. (1985) 'The importance of process in resolving environmental disputes', *Environmental Impact Assessment Review*, 5: 341–56.

Wood, D.J. and Gray, B. (1991) 'Toward a comprehensive theory of collaboration', *Journal of Applied Behavioral Science*, 27 (2): 139–62.

PART THREE

COLLABORATION IN PRACTICE: KEY ISSUES

5

Collaborative Working and the Issue of Sustainability

Steve Cropper

> You will build effective and sustainable partnerships between public and private
> organizations . . .
>
> *Guardian 'Society'*, 16 November 1994*

The initiation and regulation of collaborative arrangements are important, increasingly pervasive and knotty tasks of public and business management. Analyses of recent developments in public policy development and implementation and public service management (Challis et al., 1988; Harrison, 1993; Leach et al., 1994; Metcalfe and Richards, 1990; Nocon, 1994) propose a crucial, bridging or integrative role for collaborative, inter-organizational working which holds out the possibility of greater 'whole system effectiveness', or, in the terms of this volume, 'collaborative advantage'. There has been a parallel exploration of developments in collaborative business management (Kanter, 1994; Lamming, 1992). In each, there is a recognition that making collaboration work is a significant challenge.

Recent experience of work with and observation of collaborative ventures which have been developed to enhance public service provision, particularly in the area of community health and well-being, underpins the argument of this chapter. Typically, such ventures would see three or more agencies concerned with community health and welfare working together to

---

* From an advertisement for the post of Chief Executive of a company set up to support the creation of economic initiatives, employment opportunities and inner city regeneration in a UK locality.

study community needs, develop shared statements of policy, and establish joint programmes or projects. They cover the spectrum of collaborative arrangements suggested by Gray in Chapter 4, ranging from exploratory policy dialogues through advisory and confederative structures to formal, contractual relationships. In certain cases, *local* leadership and innovation have led to the creation of these collaborative interventions in such areas as community development and leadership, local service development and policies targeted at particular priority groups; in other cases, alliances have been established in the context of a powerful 'call to action' made by central policy-making bodies. Regardless of the source of initial impetus, the alliances often have no new funding, or central and local funding regimes mean that additional commitments of resource have strict time limits.

To illustrate the genre, in one such venture, a group of public and voluntary sector organizations operating within a tightly knit sub-region of England were invited by a national governmental agency to form a 'network' to support a short, anti-smoking campaign played out largely through the mass media. The invitation was to produce concerted, local action – events, services and activities which should also have publicity value. The national agency would provide funding for a part-time co-ordinator and a budget for local action for the duration of the campaign.

A sufficient number of local agencies responded to the call to action to make the local campaign viable, indeed vibrant. Each agency had a particular contribution to make, within a broad matrix of geographical 'jurisdiction' (covering either the sub-region or one of five localities within the sub-region) and 'sectoral base' (local government services, health services, voluntary, campaigning and service organizations). Whilst every agency added strength to the collaboration, the withdrawal of any one agency would not, in itself, have threatened the viability of the collaborative effort. During the first campaign, a clear pattern of active participation and passive support emerged. This was reinforced during a second campaign period, one year on, which was again supported financially by the national agency, but only after a search for local funding had produced insufficient support to continue.

To the author, as an independent evaluator of the initiative, witness to the development and subsequent renewal, under severe time pressure, of this network, the strong case for multi-agency working became clear only as the early, frenetic sharing of existing activities was replaced by more directed, collaborative action. This was most notable during the second, equally concentrated campaign period. That transition was not easy. The ability rapidly and consensually to put on to paper, at the very start, a set of broad and permissive rather than constraining objectives for the campaign deflected from a debate about the purpose of the group and the types of activity the alliance should be engaging in. For some in the network, there was one purpose – attracting media attention and coverage for the smoking issue. For others, media coverage was not the end, or even the output of most significance: their prime motivation was to secure appropriate smoking prevention activity at community level – the campaign and the media push was an opportunity to refresh or to develop links with health workers and community leaders in their patches and to work with them in shaping proposals for community activity. These latter are distinctly local purposes which would be made more potent by the support and challenges offered by membership of a wider alliance of interest.

With the conclusion of the two nationally sponsored campaigns, the issues of purpose and focus of activity of the collaborative arose sharply. Much effort has been spent in seeking local sponsorship mechanisms which will secure a future for the alliance. As with much collaborative work, this is problematic: the alliance falls between regional and local levels of organization; it is neither 'big enough' nor 'local enough' to provide a natural rallying point for support. The alliance wishes to continue, but requires support to do so. The search for an expression of rationale which commands real support from all necessary quarters and which reflects the commitment and capacity of the members of the alliance has been difficult: implications for the form, intensity and resourcing of collaborative behaviour in the future are serious.

The survival of such alliances depends, heavily, on their ability, judiciously, to create and to command value. It is in terms of the bases of value and the processes of creating and managing value, then, that the following discussion of collaborative working and sustainability is couched.

Collaboration

Collaboration implies a positive, purposive relationship between organizations that retain autonomy, integrity and distinct identity, and thus, the potential to withdraw from the relationship. Between the extremes of independence and fusion, the spectrum of structural form within which collaboration falls is nevertheless wide. It ranges from wide networks through loose alliances and tight federations to the creation of novel organizational entities, sometimes separate from the partner organizations, sometimes vested in one partner. In terms of texture rather than structure, collaboration is a distinct mode of organizing. Huxham and Himmelman (see Chapters 1 and 2), characterize collaboration as an intense form of mutual attachment, operating at the levels of interest, intent, affect and behaviour: actors are bound together by the mutually supportive pursuit of individual and collective benefit.

In exploring principles and practices for the achievement of collaborative advantage, a number of behavioural qualities could be argued to be critically important. Comparative studies of modes of organizing emphasize such qualities as the reliability, accountability and adaptability (Hannan and Freeman 1984), legitimacy (Meyer and Rowan, 1977) and efficiency (Williamson, 1985) of different forms of organization. Cross cutting these is the quality of sustainability.

Sustainability

Sustainability is a behavioural quality which connotes *future* persistence, continuity and continuing viability: it is both an outcome of, and a consideration in, the design and regulation of collaborative working; something to be explained and something which bears directly on organizational practice.

Sustainability has been treated, within work on strategic management (for example, see Ghemawat, 1989 and Kay, 1992), as a quality of competitive advantage, both at the product level and the level of the firm. Analysis of sustainability may suggest ways in which the advantage gained through innovation and market position and other distinctive competencies can be protected from erosion, by competitors, through imitation or substitution, from loss of privileged access to scarce factors of production, and so on. Without these sources of advantage, the benefit which can be appropriated by the company is reduced, so sustainability is a critical concern in assessing current and expected future performance.

Both Gray and Sink (Chapters 4 and 6) raise sustainability as an indicator of positive performance in the evaluation (and design) of co-operative inter-organizational relations. For various reasons, the length of a collaborative relationship *is* likely to be associated with positive performance. It is important, however, to distinguish between the behavioural outcome of longevity and the behavioural quality of sustainability of collaborative working: where longevity indicates past success, sustainability is inherently future-oriented. Yet, any judgement about the future state of collaborative action must be based on the assessment of other, present qualities and characteristics, including scale, complexity, and robustness, or alternatively, vulnerability (Hardy et al., 1992; Wistow and Hardy, 1991) of organizational arrangements and of commitment. An initial proposition, then, is that sustainability should be conceived not as a measure of performance, in itself, but, rather, as an expression of the value which collaborative working commands and of the processes by which collaborative efforts construct their value.

This chapter focuses on the forms that value can take, distinguishing broadly between the consequential value and the constitutive value of collaborative working. Each type of value has its own distinct bases, and these are briefly explored. Consequential value is expressed in claims about, *inter alia*, the relative efficiency, security and productiveness, legitimacy and adaptability, either of collaborative working in general, or of collaborative efforts in particular. These behavioural qualities may be a reason for the selection or emergence of collaboration in the first instance. They may also help to explain and promote the continuation or sustainability of collaboration (Hannan and Freeman, 1984). Whilst they are powerful claims to make about collaborative efforts, they are derivative, evaluative products of the way collaborative ventures are constituted. None is susceptible to direct manipulation or intervention, but each is, nevertheless, central to the interpretation and evaluation of those efforts. The primary, constitutive value of collaborative working is found in the character of collaborative efforts as they are constructed as expressions of purpose, as capacities, as a coherent, or as a disruptive, part of the institutional context, and as a form and standard of conduct. The nature and value of these four facets of character are constantly changing, defined, established and maintained through the processes of interpretation, negotiation and enactment which drive collaborative working. Thus, they are powerful levers which enable direct intervention and manipulation in the regulation of collaborative working and in the maintenance of collaborative relations and which may, too, hold value in themselves.

Bases of consequential value

Collaborative working is evaluated against alternative modes of organizing: the argument, below, is that it may be valued for any of a variety of behavioural qualities. These bases of evaluation are not necessarily mutually compatible, nor is there any necessary a priori ordering of the qualities. All things being equal, however, collaboration (both in general and in particular instances) is likely to be valued and to persist where it is, for example, comparatively productive, efficient, secure, legitimate and adaptable. These five bases of consequential value are considered, below, in order to highlight and illustrate the relationship between the behavioural qualities and the sustainability of collaborative efforts. The review is not exhaustive. The 'reliability' of collaborative forms of organization, for example, is not adequately addressed in the discussion of 'security': nor is the quality of 'accountability' properly raised in the discussion of legitimacy. Nevertheless, as the review suggests, the five qualities considered are important derivative or consequential bases of evaluation.

Productivity

There is broad agreement that the structural basis of collaboration lies in relations of interdependence between organizations, the functions they serve and the resources they control. In addition to goods and money, information, skills and technologies, access to publics and markets are common currencies of exchange; legitimacy and reputation – invisible assets – can also be seen as resources for exchange.

Pennings (1981) distinguishes three types of interdependence: vertical, horizontal and symbiotic. Each form of interdependence is the basis for a distinct type of exchange, with particular implications for the sustainability of collaboration.

The first (**vertical**), characterizes interdependencies between organizations at different stages in the process of 'production'. The creation of separate organizations responsible, respectively, for purchaser and provider roles in the newly formed 'internal market' for health care in the UK, the introduction of compulsory competitive tendering for an increasing number of public service functions, and the use of other forms of 'contracting out' have created new vertical interdependencies in public services (Harrison, 1993). In each case, client or purchasing organizations seek to ensure provision of services from a choice of possible contractors or provider organizations: provider organizations are, themselves, free to seek and enter contractual relationships with more than one client or purchaser. As a result, private sector providers compete with public service providers for the business of delivering public services and public service providers compete with one another. But, while they would normally be seen as competing for resources or custom, they may also work together to promote mutual interests, including, for example, fairness in contracting mechanisms. This second type of interdependence (**horizontal**), draws together functionally similar organizations around limited common interest, and may be reflected organizationally in, for example, trade federations and associations, lobby groups and 'cartels'.

In this perspective, collaboration allows for the very possibility of fulfilling organizational purpose or function. But it may also allow for the elaboration of new purpose and capability. Work on social problem-solving (Gray, 1989; McCann, 1983; Trist, 1983) explores the formation and maintenance of inter-organizational 'fields' or 'domains' through the definition, shaping and regulation of more extensive networks of interdependence. In such fields as economic development, crime prevention and community health and well-being, organizational interdependencies (of various types) are defined in relation to problems which are distinctly supra-organizational.

The third type of interdependence (**symbiotic**), extends this principle. It is comparable to 'productive' exchange or incorporation, which Emerson describes as follows:

> It takes two to dance the tango. If it is done well by both parties, both parties benefit from a single, socially-produced event. If either one fails to perform properly, neither one will benefit. Value is produced in the social process from behavioural contributions that have little or no value taken by themselves. (1981: 34)

There are a number of variants on this theme which emphasize, on the one hand, the emergence of group or collective gain, and on the other hand, the benefits to individuals that derive from group action. Thus Kay, for example, distinguishes two broad categories of joint venture, 'common objective' and 'mutually beneficial exchange'.

> The common objective venture is typically one in which ... two distinctive capabilities complement each other ... Mutually beneficial exchange is where each party has skill or information or expertise which is of value to the other. (1992: 152)

In terms of sustainability, 'common objective' collaborative relations will persist, all things being equal, so long as additional value is realized and/or anticipated through the juxtaposition and exploration of complementary resources. The anticipation of benefit is uncertain, but a sustained commitment of assets to a particular collaborative relationship may enable new and improved productivity. Dodgson (1993) and Lamming (1992), for example, argue that more extensive, more powerful and novel combinations of resources and technologies may become possible only as partners learn together about the potential for synergy.

Efficiency

Economic analyses of forms of organization now recognize the distinctive logic of a mode of governance of transactions that stands between markets and hierarchies (Thompson et al., 1991; Williamson, 1985). Such analyses recognize the economies of scale and scope that are afforded by pooling resources and efforts, but of central concern are the relative costs incurred in transactions. Where transactions are relatively frequent, where there is relatively great uncertainty and where durable transaction-specific investments are incurred by partners, then an emergent, adaptive process of agreement and production (collaboration) is an appropriate way of governing transactional relations between organizations (Williamson, 1985). The implication is simply that collaboration will persist where it demonstrates its efficiency as an instrument for governing transactions compared to hierarchy or market, and so long as those starting assumptions remain valid.

At the micro level, collaboration (labelled as relational or, more specifically, obligational contracting) has a particular binding mechanism. Thus, 'both parties have an incentive to sustain that relationship rather than to permit it to unravel, the object being to avoid the sacrifice of valued transaction-specific economies' (Williamson, 1985: 115). Williamson's argument turns in part on a consideration of sunk costs – collaboration is expected to develop efficiencies over time as developing trust and shared understanding between partners lead to reduced costs of conducting transactions – but it also rests on the relative cost of establishing and maintaining alternative mechanisms, collaborative or otherwise. These are central issues in work which takes the exchange relationship rather than the transaction as its central unit of analysis. Thus social exchange theorists argue that rather than efficiency, it is a preference for security and aversion to uncertainty which are the basic forces that tie organizations together in relationships of exchange.

Security

At a gross level of analysis, exchange theoretic analyses draw arguments about efficiency and productivity together to suggest that where partners secure needed resources and thereby realize benefits which outweigh costs over a number of transactions, development of resource dependence on the exchange partners may occur. The tensions between collaboration and competition in situations of horizontal interdependence may mean that collaborative efforts of this type are likely to take the form of a temporary 'coalition' or action set (Alter and Hage, 1993). In such cases, collaboration is purely instrumental and security is not expected. If, or as, partners develop trust in and commitment to one another, however, an exchange relationship may deepen to lock partners into a long-term relationship – for example, where exchange eventually involves a variety of resources, that package of resources may not be obtainable from any other potential partner. Recent accounts of collaboration to manage vertical interdependence – (for example, Lamming's (1992) work on supply chain management) – have emphasized the importance of longevity of relationships between suppliers and customers. Dodgson's (1993) work on technology innovation has similarly argued that collaboration is a long-term process. Finally, the relationship may come to dominate exchange considerations *per se*: this is expressed as particularism in which only certain partners are acceptable for reasons which may go considerably wider than the exchange of resources (Cook, 1977; Foa and Foa, 1980).

The sustainability of exchange relationships, at least as mediated by relations of dependence, is not solely a function of the value placed on resources made available by exchange partners, but also by the availability of potential alternative partners. Where particularism is extreme, then alternatives are unlikely to exist. Where dependencies are based on the security of resources and on the exchange ratio offered, then alternatives may challenge exchange ratios by offering either equivalent or substitutable resources. Thus sustainability is not simply a function of the particular relationship, but of the wider organizational context in which any particular exchange relationship is set.

Legitimacy

While social exchange theories remain the dominant framework for conceptualizing the rationale and structural basis for collaboration, social exchange theory applies most clearly to the explanation of *voluntary* exchange relations. Thus, organizations are willing to give up degrees of freedom, or autonomy, in order to secure needed resources, ranging from the material and financial to the symbolic, through exchange transactions.

Exchange theory and its close relation power dependence theory, can also depict and account for relationships in which power differentials exist between actual or potential exchange partners and where coercion may be a contributory factor in the formation and maintenance of exchange. A special form of 'external' coercion occurs when exchange and collaborative relations are mandated (Raelin, 1980). The term mandate is commonly used in such a way as to imply prescription, that is, to set out legally binding obligations and responsibilities. Mandates often are prescriptive, if incomplete and imprecise as instruction sets, but there are also many weaker signals, strategies, policies and guidelines, and accompanying incentives, for example, which legitimize and encourage particular forms of organizational activity and behaviour. Such instructions are permissive or enabling and have the status of *authorizations* rather than obligations. Authorizations, for example in the form of policies or guidelines, are likely to be ambiguous (Baier et al., 1986; Barrett and Fudge, 1981) and to allow significant discretion both in response and the form and extent of collaborative working which may result. Members of organizations seeking external sources of value – flags and symbols – to further their own interests will look to such authorizations as ways of managing meaning within and between organizations (Pettigrew, 1977).

Many accounts of collaborative working emphasize the process by which collaborative action may legitimately be undertaken in the name of a problem domain. But collaboration, as a mode of organizing, may itself acquire and imbue legitimacy. Thus, Meyer and Rowan argue that:

> . . . organizations that omit environmentally legitimate elements of structure or create unique structures lack acceptable legitimated accounts of their activities. Such organizations are more vulnerable to claims that they are negligent, irrational or unnecessary. (1977: 349–50)

In this view, collaboration will be sustainable, then, so long as it serves as a defence against critique or as a currency which may be used to strengthen claims to retain role, to extend functions, or simply, to survive.

Survival may have its own self-reinforcing quality of legitimacy, as Hannan and Freeman argue:

> Processes of external legitimization also take time. Although an organization must have some minimal level of public legitimacy in order to mobilize sufficient resources to begin operations, new organizations (and especially new organizational forms) have rather weak claims on public and official support. Nothing legitimates both individual organizations and forms more than longevity. Old organizations tend to generate dense webs of exchange, to affiliate with centres of power, and to acquire an aura of inevitability. (1984: 158)

Whilst the shape and legitimacy of an inter-organizational domain will alter over time, collaborative activity, initially undertaken to address a specific problem, may nevertheless become institutionalized, selected, defined and cemented, for example, in an annual cycle of joint planning, a protocol for exchange of resources, in job descriptions, and in shared facilities and initiatives.

Adaptability

While the qualities of legitimacy, efficiency, security and productiveness of collaboration are important points of reference, sustainability, it may be argued, also lies in the ability of organizations, collectively and in concert, to adapt to changes in circumstance. Continuity in collaborative working can be promoted through change and adaptation in a variety of ways.

First, the capacity to maintain, or repair, collaborative relationships is an important form of adaptability which bears directly on the sustainability of collaborative working. The idea of maintenance or repair is not intended to imply the specification and preservation of a particular state – of purpose, membership, structure and so forth – of a collaborative effort. Instead, it is intended to suggest a process of change and adaptation which involves, nevertheless, the conservation of identity and integrity. This follows Selznick's argument that:

> The leadership of any polity fails when it concentrates on sheer survival: institutional survival, properly understood, is a matter of maintaining values and distinctive identity. (1957: 63)

A particular form of maintenance occurs where the terms of exchange, or partnership are left incomplete by design and are the subject of periodic review and redefinition rather than simply used as a basis for enforcement (Williamson, 1985). However, such adaptation is simply a part of the warp and weft of collaborative working (Gray, 1989; Ring and Van de Ven, 1994; Strauss, 1982). As Ring and Van de Ven, for example, argue:

> . . . co-operative IORs [inter-organizational relationships] are socially contrived mechanisms for collective action, which are continually shaped and restructured by actions and symbolic interpretations of the parties involved. Thus just as an initial structure of safeguards established a context for interparty action, so also do subsequent interactions reconstruct and embody new governance structures for the relationships. (1994: 96)

But many accounts of collaborative working go further to emphasize the capacity for responsiveness, adaptation and innovation that emergent collaborative arrangements afford. In their recent analysis of action-oriented networks, for example, Carley and Christie argue that:

> organizations are forced increasingly by turbulence and complexity into a range of *temporary* alliances, formal or informal, with other organizations. The capacity to do this productively is called 'connective capacity', which results in collaborative problem-solving. (1992: 171)

This sees collaboration as an innovatory, tactical mode of working (Gray, 1989; Lamming, 1992) where alliances are forged, reshaped and ended in response to pressures from the wider environment. The value of such a practice is in its responsiveness at the level of populations of organizations rather than its enduring presence in any specific situation; indeed, the sustainability of specific collaborative ventures is not, itself, a desirable characteristic of this mode of organizing. Where specific collaborative arrangements are disbanded, traces of organization are, none the less, likely to remain, more loosely formed than before, but potentially capable of generating and pursuing collective strategies. Professional, role and social networks and networking practices, re-usable learning about effective procedures and management methods and enhanced understanding of the interests and capacities of others are examples of such traces (Friend and Hickling, 1987). Adaptability, in this sense, might be seen almost as the antithesis of sustainability, and more strongly associated with the replication or diffusion of collaboration as a general response to societal or business issues. So long as adaptation is not simply interpreted as opportunism, collaboration as a strategy for organizing may remain in good currency.

The constitutive bases of value

It is tempting to argue that the five consequential bases of value reviewed above, and others, provide general decision and evaluation criteria which are powerful in explaining the initiation of collaborative activity and indicative of the sustainability of that activity. All things being equal, the greater the presence of these qualities, the more likely collaborative working is to be sustained. They are, however, only indicative. Even among the five qualities reviewed, there are potentially incompatibilities; for example, high levels of security may be inconsistent with adaptability. The importance placed on each quality and the balance of value which holds at any point in the life of a collaborative venture will, therefore, be critical mediating factors. Loss of legitimacy may be fatal; or it may simply mean that collaboration is driven 'underground'. Inefficiency may be tolerated for the security and legitimacy collaboration brings; or it may lead to loss of members, functions and critical mass.

Any practical judgements about the sustainability of collaborative working, or affecting its longevity, will be grounded against an account of particular collaborative activity. While the behavioural qualities will intrude as points of reference, the first line of judgement is with that account and with its various elements which form 'constitutive' bases of value. Each of the four elements proposed is, itself, complex, and will have its own life cycle or 'biography': taken together, however, they define the basis on which the identity and value of collaborative activity is negotiated. Together, they characterize collaboration so that it may be evaluated in terms of the consequential bases of value. Thus, it is argued, expectations and decisions about collaborative futures are likely to be influenced by the extent to which collaborative efforts are, or would be, valued as: (i) expressions of purpose; (ii) a part of a wider institutional context; (iii) channels and capacities; and (iv) a mode and standard of conduct. Yet, each, where it is possible to disentangle them, might be a source of value in itself.

Selznick's observation is apt here; that organizations can become valued for what they are, and what they represent, a source of direct personal gratification and as a vehicle for group integrity and perpetuation, rather than for what, instrumentally, they can do.

> . . . to institutionalize is to infuse with value beyond the technical requirements of the task at hand . . . From the standpoint of the committed person, the organization is changed from an expendable tool into a valued source of personal satisfaction . . . The test of infusion with value is expendability . . . organizations become infused with value as they come to symbolize the community's aspirations, its sense of identity . . . An organization that does take on this

symbolic meaning has some claim on the community to avoid liquidation or transformation on purely technical or economic grounds . . . All this is a relative matter and one of degree . . . For the group that participates directly in it, an organization may acquire much institutional value, yet in the eyes of the larger community the organization may be readily expendable. (1957: 17–20)

Collaborative action as an expression of purpose

Attachment to collaborative efforts is both driven and constrained by prior attachment and accountabilities to reference groups and their purposes outside the immediate context of collaboration; in particular, groups within 'parent' organizations demand a duty of reference (Friend, 1993). These groups may be other established task groups, functional groups or sentient groups to which accountability or loyalty is due (Miller and Rice, 1990). To be sustainable, collaborative arrangements must be able to recognize, reconcile and extend, or at least mediate, these interests with those the collaborative effort comes to assert.

The way in which an inter-organizational domain of activity commands energy and becomes organized has been well explicated by Trist (1983) and others (Gray, 1989; McCann, 1983; Pasquero, 1991). Through the act of appreciation of a meta-problem, common purpose is defined, although it may only become fully articulated through a continuing process of institution-building and 'direction-setting'. Trist thus links the expression of purpose to the emergence of organization and leadership within an inter-organizational domain.

As an identity is acquired the domain begins to take a direction which makes a path into the future . . . Once a referent organization appears, purposeful action can be undertaken in the name of the domain . . . (1983: 274–5)

While there has been less attention paid to the continuation of collaborative action, the maintenance of consensus, regulation of conflict and continuing process of appreciation of future problems – all functions of the referent organization – are likely to be critical. The evaluation of collaboration as an expression of purpose plays a role in each of these processes.

Purpose may be expressed in processes of dialogue, in patterns of involvement and commitment, and in the way leadership functions are fulfilled. It may be found, too, in the pattern of decisions and actions taken on behalf of and as a result of the collaborative and in shared understanding that develops as collaborative working is pursued. In short, collaborative activity can express purpose without declaring intent explicitly. The purpose inferred from the existence, and activity, of a collaborative endeavour forms a base of constitutive value.

The argument for the specification of explicit, shared, or common, purpose which attaches specifically to the collaborative effort is based, in part, on the need for a mutually agreed mechanism for regulation of collaborative arrangements (Astley, 1984; Huxham, 1993a). Explicit statements of purpose have value in a number of ways. First, they are a source of identity for collaborative organizations, helping to clarify boundaries and commitments and to define the scope and scale of joint work. They also serve as a way of raising and evaluating claims to membership of the collaborative organization. Secondly, purpose provides a control against drift by the collaborative, against inappropriate action and against deviation or opportunism by partners – it serves as part of a contract between partners. Thirdly, explicit statements of purpose also provide a reference point for external dealings – both a language for mobilizing resources, influencing others' activity, and a way of reckoning. As Hannan and Freeman have argued: 'the basis on which organizations mobilize resources initially and gain support from society is their claim to accomplish some specific set of ends' (1984: 152).

In each of these ways, collaborative efforts may be valued as and for their expressions of purpose. They may serve to include or to exclude organizations from responsibility to act, or otherwise help to define the scale of work to be undertaken by the collaborative effort and by responsible organizations under their own mandates. They may provide leadership and focus in complex, contested domains. And they may serve as rallying points enabling new forms of linkage, or the alteration or renewal of existing relationships. Collaborative action, as an expression of shared purpose which lends coherence and identity to its component parts, is thus a basis of constitutive value. Individuals, and their organizations, may value collaborative activity simply as a statement of purpose. The specific content of the espoused purpose, and the manner of its expression, will, then, fundamentally affect judgements about the collaborative effort.

Collaborative action as an element of the institutional framework

In his paper on designing precarious partnerships, Metcalfe (1981) draws on the idea of the 'corporate group', whose task is to cope with two interrelated sets of problems: the integration of the parts into the whole; and the integration of the whole with the wider environment. Collaborative organizing efforts tend to blur the boundaries between these two problems in that each constituent organization is also a channel to, and part of, the wider environment. Nevertheless, the viability of a collaborative venture is likely to be significantly affected by the degree to which it is valued as a component of the organizational matrix into which it is set, or from which it emerges.

The institutional context or framework can be depicted as the existing arrangement of territories, functions and practices, and the ways in which these are organizationally, professionally and politically demarcated and defended. Such a framework has many dimensions, including purpose and functions of organizations, geographical territory and mandate, lines of accountability, and so on.

While they are sources of stability, institutional contexts do change, often through changes in and repairs to practices. Collaborative efforts contribute both to the support or to this gradual refashioning of the institutional framework. For example, an informal network established to share professional best practice may become formalized and extended by 'bidding' to develop a new service or rationalize existing services. Occasionally, collaborative efforts may demand radical change with a long tail of consequences, through major redesigns of the functions, mandate, structure and working practices of partners, and, indeed, of other organizations which are not within the boundaries of the collaborative organization. Differences in culture, structures, working methods between organizations (Wistow and Hardy, 1991) all jeopardize collaborative efforts as they demand realignment. The reconstruction of local authority services into one-stop shops is an example of radical change (Bostedt and Rutqvist, 1994); the changes in function of health and local authorities in England, from direct service providers and managers to service commissioners and enablers is another example of wholesale institutional change (Harrison, 1993; Leach et al., 1994).

Purpose is one form of linkage between collaborative efforts and the institutional context. The expression of purpose has implications for the way in which the boundaries of the collaborative effort overlay, nest within, or link those of existing organizations; and conversely, the membership of the collaborative organization influences the purpose it can claim (see Finn, Chapter 10). As well as the specific content of a claim, the 'level of resolution' at which collaborative purpose is specified (that is, more or less encompassing) is thus important in determining the fit with the framework around (Friend, 1977; Huxham, 1993b). The institutional framework similarly constrains the distribution of functions among organizations (Carley and Christie, 1992; Trist, 1983). Trist (1983), for example, argues that a referent organization, the most tangible expression of collaborative function, is sustainable only where it does not usurp the functions of its constituent organizations.

The value of collaborative working, as an element in the institutional framework, is reflected in commitments to new patterns of relating between organizations one order removed from its primary relations. In the way that collaborative efforts may be valued for their expression of purpose, so too collaboration may be valued for its elaboration of the existing pattern of function and territory.

Collaborative action as a capacity

By the capacity of a collaborative venture, is meant the ability to acquire and organize resources to deliver activity against purpose or task. Capacity may be latent, where, for example, purpose or tasks are not clear or decided, and yet it may still have value. Judgements about capacity will include the membership and potential membership of the collaborative, size and the specialization of function, the decision-making and communication structures and processes within which interaction occurs – formal and informal – and so on. It is as an infrastructure with the potential to deliver appropriate benefit that collaborative capacity is valued.

The resourcing of collaborative efforts is often a significant point of vulnerability. Within public services, collaborative efforts may, at least initially, be stimulated by external funding. Sustainability, then, has a strong connotation of independence from or capacity to maintain identity without external support (Stefanini and Ruck, 1992). As a hedge against risk, collaborative ventures are often started by resourcing at the margin of core organizational activities, for example, by adding the collaborative task to existing workload of managers and professionals. Marginal resourcing means that little is lost if the collaborative effort fails, and that the effective creation of capacity is highly valued. The difficulties inherent in the 'co-ordination of many margins', however, mean that capacity within the collaborative effort can be weak. A common response is to focus the collaborative effort organizationally. As Carley and Christie observe:

> It would be misleading to imply that successful, task-oriented networks do not require considerable nurturing and maintenance to survive and prosper . . . some administrative support, financial control and most important some central focus. (1992: 200)

Trist (1983) proposes the referent organization as a 'centre' of leadership, co-ordination and regulation of the production capacity of an inter-organizational domain. In more bounded networks and partnerships, a 'lead partner' commonly holds such responsibilities.

Once a critical mass or organized resource is established, however, the capacity represented by the collaborative effort can be used in a variety of ways to generate new collaborative relationships and new collaborative activity. As Ring and Van de Ven have argued:

> . . . most co-operative interorganizational relationships emerge incrementally and begin with small, informal deals that initially require little reliance on trust because they involve little risk . . . As these transactions are repeated through time, and meet basic norms of equity and efficiency, the parties may feel increasingly secure in committing more of their available resources . . . (1994: 101)

The availability of an infrastructure, or a capacity, within which new activities can be lodged and from which new activity can be spawned is a source of constitutive value.

Secondly, while initiating and stabilizing capacity is a significant challenge, regulating collaborative activity so that it does not exceed the 'carrying capacity' of the collaborative itself and the agents that make it up is a continuing concern. Demands on capacity can over-reach thresholds of tolerance – too great a yield can be sought, too many tasks or functions loaded into the system, or too fast a pace of change set. The carrying capacity refers to the level of activity or the degree of change a collaborative relationship (or set of such relationships) is able to sustain without any partner organization losing its sense of security in the relationship. The tolerance of organizations to the level of activity or its rate of change may relate to the organization's own sense of identity, as expressed in strategy statements and level of development of management processes, and to its awareness of a need to collaborate (Huxham, 1993b). Some issues concerning the conduct of collaborative working and its impact on sustainability are considered in the next section.

Collaborative action as a model of conduct

As with each of the bases of constitutive value, the manner in which collaboration is conducted may be a source of value, both instrumentally, and for itself. Instrumentally, principled conduct may serve, as Kanter (1994) has argued, to create reputation as a good partner: conduct may equally be valued as and for itself, as a form and standard of relating to others. Conduct forms the texture (Hosking and Fineman, 1990) of two sets of relationships: those between partners in a collaborative arrangement and those between the partner organizations and their representatives or agents. Each is important in creating and sustaining value, but only the first is considered here.

Ring and Van de Ven (1994) argue that co-operative inter-organizational relations may dissolve for four reasons relating to conduct:

1   excessive legal structuring and monitoring of the relationship;
2   conflicts between role and interpersonal behaviours of organizational parties;
3   conditions for violations of trust;
4   escalating commitments to failing transactions.

Of these, the issue of trust has tended to receive most attention.

The ability to presume that partners are acting responsibly towards and within a collaborative relationship is highly valued and likely to influence where commitment to collaborative activity is directed. To presume, however, that others are being open about their motives, interests, information, decision-making and changes in circumstance, at least as they affect the collaboration, requires heroic thresholds of trust, or acceptance of risk. A particular preoccupation in the literature has been how 'opportunism' may be forestalled. As Selznick warned:

> To take advantage of opportunities is to show that one is alive, but institutions, no less than persons must look to the long-run effects of present advantage. In speaking of the 'long-run' we have in mind not time as such but how change affects personal or institutional identity. Such effects are not usually immediately apparent, and therefore we emphasize the lapse of time. But changes in character or identity may occur quite quickly. (1957: 143)

Discussion of opportunism has focused on the conditions under which, and the extent to which, trust may replace explicit agreements, or contracts, as the basis of a relationship between organizations. Here, the issue is the reverse – how and to what extent can the terms of collaboration be spelt out explicitly in order that they may underpin collaborative conduct which holds value. Reliance on tacit agreement and trust is inevitable since 'contracts' cannot specify all contingencies, but this is the result of experience, as Ring and Van de Ven argue:

> Congruent expectations [are] a cumulative product of numerous interactions; through these interactions emerge trust in the goodwill of others and an understanding of constraints on the relationship that may be imposed by a person's organizational role. (1994: 100)

Explicit ground rules cannot substitute for trust which results from shared experience of expectations met. The discovery and articulation of shared beliefs and values about conduct can, however, help to promote a sense of inclusion, of predictability or dependability, and of unequivocality in relationships, all of which, as Ring and Van de Ven (1994) have noted, are fundamental pre-requirements for continuing motivation and commitment. It may also provide an early opportunity to model and evaluate collaborative conduct.

What areas of practice should ground rules address? Agreements could cover a wide range of matters, from criteria for entry into and membership of the collaboration and status as a member, through information sharing and disclosure, to 'exit strategies'. Two 'headline' areas of conduct are, first, fair dealing in the distribution and appropriation of benefits arising from collaborative working, and secondly, issues of fairness in procedure.

The manner of distribution of costs and of benefit are significant concerns in the conduct of collaborative working. Carley and Christie note that:

> Organizations will often act in unco-ordinated and dissonant ways in attempting to meet their individual objectives, typically externalising as many of the costs and internalising as many of the benefits, of their actions as they can. (1992: 165)

Where such opportunistic conduct dominates, then collaborative action is unlikely to be sustained. Ring and Van de Ven's (1994) analysis is important in highlighting the need for explicit and principled agreements about the distribution and appropriation, suggesting the overriding principle of 'fair dealing'. Commitment to the collaborative effort is clearly dependent on the realization of benefit by the collaboration. The manner of distribution of benefit, however, depends on the nature of the work of the collaborative and on the 'accounting' procedures by which benefit is defined. In public service collaboration, the added value from collaboration is expected to be returned to the clients of those services or to the citizens. Where various client groups are to be served, each by a partner organization, there may be an issue about the sequence in which organizations, and hence their clients, realize the benefits. Acceptance that equity will only be seen over the long run, and that, at any point in time there may be an uneven distribution of benefit is thus a principle of importance. Value lies in a confidence that obligations will be met, particularly when collaborative efforts fall into the large area between fixed point collaboratives and permanent, institutionalized relations, where expectations of collaborative futures are ambiguous, tilted one way or the other by presumptions of permanence or of temporariness. Thus, Boon proposes that:

> A charitable orientation towards evaluating the partner's actions is perhaps the hallmark of a trusting relationship. In part, this liberal view of the partner's behaviours and underlying motives is due to the long-term nature of the accounting process that trusting individuals employ to track their partners' contributions to the relationship. Evaluated in the broader context of positive events and experiences . . . occasional negative behaviours inevitably pale in significance. (1994: 102–3)

While the distribution of direct benefit may be manageable, other, residual benefit created through the process of collaborative action – experience gained, skills developed, networks catalysed, knowledge transferred, glory, and so on – may be more problematic. The distribution and appropriation of these benefits is less easily regulated. Where passive association with a successful collaboration may be sufficient to enable, if not to justify, appropriation of information and glory, active contributors may feel their efforts devalued.

Agreement over a form, or forms, of distributive justice is bound up inextricably with agreement and control over procedures; attempts to secure procedural justice are likely to be equally important to the value individual agents and their organizations place on collaborative working (Lind and Tyler, 1988). Procedural principles cover such matters as rights of access to information and to decision-making forums, but they may also seek to establish expectations of openness between partners about motives, interests and the implications of any changes in circumstance for the collaborative effort. While, 'pessimistically', collaboration may simply be another political arena in which sectional interests are defined or obscured but nevertheless pursued (Challis et al., 1988), the seeds of sustainability lie in beliefs and values which make for a 'way of looking' (Castaneda, 1990), an appreciation of collaboration and its potential and the conduct and symbols these engender or support.

Conclusion

This chapter started with an assertion that the sustainability of collaborative organizing efforts lies in their ability to create and command value. With value comes commitment and with commitment, continued existence. The argument has been that collaborative efforts may be valued for a variety of reasons, or in a variety of ways. In the processes of creating and maintaining value, it may be helpful to distinguish the bases of value. In this chapter, two distinct types have been proposed. The first, bases of consequential value are derivative, behavioural qualities of collaborative organizational arrangements: they include such qualities as legitimacy, security and efficiency. While they are important reference points in evaluation of collaborative efforts, they are not susceptible to direct manipulation, in part because they are used to make comparative judgements. The second, bases of constitutive value, see collaborative efforts may be valued for, and as expressions of purpose, fit within an institutional context, capacity and conduct. Each of these, alone, or together, may be directly manipulated to create identity for a collaborative effort.

Collaborative working is a complex phenomenon. To argue, then, as this chapter has done, that collaboration may be reduced to a set of elements without elaborating the relationships between those elements may be to oversimplify grossly. Yet, the attribution and maintenance of value is dependent on the political economy of organization. Active agents and passive agents, their reference groupings, especially within their parent organizations, and the wider communities of stakeholders and of interested observers are all of relevance in the construction of the value of collaborative action and of its future sustainability. They are all likely to do so in different ways. This chapter has sketched a framework setting out some elements in terms of which that process of construction of value can be considered.

Acknowledgements

Thanks are due to many collaborators for their tolerance of observation and feedback, and for their willingness to talk frankly and with great insight about their practice. Special thanks to colleagues at the Centre for Health Planning and Management at Keele University who were involved in the research or who commented on the text, and to Ben Corr for many thought-provoking discussions. This chapter is based, in part, on research funded by the Health Education Authority of England.

References

Alter, C. and Hage, J. (1993) *Organizations Working Together*. Newbury Park, CA: Sage.
Astley, W.G. (1984) 'Toward an appreciation of collective strategy', *Academy of Management Review*, 9 (3): 526–35.
Baier, V.E., March, J.G. and Saetren, H. (1986) 'Implementation and ambiguity', *Scandinavian Journal of Management Studies*, 2: 197–212.
Barrett, S. and Fudge, C. (1981) *Policy and Action: Essays on the Implementation of Public Policy*. London: Methuen.
Boon, S.D. (1994) 'Dispelling doubt and uncertainty: trust in romantic relationships', in S. Duck (ed.), *Dynamics of Relationships*. London: Sage. pp. 86–111.
Bostedt, G. and Rutqvist, H. (1994) 'One stop shops'. Paper presented at the International Workshop on Multi-Organizational Partnerships: Working Together Across Organizational Boundaries. EIASM, Brussels, September.
Carley, M. and Christie, I. (1992) *Managing Sustainable Development*. London: Earthscan.
Castaneda, C. (1990) *A Separate Reality*. Harmondsworth: Penguin.
Challis, D., Fuller, S., Henwood, M., Klein, R., Plowden, W., Webb, A. and Wistow, G.

(1988). *Joint Approaches to Social Policy: Rationality and Practice.* Cambridge: Cambridge University Press.

Cook, K. (1977) 'Social exchange as the basis for inter-organizational relations', *Sociological Quarterly*, 18: 62–82.

Dodgson, M. (1993) 'Learning, trust and technological collaboration', *Human Relations*, 46 (1): 77–95.

Emerson, R.M. (1981) 'Social exchange theory', in M. Rosenberg and J. Turner (eds), *Social Psychology: Sociological Perspectives*. New York: Harper & Row. pp. 30–65.

Foa, U.G and Foa, E. (1980) 'Resource theory: interpersonal behavior as exchange', in K.J. Gergen, M.S. Greenberg and R.H. Willis (eds), *Social Exchange: Advances in Theory and Research*. New York: Plenum Press. pp. 77–101.

Friend, J.K. (1977) 'The dynamics of policy', *Long Range Planning*, 10: 40–7.

Friend, J.K. (1993) 'Searching for appropriate theory and practice in multiorganizational fields', *Journal of the Operational Research Society*, 44 (6): 585–98.

Friend, J.K. and Hickling, A. (1987) *Planning under Pressure*. Oxford: Pergamon.

Ghemawat, P. (1989) *Commitment: the Dynamic of Strategy*. New York: Free Press.

Gray, B. (1989) *Collaborating: Finding Common Ground for Multiparty Problems*. San Francisco: Jossey Bass.

Hannan, M.T. and Freeman, J. (1984) 'Structural inertia and organizational change', *American Sociological Review*, 49: 149–64.

Hardy B., Turrell, A. and Wistow, G. (1992) *Innovations in Community Care Management: Minimising Vulnerability*. Aldershot: Avebury.

Harrison, A. (ed.) (1993) *From Hierarchy to Contract*. Oxford: Policy Journals, Transaction Books.

Hosking, D. and Fineman, S. (1990) 'Organizing processes', *Journal of Management Studies*, 27 (6): 583–604.

Huxham, C.S. (1993a) 'Pursuing collaborative advantage', *Journal of the Operational Research Society*, 44 (6): 599–611.

Huxham, C.S. (1993b) 'Collaborative capability: an intraorganizational perspective on collaborative advantage', *Public Money and Management*, 12 (July–Sept): 21–8.

Kanter, R.M. (1994) 'Collaborative advantage: the art of alliances', *Harvard Business Review*, July–August, 96–108.

Kay, J. (1992) *The Foundations of Corporate Success*. Oxford: Oxford University Press.

Lamming, R. (1992) *Beyond Partnership: Strategies for Innovation and Lean Supply*. New York: Prentice Hall.

Leach, S., Stewart, J. and Walsh, K. (1994) *The Changing Organisation and Management of Local Government*. Basingstoke: Macmillan.

Lind, E.A. and Tyler, T.R. (1988) *The Social Psychology of Procedural Justice*. New York: Plenum.

McCann, J.E. (1983) 'Design guidelines for social problem solving interventions', *The Journal of Applied Behavioral Science*, 19 (2): 177–92.

Metcalfe, L. (1981) 'Designing precarious partnerships', in P.C. Nystrom and W.H. Starbuck (eds), *Handbook of Organizational Design*, vol. 1: *Adapting Organizations to their Environments*. Oxford: Oxford University Press. pp. 503–30.

Metcalfe, L. and Richards, S. (1990) *Improving Public Management*. London: Sage.

Meyer, J.W. and Rowan, B. (1977) 'Institutionalized organizations: formal structure as myth and ceremony', *American Journal of Sociology*, 83: 340–63.

Miller, E.J. and Rice A.K. (1990) 'Task and sentient systems and their boundary controls', in E. Trist and H. Murray (eds), *The Social Engagement of Social Science*, vol. 1: *The Socio-Psychological Perspective*. London: Free Association Books. pp. 259–71.

Nocon, A. (1994) *Collaboration in Community Care in the 1990s*. Sunderland: Business Education Publishers.

Pasquero, J. (1991) 'Supraorganizational collaboration', *Journal of Applied Behavioral Science*, 27 (1): 38–64.

Pennings, J.M. (1981) 'Strategically interdependent organizations', in P.C. Nystrom and W.H.

Starbuck (eds), *Handbook of Organizational Design*, vol. 1: *Adapting Organizations to their Environments*. Oxford: Oxford University Press. pp. 433–55.

Pettigrew, A.M. (1977) 'Strategy formulation as a political process', *International Studies of Management and Organization*, 7 (2): 78–87.

Raelin, J.A. (1980) 'A mandated basis of inter-organizational relations: the legal-political network', *Human Relations*, 33: 57–68.

Ring, P.S. and Van de Ven, A.H. (1994) 'Developmental processes of cooperative interorganizational relationships', *Academy of Management Review*, 19 (1): 90–118.

Selznick, P. (1957) *Leadership in Administration*. New York: Harper & Row.

Stefanini, A. and Ruck, N. (1992) 'Managing externally-assisted health projects for sustainability in developing countries', *International Journal of Health Planning and Management*, 7: 199–210.

Strauss, A. (1982) 'Interorganizational negotiation', *Urban Life*, 11 (3): 350–67.

Thompson, G., Frances, J., Levacic, R. and Mitchell, J. (1991) *Markets, Hierarchies and Networks: the Coordination of Social Life*. London: Sage.

Trist, E. (1983) 'Referent organizations and the development of interorganizational domains', *Human Relations*, 36 (3): 269–84.

Williamson, O.E. (1985) *Economic Organization: Firms, Markets and Policy Control*. Brighton: Wheatsheaf Books.

Wistow, G. and Hardy, B. (1991) 'Joint management in community care', *Journal of Management in Medicine*, 5 (4): 44–8.

6

Five Obstacles to Community-Based Collaboration and Some Thoughts on Overcoming Them

David Sink

A statement in an article by Chris Huxham suggests the tenuous nature of collaboration:

> There is a fine balance to be struck between gaining the benefits of collaborating and making the situation worse. (Huxham with Macdonald, 1992: 50)

Keeping this balance in mind, facilitators must be careful in calling for collaboration when a community is unprepared for it or when collaborative effort is inappropriate. Facilitation of successful collaboration faces significant obstacles which may prevent successful implementation (Gray, 1989).

The purpose of this chapter is to discuss five obstacles that frequently confront community-based collaboration attempts. Although not intended to be an exhaustive listing, the discussion focuses on five of the most difficult barriers to overcome and reflects extensive experience of the author in facilitating collaboration among various combinations of the following organizations in US cities: local governments, private businesses and business associations, local police departments, neighbourhood associations, churches, health-related agencies, universities, and youth-serving non-profit organizations.

In the United States, many health and human services are delivered not by government but by private, non-profit agencies which contract with government to provide those services. Public funding is rarely adequate and the non-profit agencies frequently must generate a portion of their own revenues through grant writing and fund raising. Likewise, these agencies are encouraged to build alliances with other agencies that have a stake in a particular service or domain in order to generate other forms of support and reduce unnecessary duplication of effort. The difficulties experienced in such collaborative efforts, many of which cross sectoral lines, spawn from the following obstacles:

1   Involving government officials is often critical to a collaborative's success but frequently problematic. Their relationships within government as well as with the citizenry seem to get in the way.

2   Most collaboration appears to take a sequential or incremental approach which may be ill-suited for emergency crises which demand non-incremental efforts.
3   The shift from a betterment to an empowerment collaborative is a difficult journey which involves social learning, building respect and trust, and much risk-taking.
4   A major challenge in facilitating collaboration is dealing with individual representatives' idiosyncrasies, egos, personal agendas and interpersonal quirkiness.
5   Collaboratives whose members represent different and differing work and social sectors face extraordinary bridging challenges.

Each obstacle is discussed in terms of its characteristics, its significance, and its implications for stakeholders and others who attempt to facilitate collaboration.

Public officials as collaborators

1   Involving government officials in collaboratives is often critical to success but frequently problematic. Their relationships within government as well as with the citizenry seem to get in the way.

Collaborative advantage is vital to the growing practice of public–private partnerships. It often is difficult to make happen because of lack of tradition, past failures, uncomfortableness, and/or unwillingness associated with the roles played by public officials (both elected and appointed) and public institutions (national, state and local). Officeholders express a keen interest in 'working more closely with the people and their organizations', especially when the people are registered voters and the organizations willing to finance re-election campaigns! Some actually do instigate meaningful change through sustained partnerships with citizen groups, but the need to sustain one's political career often gets in the way. Ironically, those with secure political futures (that is, those representing 'safe' districts), whom we would assume could take some political risks in reaching out, seem least likely to do so. Conversely, the relatively short timeframe that constrains public officials (that is, two- or four-year terms) also may account for many elected leaders being unwilling to invest the time and energy necessary to make a collaborative effort work.

Bureaucrats, even enlightened ones, may have even less incentive to participate in collaboratives. Because public administrators generally have little flexibility and autonomy in defining the purposes of their organization and programmes, and because their objectives are more diverse and harder to specify, collaborative behaviour (both inside government and with external organizations) is usually subject to a more complex set of influences and is more difficult to facilitate. Reward systems are generally standardized and discourage risk-taking and going beyond the explicit tasks assigned. Unless the job description calls for actively working with elements of a shared domain, the public administrator appears unlikely to take the initiative and invest in collaborative formation. Barr and Huxham shed light on this topic in their discussion related to government officials and community representatives collaborating for community development in Chapter 7 of this volume.

Despite these obstacles to public-sector involvement, the need is greater than ever. Resource scarcity in many local governments, caused by declining tax bases and a general unwillingness of people to tax themselves more, argues for collaborative effort. Many public and non-profit agencies lack the wherewithal to go it alone. Yet, ironically, facilitators are finding that a fewer-than-expected number of collaboratives forms in response to crisis scarcity (Sink, 1987). That may be because the need to reduce uncertainty and enhance resources is outweighed by an unwillingness to increase an agency's dependence. A fear of lost autonomy seems to dominate the thinking. From a rational perspective, such decision-making appears absurd. And, at some point, imminent demise does tend to jump-start even the most reticent to reach out. Still, many agencies exercise a so-called 'bunker mentality' where one keeps the head down, the neck tucked in, and the shelter door closed tight until the storm blows over. They lack what Barbara Gray calls a 'domain focus,' displaying an: 'inability to conceptualize problems and organize solutions at the domain level' (1989: 15).

Other key players in municipal level politics include prominent business interests. In a larger context of 'urban regimes' – an intriguing explanation of community power developed by Elkin (1987) and Stone (1989) – purposive collaboration may formalize the informal power arrangements between public and private-sector actors that characterize an urban regime and provide a mechanism for strategic choice to be exercised. As a 'governing coalition', an urban regime makes and carries out governing decisions. Economic interests may dominate most urban regimes and favour the market model of planning and decision-making. However, collaboration among public, private and non-profit sector organizations can improve the quality of planning and decision-making and enhance ultimate outcomes.

Put another way, private sector stakeholders prefer reliance on the market to determine the future of a city; hence, it is incumbent upon officials in municipal government, in concert with non-profit agency directors, to balance this bias and strive for equal voice for the people. Aggressive collaboration is one method to accomplish that. Collaborative advantage may be a process of transforming power relations (see Himmelman, Chapter 2, Eden, Chapter 3 and Finn, Chapter 10), so that less powerful elements of society have a voice in policy-making. Left to the devices of the market, minorities and the poor in most cases are locked out.

The task for facilitators of collaboration can be daunting when elected and appointed government officials remain aloof from building inter-

organizational relationships. Since these stakeholders speak with an authoritative voice, merely ignoring them or bypassing them in the formation of
community-based collaboratives solves little. Creating meaningful incentives to attract local government officials to collaborate with non-profit and
private-sector organizations is the real challenge.

Collaboration as a non-incremental strategy

2   Most collaboration appears to take a sequential or incremental
    approach which may be ill-suited for emergency crises which demand
    non-incremental efforts and systemic change.

Another way of stating this obstacle is that many collaborative efforts
appear to bog down in the transition from start-up to maintenance stages.
They often fail to get past addressing symptoms and solving primary
problems and into causing systemic change. They fail to operationalize a
comprehensive, effective change technique. Even relatively successful collaboratives which have accomplished their initial goals often fail to sustain
themselves because they lack useful evaluation capacity. Cropper discussed
the challenges of sustainability in collaboratives in Chapter 5 of this book.
Non-incremental approaches require an ability to anticipate change. They
must be able to redesign and change, adapt to a turbulent environment,
and recognize important alterations in inter-organizational boundaries and
stakeholders. Importantly, they must be able to accumulate adequate
resources.
    Incremental behaviour demonstrated through successive marginal
readjustments in policy-making is a fact of political life because it results
from a limited capacity to anticipate change and predict the future. As a
decision-making strategy, it may help officials avoid major, expensive
errors, and allow erroneous decisions to be reversed. In bounded
rationality, incrementalism appeals to common sense, even though major
problems facing communities, such as violence, crime and poverty demand
otherwise.
    The implications for facilitators should be noted. Perhaps unwittingly,
some facilitators have applied a sequential or incremental approach to
collaboration. On one hand, we argue for comprehensive, strategic analysis,
but prescribe our process models and checklists which lead a facilitator
through the collaboration routine. To be sure, students of collaborative
advantage warn change agents of the potential pitfalls in terms of necessary
preconditions, complexities and dilemmas, but appear to want it both ways;
think rationally and comprehensively, but act incrementally. That may
make sense, actually, but seldom achieves big victories. Although many of
the goals which community collaboratives seek to accomplish are relatively
small (and highly worthy) goals, those problems which face society today
are truly monumental and defy incremental approaches.
    In the US, local governments in areas highly vulnerable to natural and

human-caused disasters often exhibit truly comprehensive, non-incremental responses to incidents. To be successful, these units of municipal or county governments must muster an incredible array of resources, deploy them in timely fashion and co-ordinate among a multitude of agencies. In effect, the most accomplished of this special form of collaborative effort overcome organizational thresholds of programme implementation, are able to consolidate control over suboperations upon which success heavily depends, and regularly attain support and resource commitment from all stakeholders.

Proposing comprehensive, non-incremental change strategies may be unrealistic because of the massive commitments of resources necessary. In this case, however, it may be a chicken-and-egg dilemma of needing a collaborative to seek support, but needing a broad commitment to engage stakeholders in a collaborative effort.

A difficult transformation

3   The shift from a betterment to an empowerment collaborative is a difficult journey which involves social learning, building respect and trust, and much risk-taking.

As Arthur Himmelman writes:

> The transformation of betterment processes into empowerment processes is often quite complicated even if those involved have the best intentions. (1992: 53)

His writing in Chapter 2 of this volume expands on this point. One reason is that the community's most powerful business leaders just don't know how to do it. Government leaders aren't much better.

Two community-based examples illustrate. The largest banks in one US city have stumbled awkwardly toward some sort of involvement with grassroots neighbourhood associations (largely consisting of black residents), not because they really wanted to, but because of a federal government mandate. Among other requirements, banks must make an extraordinary effort to assist minorities and the poor buy homes by pooling resources in a high-risk lending reserve. They must invest in neighbourhood and housing rehabilitation. Although some of the bank leaders are well intended, the social gulf between them and the neighbourhood activists is so great as to discourage even the most mundane conversations.

After initiating a series of meetings, the white bankers and neighbourhood leaders retained a strong suspicion of each other. The largest bank in the city quickly promoted an up-and-coming black vice president so that he could talk to the neighbourhood folks! Although truly a wise move, it reflects just how uncomfortable and how unable the bankers are to be personally involved. Not only were they personally ill-at-ease, they were unwilling to empower neighbourhood leaders because they didn't trust them to do it right.

The second example involves a planning collaborative, initiated by one local government to chart its city's course over the next decade. The make-up reflected the racial make-up of the city (34 per cent black), but woefully failed to involve an adequate number of women (nine of 37). From the start, the collaborative fell into two camps, divided on the question of development and growth policy. Interestingly, participants in the two main camps used the strategies they knew best: the bankers and developers approached issues from a contractual basis, while the community activists caucused among themselves and attempted to compromise. Two incompatible bargaining styles, notable differences in a vision for the city's future, and a deeply felt distrust were difficult obstacles for the facilitator to overcome. The powerful were saying, 'we don't trust our city to you,' and the community activists were accusing the business elite of, 'business-as-usual'.

Such divisions which have built over decades cannot easily be dismantled by even a skilled facilitator. In the latter case, the city government hired an expensive, out-of-town process consultant to organize the collaborative. Here part-time, she simply didn't know the territory nor have on-the-ground help. Perhaps what is needed in this case is an in-town facilitator representing an institution which is viewed with respect and trust and seen as neutral.

Another way of viewing the transformation from a betterment to an empowerment collaborative is as a 'double-empowerment' transformation, which includes both business elites and neighbourhood residents. If the corporate leaders are truly sincere about wanting to be more understanding of the problems of poor people and minorities, then the transformation can be a major empowerment for them. It takes time and risk, but is worth it in the end.

People make up collaboratives

4   A major challenge in facilitating collaboration is dealing with individual representatives' idiosyncrasies, egos, personal agendas and interpersonal quirkiness.

After all, people sit down together, not organizations. How collaborative members perceive stakeholder organizations in formation and action stages is coloured greatly by the behaviours, personalities and interpersonal skills of their representatives. Beyond making the interaction pleasant (not a minor consideration), the ability for people to get along and truly communicate strongly affects the outcomes of the collaborative. Facilitators must be aware of the ways that personalities affect group communications, behaviours and decision-making. Outside facilitators rarely have the opportunity to choose collaborative members. Inside facilitators who represent one of the stakeholder organizations more likely have some say over make-up, but often are more concerned about including stakeholder organizations rather than selecting their boundary-spanners. In most cases, whom they send is the call of the organizations.

Organizational boundary-spanners who represent their agencies in activities of collaboratives are truly caught in the middle between the demands and expectations of their own institutional leaders and the dynamics of the collaborative. David Brown's (1983) writings on conflict and organizational interfaces are instructive here. It appears to me that the nature and effectiveness of their contribution to the collaborative is affected both by their roles and their personalities. We know that they operate by such factors as how freely they can commit organizational resources, their perception of status *vis-à-vis* other collaborative members (power differential), how much potential the collaborative offers for achieving their organizations' goals, and so on. But we must be conscious of the effects of personalities and personal behaviour on the collaborative.

In one collaborative, two extremely aggressive and egoistic participants hotly competed for leadership and authority. Regularly, meetings degenerated into shouting matches between them. Attendance dwindled and little progress was achieved. Interestingly, when one of them was transferred by his organization so that he no longer represented it to the collaborative, the other antagonist quit coming. Perhaps he was challenged by the competition and lost interest without regular combat. In another case, three of four male representatives quit coming when the percentage of women representatives exceeded 75 per cent – perhaps a version of a 'tipping point'.

What can a facilitator do to anticipate and correct for the influence of personality on interaction and ultimate success of a collaborative? Perhaps individual interviews with each participant before the collaborative starts up would familiarize him/her with individual personalities. Huxham's chapter (Chapter 9) in this volume emphasizes this approach. Shaping perceptions and communications of the participants might be accomplished at a retreat on which collaborative members can see each other as individuals rather than organizational representatives. Considering the role of personality and the mix of distinct types, rather than just taking it as it is, will aid the facilitator in organizing a collaborative.

Multi-sector collaboration

5   Collaboratives whose members represent different and differing work and social sectors face extraordinary bridging challenges.

This obstacle is reflected, in part, in the previous discussions, especially on the first and third points. Elected officials and corporate leaders frequently operate on much different agendas and styles than potential collaborators from the streets. For that matter, corporate CEOs frequently find working with rank-and-file difficult. But, this point goes beyond class, positional and racial differences to the problems that different methodologies, theories and basic approaches (even terminology) can cause in multi-sector collaboration.

For example, police officers and social workers experienced great difficulty collaborating on youth violence prevention because of their differing theories about dealing with youth gangs. The cops wanted to bust them up; the social workers wanted to redirect them, contending that the kids are seeking affiliation and belonging. The police were responding not only to their own methodology but to their perception that the citizenry supports this tough, no-nonsense approach. Unfortunately, the collaborative could not come to a compromise between two such radically different approaches. As a result, the police kept on doing what they know best and the social workers counselled gang members about directing their destructive tendencies toward community-help projects. A parallel collaborative dealing with alternatives to incarceration of youth who commit violent crimes wrestled with similar variances among proponents of restrictive to lenient treatments.

Other differences exist. Collaborative members from the private sector with the profit motive paramount have difficulty understanding basic motivations of non-profit and public agencies. One collaborative convener from the non-profit sector admitted in private that she was hesitant to invite a corporate stakeholder to send a representative to her collaborative for fear of not being taken seriously. 'After all,' she said, 'they're too busy making money to care about domestic violence.'

How does a facilitator educate and enhance communication across sector lines? Are basic glossaries necessary? Should formal classes be required? Should different assignments be made to capitalize on specific expertise? With the growing demand for multi-sector collaboration to solve community problems that defy treatment by just one sector, these issues should be addressed.

A closing comment

A risk for change agents and empirical researchers alike is that we too often assume rational behaviour by collaborators. The need and desire to build models of collaboration which will work in many diverse settings is worthwhile, but may lead us into unconsciously standardizing approaches and overlooking critical exceptions. An emphasis on designing preparation strategies as well as implementation strategies, for example, might pay dividends. Given the severity and intractability of sociopolitical problems which confront our society, the scarcity of resources with which to address them, and the multi-sector nature of response which is necessary, the importance of collaborative advantage is evident. As proponents and practitioners, we must anticipate potential obstacles and prevent them from defeating our efforts.

References

Brown, L.D. (1983) *Managing Conflict at Organizational Interfaces.* Reading, MA: Addison-Wesley.

Elkin, S.L. (1987) *City and Regime in the American Republic.* Chicago: University of Chicago Press.

Gray, B. (1989) *Collaborating: Finding Common Ground for Multiparty Problems.* San Francisco: Jossey Bass.

Himmelman, A.T. (1992) *Communities Working Collaboratively for a Change.* Minneapolis, MN: The Himmelman Consulting Group.

Huxham, C. with MacDonald, D. (1992) 'Introducing collaborative advantage: achieving interorganizational effectiveness through meta-strategy', *Management Decision*, 30 (3): 50–6.

Sink, D.W. (1987) 'Success and failure in voluntary community networks', *New England Journal of Human Services*, 7: 25–30.

Stone, C.N. (1989) *Regime Politics: Governing Atlanta, 1946–1988.* Lawrence, KS: University of Kansas Press.

7

Involving the Community: Collaboration for Community Development

Catherine Barr and Chris Huxham

Community development refers broadly to the social and economic development of places where people live and work through the involvement of those directly affected. The idea is that local people's capacity to help themselves is stimulated by the intervention of some kind of 'community worker' (CPF, 1982). Thus, community development involves people from different sectors and organizations collaborating to improve a specific area. There may be a general focus on regeneration, or a more specific focus on an issue such as tackling poverty or improving housing. Either way, the concern with the local area is fundamental.

In the UK, government policy is promoting community development through initiatives such as area regeneration partnerships. Hence cross-sectoral collaborations involving community representation will become increasingly common. This book has stressed that successful collaboration between organizations is difficult to achieve, even when the individuals involved are experienced managers and there is parity of status between the organizations (see, for example, Chapters 1 and 5). These difficulties are likely to be exacerbated in collaborations involving both community organizations and organizations from other sectors because those involved perceive large power differences between the organizations and there will be perceived, or actual, differences in managerial skill levels between the individuals involved (Huxham and Vangen, forthcoming). There will also be inherent cross-sectoral cultural differences between the collaborating organizations. In the context of community development, additional issues become significant arising from the involvement of local people and the degree to which they may represent the wider community.

The ideas which are discussed in this chapter derive from an 'audit' of four community development collaborative groups located in the West of Scotland. They are each concerned, in different ways, with addressing poverty in their local area. Each is run by a **core group** of five to ten individuals and in some cases a wider group of individuals also attends meetings occasionally, sometimes on a one-off basis. The collaboratives have varying compositions and aims. Two of them consist both of individuals who work as employees for public agencies and other non-profit community organizations and of individuals who are unpaid members of community organizations. Unusually for a collaborative with community development aims, the third core group presently consists only of individuals who work for public and non-profit organizations although they are reviewing whether or not to involve the community in the collaborative. The fourth collaborative consists only of unpaid representatives of community organizations although public sector employees provide support. Their aims and purposes range from addressing poverty in their area to providing a forum for local people to tackle local issues and to provide community representation for the government's area regeneration initiative. Interestingly, none of those interviewed actually used the term 'community development' to describe the activities of their collaborative although their purposes and structures are consistent with the principles of community development.

The intention of the audit of these collaborative groups was to collect the views of their members on whether and why they are successful (or not). The work formed part of a local authority funded project to develop an 'anti-poverty pack' to be used by community-based groups wishing to develop local anti-poverty strategies or by those wishing to set up a local anti-poverty collaborative group (SRC, 1994). The audit was carried out using in-depth semi-structured interviews with 27 individuals across the four collaboratives. All of the individuals were members of their collaborative's core group – that is, of the group of individual representatives of the participating organizations which managed the collaborations. The audit process is outlined in the Appendix.

Obviously an audit of this type raises a vast variety of issues about collaboration (Barr, 1993a, 1993b; Vangen, 1992; Vangen and Barr, 1992). 'Involvement of the community' – whether or not this is valuable, what the problems are and how to go about it – however, emerged as a central theme running through almost all of the other issues. This theme was particularly significant because it was neither prompted by the interviewer nor – given that the interviewees did not use the term – by 'official' definitions of community development.

This chapter, therefore focuses on how this one significant concern is enacted in practice. The focus is on what appears to be actually happening in the collaborative groups rather than on trying to prescribe what might be good practice. It may be important to stress here the UK context of this work, since it is likely that other national cultures will engender different implications for community involvement.

Involving the community – the issues

Many authors comment on the importance of the issue of membership of collaboratives and it is indeed a key theme in many of the chapters in this book (see Chapter 12 for a summary of the issues). Much conventional wisdom about collaboration over social issues suggests that involvement of all who will be affected by the purpose of the collaboration should be members of it (see, for example, Mattessich and Monsey, 1992). While it can be argued that this is an ideal position, it is clearly not a practical one; issues such as who decides who will be affected, who decides on the nature of the collaborative purpose and what is a manageable size of core group ensure that this is so (Huxham, 1993a). Indeed, Finn's approach to getting started with collaborative groups in Chapter 10 focuses centrally on which stakeholders should be in the collaborative and which should be left outside as part of the environment that it has to deal with.

Our experience with other community sector collaborations suggests that while considerations of who to involve in general are of some concern to participants, if left to their own devices they will rarely formally address the issue. By contrast, in this context of community development, experience with the four core groups suggests that the particular issue of how to involve *the community* in the collaborative group's efforts to tackle its objectives is a fundamentally important concern which exercises them considerably. This, in itself, is not surprising; the community sector tends to be, by its very nature, concerned to involve its constituents in its work. What is unusual – at least in the UK context – in the case of these community development collaboratives is that the concern is not with providing some external forum through which members of the community can be consulted or become involved, but with whether or not it is possible actually to get good community involvement through inclusion of community groups in the collaborative core group itself. This is perhaps a first stage in achieving **collaborative empowerment** (see Chapter 2).

Everyone interviewed raised the concept of **involving the community** and many dwelt upon the issue at some length. They did not all consider the issue in the same light but they all argued that involving the community, *or not*, in the activities of the core group, was important to the achievement of the substantive aims of the collaboration. References to involving the community were not always explicit and were sometimes obliquely implicit in other issues. For example, having status with funders was an issue raised by some people, who felt that being seen to be involving the community was essential to achieving this. Others were keen that their collaborative should campaign on specific poverty issues, but noted that campaigning was an inappropriate activity for public officials to be involved in. In these collaboratives, involvement of people or organizations who could legitimately campaign against the government was seen as essential.

However inexplicit, taken together these references to community involvement raise several interesting issues: the ways in which notions of 'community' and 'community involvement' are conceptualized; the ways in which collaboratives can be representative of a community; the tensions in deciding what kinds of organizations or people should be part of the core group; and concerns of how to work in practice across a significant sectoral divide. Discussion of these issues is the focus of the remainder of this chapter.

What is meant by 'community'?

The people we interviewed all used the term 'community involvement' freely and comfortably. However, their conceptualizations of what this means in practice are rather ill-defined. A first point which is striking to an outsider but which seems not to be acknowledged by those involved is a lack of clear definition of what they meant by 'the community'. This lack of clarity has been reported on by others (for example, Chanan and Vos, 1990; Willmott 1989) who confirm that the term tends to be used as a catch-all with different implied meanings depending on its context of use. For example, a community may be identified spatially in terms of a well-defined area or in terms of an interest group such as single parents or the elderly. In the former case there can be additional confusion about whether the term is used to refer only to people who live there or whether it is also used to include employees who work in the area and the employing organizations themselves.

In practice, members of the collaborative were happy to use the term 'community' without explicitly identifying its meaning. More particularly, they did not apparently try to identify the nature of the specific community that they were aiming to involve. Whether members meant the same thing by 'the community' was unclear.

Conceptualizing 'community involvement': distinguishing types of participant

While the term 'community' is thus used somewhat vaguely, the concept of 'community involvement' in this context seems even more nebulous. Surprisingly, rather than referring to it through a focus on the community *per se*, the core group members frequently conceptualized it in terms of a distinction between those members of their collaborative who were referred to as 'community representatives' and those who were regarded as 'officers'. The implication was that effective participation of community representatives in the core group was synonymous with the notion of community involvement.

The distinction between these two types of participants is one which members of all four collaboratives appeared to have internalized and it arose frequently in comments that they made about many aspects of their experiences other than simply those concerned with 'involving the community'. They used the terms without feeling a need to explain or define them and appeared clear and in agreement about how any individual member of their core group should be categorized. Viewed from the outside, however, the distinction is less clear.

Interestingly, the main way in which differentiation between community representatives and officers appears to take place is on the basis of how the individual concerned perceives him or herself; others' perceptions are thus influenced by the self-perception. In turn, this appears to be influenced by factors such as:

- whether members of their organization act in an unpaid capacity *or* are seconded to the collaborative from their paid job and deal with core group business during their employer's time;
- whether *or* not members of their organization live in the community;
- whether the experience that they bring to the collaborative is directly of the types of problems that locals have and of the issues which the collaborative is tackling *or* derives from professional expertise;
- whether members of their organization have social relations with community members *or* only professional relations with community members.

Clearly these criteria sometimes contradict each other. For example, someone who is seconded to the core group from their paid job may also live in the community. Similarly, someone who works in a community organization within a community but does not live there may nevertheless have both social and professional relationships with community members. In general, living in the community seems to override all other criteria in terms of defining someone as a community representative rather than an officer, but even this is not clear-cut.

What do community representatives represent?

The discussion so far suggests that while community involvement is central to the thinking of those involved, it is an extremely difficult concept to operationalize in practice. It is defined only obliquely through making a distinction between community representatives and officers, and this distinction in itself is ill-defined. Furthermore, the very notion of 'community' is used ambiguously.

The implication to be taken from the emphasis on the distinction between community representatives and officers, however vaguely that may be enacted in practice, is that community involvement is regarded as taking place only if there are community representatives in the core group. It might therefore appear reasonable to assume that the degree to which those coming to the core group from community organizations and groups are actually representative of the community would be indicative of the level of community involvement in the collaborative. This then leads to the question of the sense in which they are representative.

In the core groups interviewed, most of the community representatives represent a community group such as a tenants' association or a forum for issues of local concern such as housing or safety. There appear to be two main ways in which community representatives become part of the core group. Most commonly, **well-known individual activists** – that is, members of the public who play a prominent role in many community groups – are targeted. One of these community groups therefore becomes a part of the collaborative **on the back of the targeted individuals**.

Often the very nature of these activists means that they are in the collaborative's core group in an individualistic capacity. On the one hand, the degree to which they see themselves as representing the particular community group which is officially a member of the collaboration may be minimal. On the other hand, they often tend to regard themselves as representing a wider constituency of those who live in the area. Indeed, they are often approached by local people 'in the street' and asked to represent their views in the collaborative. They do not, however, have a formal role in this respect.

This begs three questions: to what extent can community groups brought into the collaborative in this rather random way be regarded as representative of key areas of the community? To what extent do the community activists who notionally represent those community groups take this organizational representative role seriously rather than as a means of legitimizing their involvement in the collaborative group? To what extent can these same activists be regarded as representative, either individually or collectively, of the wider community? Looked at in this way, it is tempting to conclude that the degree to which either these community groups or the activists are representative may be small.

Not all community organizations become part of the collaborative in this way, however. Some are deliberately invited to be part of the collaboration and the individuals that become involved in the core group do so as nominated representatives. However, these organizations are often targeted on a somewhat ad hoc basis; that is, they are those which happen to have been heard of by the initiators of the collaboration. Furthermore, they tend to be invited on the strength of their 'communityness' rather than because they are relevant to the substantive goals of the collaboration. There is little sense that organizations are targeted because they have a stake in the issue or because they have resources to bring. Thus even when there is a deliberate policy of involving organizations, it is unlikely that the community is fully represented. The degree to which the organizations may provide a representative range of views and expertise on the substantive concerns of the collaborative is certainly questionable.

Even if these collaboratives operated a more deliberate policy about which community organizations to involve, it is doubtful that they could be fully representative of the community. Others have argued that it cannot be presumed that community groups reach everyone, particularly those who are most disadvantaged (Boaden et al., 1982; Chanan, 1992) and special efforts may have to be made to reach such individuals (Chanan and Vos, 1990). Furthermore, since any core group is unlikely to have more than a small number of community representatives, they are unlikely to be able to represent all the community interests which exist (McArthur, 1993).

It is difficult to see therefore, that the involvement of community representatives in a collaborative group *per se* is a good way of involving the community *as a whole*. However, the main concern of those interviewed seemed to be with ensuring that *some* community representatives are involved rather than creating complete or representative cover. Perhaps this apparently rather unsophisticated outlook stems from a position where getting *any* effective community representation would be a step forward compared to what has happened in the past (Colenutt and Cutten, 1994). Alternatively, perhaps the drive to include community representation is purely ideological and can be satisfied by ensuring *some* community involvement. A third possibility is that perhaps it is not the 'representative' aspect of community representatives that is at the heart of community involvement. Some of the points in the next section would suggest that the emphasis on 'community' is enough for a community representative to promote involvement whatever organization or interest they are representative of because it eases communication and engenders trust. If this is the case, the issue of representativeness is a 'red herring'.

Balancing the tension of whom to involve

It was argued earlier that community involvement appears to be conceptualized in terms of a *distinction* between community representatives and officers. The strong focus on *community* involvement, however, leads to the question of who the so-called 'officers' are and why they are involved at all. In practice, they tend to represent organizations such as the social work department of the regional council, the Department of Consumer and Trading Standards or a locally based money advice project. Some appear to be mandated by their organization to be part of the core group. Others, however, may attend purely out of personal interest and a sense of wanting to help. In these cases the officer tends to be acting individualistically rather than representing the organization. In either case, whether or not the particular organizations involved are selected by the collaborative or are self-selected is not clear, but it seems likely that some, at least, invite themselves.

Traditionally it would be expected that these kinds of people would have roles in collaborative groups of this type. Public and non-profit organizations are, after all, set up explicitly to tackle the kind of social issues which are at the heart of community development. In addition, often the initiative to set up the collaborative, as well as funding to support it, will have been generated by such an organization. In Himmelman's terms (Chapter 2) these officers may be viewing the collaborative from a 'betterment' perspective rather than an 'empowerment' one, and may hence see their role as one of helping the community rather than involving it. However, in Chapter 6 Sink has made arguments for why officers are important members of community collaboratives. Certainly, community representatives as well as officers in our collaboratives were well conscious of the values – and hazards – of involving officers in their core groups. They were also able to articulate what it is that community representatives have to offer that officers alone cannot contribute. Yet all were acutely aware of the difficulties of involving *both* kinds of participants.

This leads to the issue of whether it is in fact worthwhile to include both community representatives and officers in the collaborative. Many of the people interviewed appeared to have spent time considering this. Officers were generally seen to be valuable in gaining access to resources such as finance, expertise and information and would be able to draw on professional experience in implementation of plans. Community representatives, on the other hand, would be better able to communicate with local people, would have personal experience of local problems and would be able to build on the trust that other residents already have in them through their other local activities. In addition, they could play a crucial role in reducing local people's suspicions of the collaborative and in encouraging them to play a part, for example, in the development of strategy. This in turn would provide local support which would improve the chances of implementation of actions to achieve the collaborative's aims. Both types of participant are thus seen to be able to contribute to improving the chances of the collaborative taking implementable action – in the one case through their professional expertise and resources, in the other through local knowledge and trust.

While members of both sectors acknowledged the value of the other, they also put forward a number of reasons for *not* involving them. Officers argued that not involving community representatives would allow them to avoid problems such as lack of understanding of professional concepts (such as an 'anti-poverty strategy') and irregular attendance by community representatives. Based on previous painful experience, some officers also argued that it would also reduce conflict within the core group which hinders progress.

Some officers argued that it was reasonable to accept that officers' knowledge of the community gained through working in it *is* adequate on its own and thus that the involvement of community representatives is not necessary. Community representatives, on the other hand, argued exactly the opposite; that not involving officers would allow them to avoid the problems inherent in officers' lack of first hand experience of how issues affect local people. They also suggested that there was value in pulling (only) local people together. In particular, this would enable the collaborative to be recognized as the 'voice of the community'.

Not surprisingly, there was a variety of views about the way in which the values and difficulties of involving either type of participant should be weighed up. While most of those interviewed argued that the inclusion of community representatives in the collaborative was essential, some of these acknowledged that this was a recent shift in their position on the matter. A small number of 'officers' remained convinced that the presence of community representatives would hamper, rather than enhance their effectiveness. A similar range of views was evident concerning the value of involving officers in the collaborative. The diversity of these views was evident in the different compositions of the four collaboratives, for while two of them consisted of both community representatives and officers, one currently involved only the former, another primarily involved the latter.

From the perspective of work on collaborative advantage, this diversity of views and resolutions is not surprising. It is argued in Chapter 9 and elsewhere (Huxham, 1993a) that processes for collaboration cannot revolve around precise prescriptions for effective practice. Rather, they must involve a process of weighing up pros and cons around key collaboration variables. Such variables might be, for example: the involvement (or not) of certain organizations; the use (or not) of formalized communication links between participating organizations; the direct involvement (or not) of many individuals from each collaborating organization. For any particular situation, this can be thought of as a process of **balancing the tension** between the weight of the pros and the weight of the cons in that situation. In this case the tension to be balanced is the value of involving both community representatives and officers in the collaboration.

How these tensions are balanced in practice in any particular situation will involve both ideological considerations – is it *right* that either type of participant should be involved? – and practical considerations – will it *work better* or be more difficult to achieve anything if either type of participant is involved? However, in all of our collaboratives both officers and community representatives generally felt the necessity of community involvement outweighed the difficulties of including community representatives.

Managing mixed collaborations

In the discussion above it was noted that some participants were concerned to avoid problems such as lack of understanding of professional concepts and irregular attendance. In highlighting these kinds of issues these participants were beginning to articulate the kinds of problems which underlie **collaborative inertia** – the tendency of collaborative groups to make much slower progress than might be expected (see Chapter 1). If both types of participant are involved, such issues must be dealt with – and doing so takes time and patience. From the point of view of public organizations funding community development collaborations, this is the price to be paid for involving the community.

Issues such as differences in working practices, professional languages, organizational cultures and so on are significant in all collaborative groups and contribute significantly to producing collaborative inertia (see Chapter 1). Clearly such differences will be problematic between any two members of these collaboratives. The implication from our community development collaboratives, however, is that these kinds of factors are especially significant across the officer–community representative divide because community representatives may not have professional backgrounds of any type and, being generally unpaid, operate with less constraints on what opinions it is acceptable to put forward relative to most people involved in inter-organizational collaboration.

Many of the people interviewed elaborated upon the practical problems of working together when both categories of participant are involved. Specifically, they argued that there are likely to be stresses which arise between community representatives and officers due to differing backgrounds, stereotypical images of each other and so on. Among the concerns, one that seemed particularly potent was the need to ensure that everyone feels confident about actively participating in meetings. A good deal of wisdom was expressed about factors that need to be attended to in order to allow this to happen.

Issues concerned with the use of language were prominent. 'Take care to use non-exclusive language', 'remember that some members are likely to be more articulate than others', 'ensure that things are explained in terms that everyone can understand but do not talk down to anyone' and 'take care not to suggest that officers feel as if they know better than community representatives' were among the pieces of advice given. Some of these points relate to the use of specific professional language or jargon. However, collaborations involving non-professional community representatives often encounter an additional problem because these people sometimes are not skilled at understanding or articulating what most professional people would regard as non-specialist language. Many of the concerns about language therefore require professionals to be especially thoughtful both about the specific words that they use and about the way in which they deliver what they have to say.

Cultural differences also provide particular difficulties across the officer–community representative boundary. Obviously it is not sensible to provide rigid typecasts, but the two groups do tend to look at issues from different perspectives. Community representatives tend to come from ideological or emotional perspectives. Officers – whatever their particular professionalism – tend to come from professional and pragmatic perspectives. Some argued that such differences need to be openly addressed if progress is to be made on issues. However, this is not necessarily an easy thing to do and may, through making differences explicit, in itself create conflict.

Designing individual behaviour and meetings so that these language and culture problems can be managed rather than providing continual difficulties was a concern of many of those interviewed. Examples of pieces of advice in this are: 'arrange meetings in a friendly, organized style so that people feel happy to ask for clarification or to disagree'; 'ensure that a paid–unpaid divide does not arise'; 'allow for the collaborative's agenda to be open to change and influence'; 'be prepared to accept explanations when things cannot be done'; and, 'ensure views are demonstrably listened to'.

While some of our collaboratives appeared to have achieved a reasonably high degree of success in working across the community representative–officer divide, it is clear that others had had very difficult experiences. Indeed many of the points mentioned above arise out of people's reflections about frustrations, rather than out of successes. Operationalizing the advice above is obviously not a trivial task. Despite all these frustrations, however, the overriding view is that it is essential that community representatives are involved.

Summary and discussion

This chapter has aimed to explore the nature of community involvement in the context of collaborations for community development. It has been argued that although notions of 'community', and 'community involvement' are used vaguely by those involved, they are very important to them. In practice, community involvement seems to be conceptualized through the distinction between community representatives and officers and enacted through the inclusion of community representatives in the core group of a collaborative. However, the notion of a community representative is, in itself, ill-defined and in addition it is unclear how the community as a whole becomes involved through them. Community representatives certainly do not seem to be very representative of the community. It has been suggested here that their role in achieving community involvement may therefore stem from their ability to relate to the community and to be seen to be a part of it. They may thus be able to create a sense of involvement for a wider constituency than that which they actually represent.

However important community representatives are to achieving community involvement, it is difficult to imagine that there will come a time when there is no role also for officers in most community development initiatives because their professional expertise and resources *are* valuable. Therefore, despite the difficulties inherent in doing so, which stem from the potentially very large differences in background, culture and constraints, community representatives and officers will have to work together.

The identification of the community representative–officer distinction as a way of conceptualizing community involvement is novel and has particular implications for community development. Neither the distinction itself nor the difficulties it highlights are likely to be surprising to anyone who has been involved in community development, but the distinction is not one that has generally been highlighted by other work either on collaboration or community development. In addition, given that funding of community organizations – rather than, for example, local authorities – to provide community services is on the increase, it seems likely that the distinction between community representatives and officers will become more difficult for the onlooker to define. While this may have the positive effect of breaking down barriers between the two 'sides', it may equally well have the effect of *obscuring* serious barriers to effective working. It may be important therefore, to understand more about how and why the distinction continues to be made.

How to address in practice the difficulties which arise from the need to involve both community representatives and officers also remains a significant concern. A key question is how the issues raised in this chapter can be made to have practical value for those involved in collaboration. Conventional expert wisdom from the collaboration field would support a view that encouragement to review and revise their structures and processes in the light of 'good collaborative practice' identified elsewhere is central to helping such collaboratives (Gray, 1985; Mattessich and Monsey, 1992). However, some aspects of established 'good practice' may need to be reinterpreted in this context. For example, conventional approaches would involve the core groups in reviewing their membership to ensure that all those who have a stake in the issue are represented. Our discussion of the role of representatives in this context, however, would suggest that this may not be appropriate. Similarly, given that some of the core group members are there primarily as individuals rather than as organizational representatives, some normal concerns of collaborations such as allowing for the **accountability** of core group members to their own organizations (Friend, 1990) and the differences in organizations' **collaborative capability** (Huxham, 1993b) do not arise. Neither can the benefits of organizational resources be exploited (Himmelman, 1992). There may also be new issues which arise because some members are acting as individuals while others are acting on behalf of their organization. Whether or not community development core groups would benefit from moving towards conventional conceptions of collaboration is open to question.

One way of helping core groups to address the issues of community involvement and of working across the community representative–officer divide might be through the use of facilitated methods such as those discussed by Eden (Chapter 3), Finn (Chapter 10) and de Jong (Chapter 11). Such processes could be enhanced by drawing upon the specific insights of this chapter through, for example, a focus on community representation and its relation to community involvement, addressing stereotypical images of each other and developing appropriate language for communication. In this way, issues concerned with balancing the community representative– officer tension and managing the process of working together could thus be addressed explicitly.

Experiences in the UK, however, suggest two barriers to this. First, while in other countries it may be relatively common for community groups to make use of expert facilitation to help with process issues, this is rare in the UK. Without a facilitator, the question arises as to whose role it is to encourage the review process. More importantly, any such process would need to take account of a general 'ignorance' (Nocon, 1989) that collab- oratives are a different and especially difficult organizational form which requires nurturing (Huxham and Vangen, 1994; Wistow and Hardy, 1991). This means finding a way of ensuring that ignorance is acknowledged.

Despite these barriers, our own view is that these kinds of facilitated approaches are worthy of further exploration in terms of both their value and practicality and in terms of how they can be made effective in the community development context.

Acknowledgements

Our thanks are due to Siv Vangen who contributed significantly to both data collection and analysis and to the Strathclyde Poverty Alliance and the four community groups for the time they have put into this work.

References

Barr, C. (1993a) 'Community research local anti-poverty strategies: Poverty Action Group, Irvine'. Department of Management Science, University of Strathclyde.

Barr, C. (1993b) 'Community research local anti-poverty strategies: Castlemilk Umbrella Group'. Department of Management Science, University of Strathclyde.

Barr, C. (1994) 'Exploring collaboration', in C. Ritchie, A. Taket and J. Bryant (eds), *Community Works*. Sheffield: PAVIC. pp. 80–3.

Boaden, N., Goldsmith, M., Hampton, W. and Stringer, P. (1982) *Public Participation in Local Services*. London: Longman.

Chanan, G. (1992) *Out of the Shadows*. Dublin: European Foundation for the Improvement of Living and Working Conditions.

Chanan, G. and Vos, K. (1990) *Social Change and Local Action: Coping with Disadvantage in Urban Areas*. Dublin: European Foundation for the Improvement of Living and Working Conditions.

Colenutt, B. and Cutten, A. (1994) 'Community empowerment in vogue or vain?', *Local Economy*, November, pp. 236–50.

CPF (1982) *Community Development: Towards a National Perspective*. London: Community Projects Foundation.

Cropper, S., Ackermann, F. and Eden, C. (1990) 'COPE-ing with complexity: computer based storage, analysis and retrieval of cognitive maps'. Working paper 90/4, University of Strathclyde, Department of Management Science.

Friend, J. (1990) 'Handling organizational complexity in group decision support', in C. Eden and J. Radford (eds), *Tackling Strategic Problems: the Role of Group Decision Support*. London: Sage. pp. 18–28.

Gray, B. (1985) 'Conditions facilitating interorganizational collaboration', *Human Relations*, 38 (10): 911–36.

Himmelman, A. (1992) *Communities Working Collaboratively for a Change*. Minneapolis, MN: The Himmelman Consulting Group.

Huxham, C. (1993a) 'Processes for collaborative advantage: a gentle exploration of tensions', in J. Pasquero and D. Collins (eds), *International Association for Business and Society, Proceedings*.

Huxham, C. (1993b) 'Collaborative capability: an intra-organizational perspective on collaborative advantage', *Public Money and Management*, 13 (3): 21–8.

Huxham, C. and Vangen, S. (1994) 'Naivety and maturity, inertia and fatigue: are working relationships between public organizations doomed to fail?'. Presented at the Employment Research Unit Conference, 'The Contract State: the Future of Public Management', University of Cardiff, September.

Huxham, C. and Vangen, S. (forthcoming) 'Managing inter-organizational relationships', in S. Osborne (ed.), *Managing in the Voluntary Sector*. London: Chapman & Hall.

McArthur, A. (1993) 'Community partnership – a formula for neighbourhood regeneration in the 1990s?', *Community Development Journal*, 28: 3–8.

Mattessich, P.W. and Monsey, B.R. (1992) *Collaboration: What Makes it Work?* St Paul, MN: Amherst H. Wilder Foundation.

Nocon, A. (1989) 'Forms of ignorance and their role in the joint planning process', *Social Policy and Administration*, 23 (1): 31–47.

SRC (1994) *Communities Against Poverty Resource Pack*. Glasgow: Strathclyde Regional Council.

Vangen, S. (1992) 'Community research local anti-poverty strategies: Anti-Poverty Working Group, Easterhouse'. Department of Management Science, University of Strathclyde.

Vangen, S. and Barr, C. (1992) 'Community research local anti-poverty strategies: Anti-Poverty Working Group, Drumchapel'. Department of Management Science, University of Strathclyde.

Willmott, P. (1989) *Community Initiatives: Patterns and Prospects*. London: Policy Studies Institute.

Wistow, G. and Hardy, B. (1991) 'Joint management in community care', *Journal of Management in Medicine*, 5: 40–8.

Appendix: research approach

The audit of these four collaboratives was carried out through semi-structured, in-depth interviews with core group members. In the first three collaboratives with two exceptions, all core members – 21 in total – were interviewed. In the fourth collaborative – an umbrella group – six people were chosen by the chairman of the group's management board. At the start of each interview, two very general triggers were used to provoke responses from the interviewees:

- Could you tell me about your [collaborative] group, how it was formed, how it works, what it deals with and what its aims are?
- What has been achieved through collaboration? What do you think makes it work, what are its benefits and what hinders it?

The interviewee was encouraged to talk as freely as possible around these.

A set of more specific questions had also been agreed based on output from a workshop held a few months previously (described in Barr, 1994) and information which the Strathclyde Poverty Alliance (SPA), who were co-ordinating the overall project, thought might be of use. However, this was used only either as a checklist at the end of the interview to ensure that everything had been covered or when people were not forthcoming. This approach allowed people to focus on what *they* defined as important issues rather than on issues predefined by the researcher. It also encouraged elaboration around these.

The data were recorded using cognitive mapping and were stored and analysed using the software, Graphics COPE (Cropper et al., 1990). A map was created during each interview and subsequently put into COPE. An example of a section from such a map is shown in Figure 7.1. Wherever possible a second interview was set up both to check that the individual 'owned' the mapped version of their comments and to explore further areas identified from the map as poorly elaborated or areas which looked particularly interesting to the researcher.

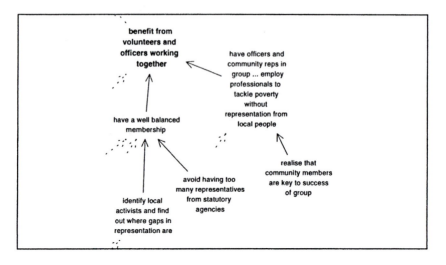

How to read a cognitive map:

- A cognitive map is a map of a person's, or a group of people's, thoughts, represented in diagrammatical form using words and arrows.
- It is basically a flow of related concepts (pieces of text) formed into a network. The meaning of each concept can be understood more completely by looking at its relationship to other concepts.
- These relationships are represented by arrows indicating how a concept may lead to or have implications for other concepts. The arrows should be read as 'leads to'.
- The map is hierarchial, with the more important concepts towards the top of it.
- A dotted arrow leading from or into a concept indicates that there are other concepts linked to this one which are not shown on the current map view.
- When a concept text has three dots followed by more text, the text after the dots is the stated (or implied) alternative to the first part of the concept. The dots may be read as 'rather than'.

Figure 7.1 *Example section of a cognitive map*

Individuals' maps were then 'merged' to provide a combined picture of the important issues concerning the success of the collaborative as seen by its members. The map was then broken down into more manageable chunks using COPE's cluster analysis facility which identifies clusters of closely linked ideas. For each core group, a report was prepared on the basis of these clusters outlining the issues which had emerged from the process. This was presented to, and discussed with the core group, both to feed back results to them and to get some sense – albeit, rather superficially – of their collective ownership of the issues identified.

These four reports provided the data used by SPA to inform the design of the poverty pack. For purposes of our own research, however, the four core group maps were subsequently merged with each other and reclustered. The clusters provided an agenda of issues in collaboration to be explored.

The use of mapping in this way has a number of advantages over other interview recording mechanisms. First, it is possible to capture a great deal of the richness and subtlety of what is said. Secondly, it is possible, through discussion of interviewees' maps with themselves, to explore and expand the argumentation beyond the often superficial points initially made. Thirdly, it is possible both to capture the interconnections between what is said at different points in an interview and to cross-relate different people's ideas. Finally and importantly, the issues that *emerge* from this process may be very different from those initially expressed and may therefore provide fresh perspectives.

PART FOUR

INTERVENTION PROCESSES FOR COLLABORATION

8

The Role of Facilitation in Collaborative Groups

Sandor P. Schuman

Many collaborative groups make use of facilitators, as illustrated in Chapters 3, 6, 9, 10 and 11. What exactly is the role of a facilitator and how is it different from the role of the participants? Why are facilitators so concerned about process versus content (as discussed in Chapter 9)? Under what circumstances should a group consider using a facilitator?

A facilitator helps a group to work collaboratively by focusing on the process of how the participants work together. Facilitators apply their expertise in leading the process, but they are not participants, have no authority to impose any action on the group, and have no vested interest in the outcome. To explore this further it will be helpful to compare the role of the facilitator to other roles that pertain to collaboration and conflict resolution, as illustrated in Figure 8.1. The participants, for example, are familiar with the issues and have pertinent knowledge. They are advocates for their own interests, values, preferences and biases. They have opinions and make judgements about what is important and what action should be taken.

In situations where the participants cannot resolve a conflict on their own they sometimes bring the problem to a higher authority, typically a government agency or the court system. Here the participants present their differing views to an administrator or judge who ensures that the decision-making process is fair, does not have a bias in favour of one party or another, but who does have the authority to make and impose a decision.

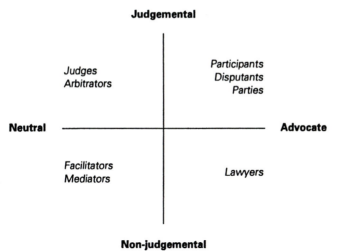

Judgemental

Judges
Arbitrators

Participants
Disputants
Parties

Neutral

Advocate

Facilitators
Mediators

Lawyers

Non-judgemental

Figure 8.1 *The facilitator's role is non-judgemental and neutral*

In such settings (as well as in formal negotiations), the participants often engage lawyers or others to act as advocates on their behalf. These individuals are skilled in the administrative or legal decision-making process and use their knowledge on behalf of their clients. In so doing they do not make judgements about their clients or the outcomes they seek.

Instead of resorting to formal negotiations, administrative remedies or legal proceedings some groups try to work out their differences by better understanding each other and working collaboratively to develop consensus. The collaborative process is complex, and their need for process expertise is great. However, they do not want process experts who will impose their own views or make decisions for them – the participants already have the necessary knowledge of the issues and want to make their own decisions. Nor do they want advocates who can represent their points of view – they can advocate on their own behalf. Instead they want assistance in constructing and implementing a process that is fair to all participants, that will ensure high quality communication throughout the group, and that will result, if possible, in creating a solution of their own making to which they agree of their own accord. Providing assistance in managing such a process is the role of the facilitator.

Process as a moral issue

Nearly everyone involved in the practice or theory of group problem-solving and decision-making seems to share some concern about distinguishing between different aspects of collaborative work. Distinctions are

Table 8.1 *Facilitator influences in collaborative activities*

Aspects of collaborating	Influence of the facilitator	
	Structure	Process
Content		Summarizing; feedback
Cognitive	Problem structure	Procedures for analytical thinking
Social	Arrangement of seating and technology	Rules of interpersonal communication
Political	Advice about who should participate	Advice about communicating results to non-participants

made between process and content (Eden, 1990; Phillips and Phillips, 1993), process, content and substance (Huxham and Cropper, 1994), process and structure (Schein, 1969), process and outcome (Rohrbaugh, 1987), context, content and process (Broome and Keever, 1989), and content, process and structure (Schein, 1987; Smith, 1988). Related distinctions are made between task and maintenance behaviours (Benne and Sheats, 1948) and task and interpersonal issues (Schein, 1987). A useful way to enlighten this discussion might be to examine why people find these to be important distinctions. One way to view their importance is because these are instrumental issues. With a better understanding and command of these issues, facilitators can design better, more successful collaborative activities. Another explanation is that these issues are just so fundamental; they are the means by which problems get solved and decisions made. In democratic systems, the means *are* the ends. These are moral issues. The way in which collaboration is practised, including the way that process and content are managed and integrated, is a moral issue, whether or not it is explicitly recognized as such by the participants.

Facilitators, and other process consultants who support collaborative activities, are largely concerned with process issues, and claim, perhaps, to intervene only in process, not in content. How exactly to say this is not a trivial turn of a phrase. Many 'process' facilitators recognize that they interpret or influence the content, although they do not contribute to it based on their substantive expertise, but rather based on their analytical expertise. That is, they listen to the participants, ask questions, analyse and integrate the different pieces of information they receive, and feed back the results of their thinking to the participants, perhaps to receive more information or to generate further discussion. This has been described as 'handing back in changed form' (Phillips and Phillips, 1993). However, by using the singular term process, we give short shrift to the role of the facilitator, and must supplement our description of the facilitator's role by saying that the facilitator delves in some fashion into content. An attempt to address these language distinctions and integrate various terms is presented in Table 8.1 and discussed in the next section.

Three types of process: cognitive, social and political

Group process has been a concern of social psychology for perhaps 30 years (for example, McGrath, 1984; Steiner, 1972). Process is generally used as a singular term, but its meaning is sometimes confusing, or takes a great deal of effort to explain. Consequently it will be useful to differentiate three types of process: social, cognitive and political.

Social process

Social process is what is typically, though loosely meant when people talk about 'process' issues. This is a concern with interpersonal interaction, group dynamics, communication, body language etc.

The importance of social process is increasingly recognized as essential to solving complex problems, for example:

> The push for participation by all kinds of people . . . produce[s] the modern executive's most puzzling dilemma. . . . How do you get everybody in on the act and still get some action? (Cleveland, 1985: 51)

Cognitive process

To tease out the notion of cognitive process is perhaps most readily acceptable to those who use mathematical or structural models in their support of collaborative work (see, for example, Bodily, 1992; Eden and Radford, 1990). They clearly acknowledge that they do something to structure the information, values, beliefs and ideas held by the various members of the group. These cognitive concerns are illustrated by the following:

> . . . in the course of learning, something like a field map of the environment gets established in the . . . brain . . . The incoming impulses are usually worked over and elaborated in the central control room into a tentative, cognitive-like map of the environment. And it is this tentative map, indicating routes and paths and environmental relationships, which finally determines what responses, if any, will finally release. (Tolman, 1948: 191)

> . . . the things which go wrong may very well stem from the inadequacy of the structures we unconsciously impose on our available information rather than from any lack of information. No matter how much it seems to us that all of our decisions would be simpler if we only had more information, it may well be the case that we are already swamped with it, are using only a small portion of what is available, and may not be using the right portion of it in reasonable ways. (Morris, 1972: 85)

By aiding cognitive processes, facilitators help the participants develop and refine their own cognitive representations of the problem, understand the cognitive representations of others, understand the feedback presented by the facilitators, and integrate or reconcile the results.

Table 8.2   *The distinction between cognitive and social processes is illustrated by a comparison between the idea generation and organization tasks*

Task	Cognitive process	Social process
Idea generation	*Cognitively simple* Relies on individual creativity; ideas are considered independently	*Socially simple* Little social interaction required; ideas are merely exchanged
Idea organization	*Cognitively complex* Ideas are considered in relation to each other; everyone must understand each idea in the same way	*Socially complex* Much social interaction required; requires collective understanding, evaluation, and agreement on the meaning of each idea and its relationship to other ideas

Cognitive and social processes

The demands placed on collaborative groups are both cognitive and social. The extent of these demands varies with the particular task at hand. Table 8.2 illustrates how these two dimensions might be differentiated for two illustrative tasks.

Cropper (1990) suggests that cognitive process (analytical or intellectual process) can be distinguished from social process (process of assisting social interaction and commitment making) as two ideal types, but that any actual approach is a synthesis of the two. Langley (1991) argues that formal analysis and social interaction in decision processes are inextricably linked. Sociocognitive analysis (Ward and Reingen, 1990) recognizes the importance of the relation between these two aspects of problem-solving and decision-making. Understanding these relationships, and developing methods to support both the cognitive and social aspects of collaborative work, is indeed a superlative task:

> One can hardly contemplate the passing scene of civilized society without a sense that the need of balanced minds is real and that a *superlative* task is how *socially* to make *mind* more effective. That the increasing complexity of society and the elaboration of technique and organization now necessary will more and more require capacity for rigorous reasoning seems evident; but it is a super-structure necessitating a better use of the non-logical mind to support it. 'Brains' without 'minds' seem a futile unbalance. The inconsistencies of method and purpose and the misunderstandings between large groups which increasing specialization engenders need the corrective of the feeling mind that senses the end result, the net balance, the interest of the all and of the spirit that perceiving the concrete parts encompasses also the intangibles of the whole. (Barnard, 1938: 322, emphasis added)

Political process

Collaborative strategy formulation can be characterized as involving social, cognitive and political processes (Bower and Doz, 1979). Bryson and

Roering (1988) note that the problem of divergence is not just conceptual, but also political. Political process might be viewed as a subset of social process in that it deals with social relationships. However, by singling it out we provide a keener focus on the larger political framework in which collaborative work takes place and the process by which the power to influence purpose and resources is shifted. The political process is responsible for the most basic issue in collaboration – who can participate and who can exercise power. The political process is much more evident in inter-organizational collaborative groups than in intra-organizational teams. Facilitators who have worked only with corporate work groups, as has been increasing in popularity with the growth of Total Quality Management (Kayser, 1990), will find another dimension of concern in working with inter-organizational groups.

The processes that go on between a participant and the organization or constituency that they represent, and the relationships between the organizations and institutions apart from the collaborative activity, are at least as important as those between the participants within a collaborative group (see Figure 8.2). Explicitly including political process keeps us mindful of the influence that one person has on another by virtue of their position, affiliation and power. Power might be based on participants' personal attributes, or on the attributes of the organization or constituency that they represent. Over the course of a collaborative process changes in the relationships among participants are the result not only of the inter-actions between themselves, but between the organizations and constituents they represent which might occur outside of the formal collaborative process. In inter-organizational settings the facilitator cannot be concerned only with the dynamics that play out at meetings between the participants, but also the dynamics between participants and their constituency organizations as well as the dynamics between the organizations.

Process versus content: why differentiate roles?

Some authors express the concern that the process be 'owned' or directed (if not at first, then eventually) by the participants (Webler, 1995). This is a highly democratic view, where decisions about the process, and not only the substance, are made by the participants. This view holds that even if roles are to be differentiated, they should still be played by members of the group. The role of an external facilitator, if any, is that of temporary guide, until the group can find its way on its own.

However, when a participant serves in the dual role as process facilitator, he or she must be able to switch hats effectively to preserve the integrity of the process (Kayser, 1990). Others contend that if the task is sufficiently complex the process decisions should be handed over to external process experts who are fair, neutral (having no vested interest in the results), and have no role in contributing content expertise (Broome and Keever, 1989).

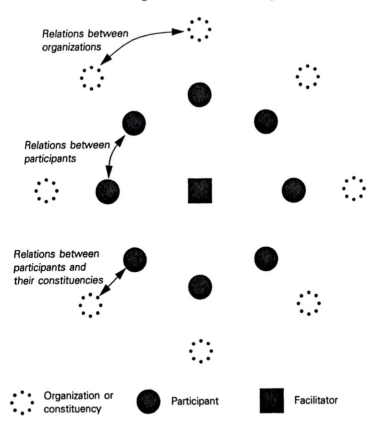

Figure 8.2   *The political process takes into account the relationship between the participants and their organizations, and between the organizations*

'Trust us with the process, with which we are expert,' says the facilitator to the participants, 'while you rely on yourselves for the content.' When should a collaborative differentiate process and content roles? On what basis is hiring an outside facilitator to be justified? This judgement can be aided by assessing the group's condition along eight dimensions (Figure 8.3).

1 Distrust or bias

In situations where distrust or bias is apparent or suspect, collaborating groups should make use of a neutral party to facilitate (and perhaps convene) the group. Those whose job it is to manage the process (the meta-decision-makers) bear an enormous influence on the process, and consequently the outcome. Their choice of participants (if they have been delegated the role of convenor as well), analytical methods, social interaction methods, and intervention into the political process have fundamental influence on the

When to use an outside facilitator

```
1 . . . . . 2 . . . . . 3 . . . . . 4 . . . . . 5 . . . . . 6 . . . . . 7 . . . . . 8 . . . . . 9 . . . . . 10
interpersonal trust          DISTRUST OR BIAS                    suspicion
```

```
1 . . . . . 2 . . . . . 3 . . . . . 4 . . . . . 5 . . . . . 6 . . . . . 7 . . . . . 8 . . . . . 9 . . . . . 10
low status                   INTIMIDATION                       high status
differential                                                    differential
```

```
1 . . . . . 2 . . . . . 3 . . . . . 4 . . . . . 5 . . . . . 6 . . . . . 7 . . . . . 8 . . . . . 9 . . . . . 10
low competition              RIVALRY                            high competition
```

```
1 . . . . . 2 . . . . . 3 . . . . . 4 . . . . . 5 . . . . . 6 . . . . . 7 . . . . . 8 . . . . . 9 . . . . . 10
well defined,                PROBLEM                            poorly or
held in common               DEFINITION                         differently defined
```

```
1 . . . . . 2 . . . . . 3 . . . . . 4 . . . . . 5 . . . . . 6 . . . . . 7 . . . . . 8 . . . . . 9 . . . . . 10
low demands                  HUMAN LIMITS                       high demands
```

```
1 . . . . . 2 . . . . . 3 . . . . . 4 . . . . . 5 . . . . . 6 . . . . . 7 . . . . . 8 . . . . . 9 . . . . . 10
simple or                    COMPLEXITY                         complex or
familiar situation           OR NOVELTY                         unfamiliar situation
```

```
1 . . . . . 2 . . . . . 3 . . . . . 4 . . . . . 5 . . . . . 6 . . . . . 7 . . . . . 8 . . . . . 9 . . . . . 10
no rush                      TIMELINESS                         pressure to
                                                                solve quickly
```

```
1 . . . . . 2 . . . . . 3 . . . . . 4 . . . . . 5 . . . . . 6 . . . . . 7 . . . . . 8 . . . . . 9 . . . . . 10
easy to get                  COST                               difficult to
together                                                        get together
```

A higher score suggests that the role of facilitator should be clearly differentiated
from that of participant and that an outside, neutral facilitator should be used

Figure 8.3 *A tool for assessing when a collaborative should differentiate
process and content roles*

collaborative effort and the collaborative itself. To give this power to any of
the participants is to give to them a great deal more power than to the
others. Consequently the collaborators might view the meta-decision-maker
(typically the chairperson) as biased – steering the process in some way to
favour their own ends. It might be true, but even if not, it might be perceived
as such.

2 Intimidation

*The presence of a facilitator can foster participation of individuals who might
otherwise feel intimidated.* In situations where participants are of disparate

educational, social or economic status, are at different levels in organization hierarchies, or are in other types of control relationships (such as
clients and service providers or small businesses and government regulators)
some participants might feel intimidated and not participate. Often the
presence of a facilitator provides participants with a neutral status person
to whom they can direct their comments without feeling intimidated. The
facilitator is also in a legitimate position to elicit information from the
group, as well as particular individuals. Intimidation and distrust or bias
might also suggest when anonymous information collection is appropriate.
This is particularly relevant in the use of electronic brainstorming tools that
have the capability for anonymous input.

3 Rivalry

*Rivalries between individuals and organizations can be mitigated by the
presence of a facilitator.* Participants are typically reluctant to exhibit
personal rivalries or attacks in the presence of an outsider. They might
want to sway the facilitator's judgement, but then realize that their claims
might not seem valid when viewed externally, and so do not even raise
them. Participants are often surprised at how polite they are to each other.
When rivalries surface, a facilitator might determine if they are relevant to
the task at hand, and if not, refocus the group on their stated purpose.
When rivalries are germane, the facilitator will ask the group to understand
them as part of the overall relationships and issues to be addressed by the
collaborative.

4 Problem definition

*If the problem situation is poorly defined, or defined differently by different
parties, a neutral listener and analyst can help to construct a complete,
shared understanding of the problem.* When people come together with
disparate views they are often more concerned with having their own point
of view understood by others, than in gaining an understanding of the
views of others. A neutral party whose sole role it is to listen to, analyse,
and integrate everyone's views is a valuable asset to such a group.

5 Human limits

*The breadth of substantive issues is so large that to think about them and
process issues is too much for any person to think about all at once.* That is,
the demand of attending to the volume of information (Bryson and
Roering, 1988), the content as well as the social, cognitive and political
processes that come into play at each moment in a collaborative meeting, is
too much to expect to be met from a single human being. Our cognitive
capabilities are not great enough. Running a meeting, and participating in
a meeting, are each sufficiently demanding tasks that we ought to focus on
one or the other. Indeed some argue that to expect a single process expert

to attend to all of the social, cognitive and political process issues in real time is too much to expect, so that we should use teams of facilitators, with each facilitator having a well-defined and complementary role (Rohrbaugh, 1992).

6 Complexity or novelty

In complex or novel situations the collaborative should employ process experts so that they might do a better job of working together intellectually to solve problems. Meta-decision-making, that is, making decisions about the problem-solving and decision-making process, is a legitimate specialty in which experts can accumulate a wealth of knowledge, expertise, judgemental capability and practical skill. 'The capacity to manage social learning is itself a form of social knowledge' (Korten, 1981). Some collaboratives have developed their own expertise for addressing recurring decisions, and so this might not be necessary. However, when approaching novel situations or tasks which they encounter infrequently, like strategic planning, it might still be valuable to call in experts who work with that type of problem frequently.

7 Timeliness

If a timely decision is required, as in a crisis situation, the use of a facilitator can speed the work of the collaborative. If the collaborative group were to make the meta-decisions as a group, it would take valuable time away from treating the substantive issues they want to address. Unlike parliamentary procedure, for which there are prescribed rules which address nearly every procedural issue that a decision-making group can encounter, there is no rule book for collaboration. Groups are faced with either making up the rules as they go along, or using the rules of the process expert as a 'collaborative parliamentarian' who will choose which rules to apply, make up new ones as appropriate, steer the group through their application and explain them as needed.

8 Cost

A facilitator can help the group reduce the cost of meeting as a barrier to collaboration. When the participants find it difficult to get together, either because of the cost of travel or other obligations, use of a facilitator can reduce the cost of collaboration. By vesting responsibility for process in the facilitator, the group reduces or eliminates the time it has to spend on meta-decisions, makes use of more effective processes known to the process expert, and takes advantage of the listening, analytical and integrative skills of a neutral party.

While the above conditions are stated discretely, in practice they all must be addressed by the facilitator. The degree to which each is addressed at any point in time is a critical judgement which the facilitator makes, and one facilitator will likely make a judgement different from that of another. These conditions compete for attention, and can be understood from four 'competing values' perspectives on decision-making effectiveness (Rohrbaugh and Eden, 1990). In brief, the conditions of distrust or bias and intimidation pertain to the consensual perspective which values participation, morale and the supportability of the decision; the conditions regarding rivalry and problem definition pertain to the political perspective which values adaptability, brokering and legitimacy; the conditions of human limits and complexity or novelty relate to the empirical perspective which values data, integration, consistency and accountability; and the conditions of timeliness and cost relate to the rational perspective which values goal orientation, directiveness and efficiency.

Moral implications of facilitation

To the extent that these conditions persist, the facilitator, or process expert, will continue to be necessary. The notion that collaboratives should or can become self-facilitating is not necessarily true or even a useful goal. So long as there are power differentials in the political process, distrust, novelty and so on, the group cannot perform this role for itself, even if it developed substantial process expertise. It would spend a lot of time arguing over process questions or rely on a 'collaborative parliamentarian' to implement those rules in an unbiased way. Institutionalizing the role of the independent, neutral process expert as facilitator could go a long way to overcoming gridlock and achieving collaborative advantage. How can we trust the role of facilitation and how can we select individuals to perform this role? If the need of a facilitator is indicated, how can the participants in the collaborative select a person on whom they can rely for a fair and competent process (Webler, 1995)?

One of the practical issues that a process facilitator must often address is that various individuals have processes in mind that they would like to see used. These process ideas might or might not be biased in some way, but the facilitator probably does not know whether or not they are. On one hand the facilitator has to be open to the group's ideas, but on the other hand must maintain his or her role as process expert, and not be seen to favour some participants over others in adopting their process suggestions. Some participants will become proactive or aggressive in pushing their process ideas, or perhaps in rejecting the process put forth by the facilitator. How can facilitators respect participants, maintain their role as process experts, and be relied on for fairness and competency?

> The stakes are now so high that there is an urgent need for cooperative engagement with these problems over a wide range of inquiry . . . there is no royal road to truth, no single perspective that offers overriding promise. Just as the sources and manifestations of human conflict are immensely varied, so too are there many useful approaches to understanding, preventing and resolving conflict. (Hamburg, 1986: 533)

These processes, social, cognitive and political, are moral. *How* we decide is subject to moral scrutiny just as *what* we decide. Participants will respond to a breach of process expectations with moral outrage, just as they will respond to a breach of outcome expectations. When participants are frustrated in their attempt to push a particular outcome, they will find fault with the process. They are concerned about the moral character of the facilitator, not just his or her process expertise. Does this place the process facilitator in a position of moral leadership in achieving the goals of fairness and competency (Webler, 1995)?

> The beginning point for sociological – and by extension organizational – analysis is not the question of how or why people go about getting what they want to get but how it is that they know what they know about the empirical world. . . . the rules and processes by which people come to agree upon as well as contest what is empirically real (i.e. social facts) are experienced in *moral* terms; cognition itself, that is to say, is a moral act. (Harmon, 1989: 147)

To maintain the morality of the process, the facilitator cannot favour any participant. To believe in what a participant says might lead to casual acceptance of that individual's version of the truth, which would undermine the faith of the other participants in the fairness of the process. It might reduce the facilitator's ability to ensure the competency of the discussion, maintain a fair process and raise valuable questions that examine the underlying values or assumptions held by 'believers'.

While not believing in the truth of any participants, it is none the less critical that the facilitator be respectful of the participants and cognizant of their sincerity. An interesting illustration is in an early recorded application of group decision-making, the debates of the rabbis of the Talmudic era in which groups of scholars sifted through the merits of conflicting interpretations of the law. The discussion first establishes that group judgement is superior to individual judgement, and then confronts the problem of deciding between judgements made by two different groups. Which group's judgement is to be followed when both groups have had high quality discussions and both have arrived at reasonable but different conclusions? The decision of one group is favoured because in rendering their decision they respectfully acknowledged the work of the other group and mentioned their findings first (Dorff, 1977).

In the field of community development a distinction is made between *felt* needs, *observed* needs and *real* needs (Goodenough, 1963). Although these needs typically are applied to community goals and activities, they can be applied in any collaborative process. The process needs perceived by participants are *felt* needs, whether they are realistic or not. The facilitator, who is not a participant, also makes an assessment of the collaborative's needs – *observed* needs – which might or might not be the same as the participants' *felt* needs. Neither should be presumed to recognize what are the *real* needs as they might be determined by some omniscient assessment (Figure 8.4). The facilitator, while listening to needs articulated by participants, independently observes and diagnoses the needs of the situation and

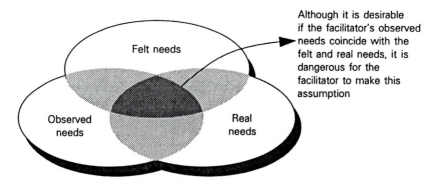

Although it is desirable if the facilitator's observed needs coincide with the felt and real needs, it is dangerous for the facilitator to make this assumption

Figure 8.4 *Facilitators cannot presume that their observed needs coincide with either the participants' felt needs or the group's real needs*

takes responsibility for making process decisions. To do so while still respecting the participants' *felt* needs, and maintaining openness to new process directions, facilitators cannot presume that they have *observed* the *real* needs of the group. They cannot believe in the participants' *felt* needs, nor can they believe in the infallibility of their own *observed* needs.

So in what can the facilitator believe? A facilitator can believe in groups, particularly groups in which all legitimate perspectives are represented, allowing all perspectives to be taken into account, striving to gain the best contributions from each member and discerning the fairness and competency of processes. But can a facilitator believe in an individual, or in a particular idea? Rather, the facilitator should believe in the participants', and their own ability, to doubt. Facilitation must 'reflect a tolerance for the ambiguity and uncertainty which are inherent in the social learning process' (Korten, 1981). Other than reinforcing the idea of self-existence, doubt reinforces the value of the group and their continuing search for solutions. Believing in a solution too soon (or believing in a 'final' solution at all), whether believed by the facilitator or by the participants, is an immoral act that discredits the facilitator, the process, the group and the complexity of the environment in which we live. Although sureness can be seductive, better that the facilitator should exercise doubt. With due respect, Karl Marx had it almost right: *Answers* are the opiate of the people.

References

Barnard, Chester (1938) *The Functions of the Executive*. Cambridge, MA: Harvard University Press.

Benne, Kenneth and Sheats, Paul (1948) 'Functional roles of group members', *Journal of Social Issues*, 4: 41–9.

Bodily, Samuel E. (1992) 'Decision and risk analysis', *Interfaces*, Special issue, 22 (6).

Broome, Benjamin and Keever, David (1989) 'Next generation group facilitation', *Management Communication Quarterly*, 3 (1): 107–27.

Bower, Joseph and Doz, Yves (1979) 'Strategy formulation: a social and political process', in C.W. Hoper and D.E. Schendel (eds), *Strategic Management: a New View of Business Policy and Planning*. Boston, MA: Little Brown. pp. 152–85.

Bryson, John and Roering, William (1988) 'Initiation of strategic planning by governments', *Public Administration Review*, 48 (6): 995–1004.

Cleveland, Harlan (1985) *The Knowledge Executive: Leadership in an Information Society*. New York: Dutton.

Cropper, Steve (1990) 'The complexity of decision support practice', in C. Eden and J. Radford (eds), *Tackling Strategic Problems: the Role of Group Decision Support*. London: Sage. pp. 29–39.

Dorff, Elliot (1977) *Conservative Judaism: Our Ancestors to Our Descendants*. New York: United Synagogue Youth.

Eden, Colin (1990) 'The unfolding nature of group decision support – two dimensions of skill', in C. Eden and J. Radford (eds), *Tackling Strategic Problems: the Role of Group Decision Support*. London: Sage. pp. 48–52.

Eden, C. and Radford, J. (eds) (1990) *Tackling Strategic Problems: the Role of Group Decision Support*. London: Sage.

Goodenough, Ward (1963) *Cooperation in Change*. New York: Russell Sage Foundation.

Hamburg, David (1986) 'New risks of prejudice, ethnocentrism, and violence', *Science*, 23 (27): 533.

Harmon, Michael (1989) '"Decision" and "action" as contrasting perspectives in organization theory', *Public Administration Review*, March/April: 147.

Huxham, C. and Cropper, S. (1994) 'From many to one and back: an exploration of the components of facilitation'. *Omega, International Journal of Management Science*, 22 (1): 1–11.

Kayser, Thomas (1990) *Mining Group Gold: How to Cash in on the Collaborative Power of a Group*. El Segundo, CA: Serif Publishing.

Korten, David (1981) 'The management of social transformation'. *Public Administration Review*, 41, (6): 609–18.

Langley, A. (1991) 'Formal analysis of strategic decision making', *Omega, International Journal of Management Science*, 19 (2/3): 79–99.

McGrath, Joseph (1984) *Groups: Interaction and Performance*. Englewood Cliffs, NJ: Prentice Hall.

Morris, William (1972) *Management for Action: Psychotechnical Decision Making*. Reston, VA: Reston Publishing.

Phillips, Lawrence, and Phillips, Maryann (1993) 'Facilitated work groups: theory and practice', *Journal of the Operational Research Society*, 44 (6): 533–49.

Rohrbaugh, John (1987) 'Assessing the effectiveness of expert systems', in J. Mumpower, L. Phillips, O. Renn and V.R.R. Uppuluri (eds), *Expert Judgment and Expert Systems*. Berlin: Springer-Verlag. pp. 251–67.

Rohrbaugh, John (1992) 'Cognitive challenges and collective accomplishments', in R. Bostrom, R. Watson, R. and S. Kinney (eds), *Computer Augmented Teamwork*. New York: Van Nostrand Reinhold. pp. 299–324.

Rohrbaugh, John and Eden, Colin (1990). 'Using the competing values approach to explore ways of working', in C. Eden and J. Radford (eds), *Tackling Strategic Problems: the Role of Group Decision Support*. London: Sage. pp. 40–47.

Schein, Edgar (1969) *Process Consultation: Its Role in Organizational Development*. Reading, MA: Addison-Wesley.

Schein, Edgar (1987) *Process Consultation*, Volume II: *Lessons for Managers and Consultants*. Reading, MA: Addison-Wesley.

Smith, Gerald (1988) 'Towards a heuristic theory of problem structuring', *Management Science*, 34 (12): 1489–1506.

Steiner, Ivan (1972) *Group Process and Productivity*. New York: Academic Press.

Tolman, Edward (1948) 'Cognitive maps in rats and men', *Psychological Review*, 55: 189–208.

Ward, James C. and Reingen, Peter H. (1990) 'Sociocognitive analysis of group decision making among consumers', *Journal of Consumer Research*, 17 (3): 245–62.

Webler, Thomas (1995) '"Right" discourse in citizen participation: an evaluative yardstick', in O. Renn, T. Webler and P. Wiedemann (eds), *Fairness and Competence in Citizen Participation: Evaluating Models for Environmental Discourse*. Boston: Kluwer Academic Press. pp. 35–86.

9
Group Decision Support for Collaboration

Chris Huxham

The introductory chapter of this book argued that most major societal issues – poverty, crime, the environment – cannot be resolved by any organization acting alone. This point has been emphasized in many of the other chapters; most notably, perhaps, by Himmelman in Chapter 2. If such issues are to be tackled at all, therefore, organizations must act in collaboration with each other.

The particular perspective on **collaborative advantage** which drives the thinking behind this chapter was outlined in Chapter 1:

> Achieving collaborative advantage requires that something unusually creative is produced – perhaps an objective is met – that no organization could have produced on its own *and* that each organization, through the collaboration, is able to achieve its own objectives better than it could alone. It may also be possible to achieve something for wider society that is beyond the remit of any of the participating organizations themselves.

This notion aims to capture the sense of synergy required for tackling societal problems while at the same time recognizing that most organizations will only be willing to be involved if there is an individual gain for them themselves.

The goal of collaborative advantage sets high targets for collaboration. Given that collaborations with less ambitious aims frequently end in frustration and failure (Bryson and Crosby, 1992; Huxham and Vangen, 1994; Webb, 1991), if collaborative advantage is aimed for, it is clear that special attention needs to be paid to the *process* of achieving it.

This chapter is therefore concerned with the design of intervention processes which may help organizations to achieve collaborative advantage in tackling major societal issues. It derives from work with a variety of organizations involved in (or contemplating) collaboration. Most significant to this chapter, however, has been a participatory action research project (Whyte, 1991) carried out over five years – with varied focuses and intensities – with a director of a UK local economic development agency. The notion of collaborative advantage itself derives from this work and much of the project has been a joint exploration into the nature of collaborative advantage as it would affect the director's own actions in encouraging his organization to act in collaboration with others (Huxham with Macdonald, 1992).

The latter stages of this work were concerned with the design of a formal process for initiating a strategic level collaboration. It is unfortunate from a research perspective – as well as, in the view at the time of the director, from the practical perspective – that other considerations led to a decision not to pursue that particular collaboration further. It was therefore not possible to try out the design in that setting. Many of the concepts have, however, been incorporated into recent work with other groups. Most particularly, they have informed a current programme of work with collaborative groups concerned with the alleviation of poverty (Huxham and Eden, 1992). The thinking behind the design thus appears to remain largely valid. The remainder of this chapter aims to outline some of this thinking.

The thinking has been driven by two, fairly distinct, themes. On the one hand, it has drawn on the precepts and practices of group decision support, and on the other, it has explored considerations which are specific to collaborative situations. These two threads are firstly introduced separately below and then integrated in the discussion of the design of a process for collaboration.

Group decision support

The particular form of group decision support (GDS) with which this chapter (like the last) is concerned is known as **facilitator-led** or **wide band** group decision support (Ackermann, 1996; Eden, 1993; Eden and Radford, 1990; Huxham and Cropper, 1994; Phillips and Phillips, 1993). Examples which typify the approach are SODA (Strategic Options Development and Analysis) (Eden, 1989), Decision Conferencing (Phillips, 1990) and Strategic Choice (Friend and Hickling, 1987). Chapters 3, 10 and 11 of this book describe similar approaches.

Designed in the first instance generally for use with teams of decision-makers in *intra*-organizational settings (though Strategic Choice is an exception in this respect), the approaches take participants through a workshop, or series of workshops, led by one or more facilitators and using a modelling method to capture, analyse and play back to participants the substance of the issues under discussion. The models so produced, which are sometimes, but by no means always, computer-based, form a focus for the workshop and help the facilitator in the management of the group processes. Where a computer is used, the data are generally entered by a facilitator rather than by the team members. The model is displayed centrally on a single screen. *The aim of this kind of GDS is to facilitate a process for tackling complex problems which encourages creativity, commitment and consensus among group members and leads to actionable decisions; it is not to provide advice.*

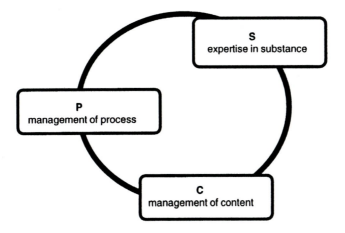

Figure 9.1   *The PCS model of consultancy practice*

P, C and S – elements of consultancy

It has been emphasized above that GDS (as this chapter is concerned with
it) is a facilitative form of consultancy. One way of understanding the
significance of this – which will be useful to later discussion – is through
the 'PCS' model (Figure 9.1), which focuses on the different kinds of input
that a consultant may put into his or her work with a client or group
(Huxham and Cropper, 1994). In this model, P, **the management of process**,
is concerned with the degree to which, and the way in which, the consultant
is concerned with managing his or her interactions with the client and
additionally, where there is a group, with managing the interactions
between participants. In terms of the model posed by Schuman in Chapter
8, P most closely relates to 'social process'. C, **the management of content**,
may be thought of as the, perhaps implicit, modelling and analysis methods
that are used to handle the content (or data) of the problem being
addressed (in Schuman's terms, this is similar to 'cognitive process').
Finally, S is the injection by the consultant of **his or her own substantive
expertise** – that is, his or her understanding of the content of the problem
area itself – into the process.

Inevitably, all consultants use all three forms of input but they will give
both different emphases and different interpretations to them. For example,
the **authoritative adviser** or **doctor–patient** style consultant (Heron, 1990;
Schein, 1969) will tend to rely heavily on S. By contrast, facilitation, in its
purest sense, might be thought of as consisting largely of P. GDS facilitation, however, focuses both on P and on C, with the modelling and
analysis of the problem content (as well as management of the group
processes) being an explicit part of the process (Eden, 1990). At face value,
S would seem to be irrelevant to a facilitative process. However, S can be

used to enhance the facilitative process in a variety of ways. For example, the facilitator's knowledge of a situation might lead him or her to question the participants' assumptions about it. *The important point for this chapter is that S can either be used facilitatively – as a way of enhancing the thinking process – or authoritatively – as a way of informing the participants what to do.* Used facilitatively, and in combination with P and C, deliberate use of S is not inconsistent with the basic philosophy of GDS facilitation.

GDS and collaboration

The relevance of GDS approaches to inter-organizational collaboration stems from two considerations. First, the social issues with which we are concerned are typical of the kind of complex problems that GDS is designed to tackle. Second, though the concern is to design collaboration processes to assist organizations to work together, in practice this will be reliant, to a large extent, upon the success with which individual members of those organizations can work with each other across organizational boundaries. In particular, it usually makes sense to create a core group (Huxham and Vangen, 1994) or working group (Friend and Hickling, 1987) of members of key organizations involved, at least to initiate the collaboration, and this group might be supported by a GDS process.

Considerations of collaboration

Our thinking in this area has evolved over time. Previous articles have focused on a variety of perspectives. For example, one focus has been on the need to consider the balance of the pitfalls of collaboration against the pitfalls of individualism (Huxham with Macdonald, 1992). Another is the need to pay attention to ensuring that the internal processes of each organization facilitate, rather than hamper, the collaboration as much as possible. In this context the notion of an organization's **collaborative capability** has been identified (Huxham, 1993a). Another thrust has involved categorizing collaboration into different types (Huxham, 1990), and in common with many other people working in the area, we have also been concerned with factors such as who to involve in the collaboration, the degree of mutual trust, the aims of the venture and so on, which would be likely to affect its success (Huxham, 1993b). More recently, we have also conceptualized the development and frequent failure of collaboration through the notions of **collaborative naivety and maturity** and **collaborative inertia** (Huxham and Vangen, 1994) and have begun to develop a taxonomy to describe the various types of goals that those in collaborations tend to need to pursue (Vangen et al., 1994).

In addition to our own work, a great deal has been written by others, based on work carried out by practitioners, consultants and researchers, which aims to give insight into the nature of collaboration. Much of this is descriptive and tends to focus on conceptualizing the factors that make collaboration work or the forces which tend to make it fail. In this book, for example, Gray (Chapter 4) discusses success factors while Sink (Chapter 6) focuses on factors likely to cause failure. At a general level such articles tend to back up the conclusions from our own deliberations. Our experience, however, would lead us to paint a more complex picture of the issues than frequently comes across.

Using collaboration expertise

If the value of this kind of understanding of collaboration – which shall be referred to here as **collaboration expertise** – is acknowledged, it seems important that it be included into the design of an intervention process. The question is, however, how should this be done?

It is useful to consider two different ways in which this can happen. First, collaborative insights can be discussed explicitly with those involved in the collaboration, to direct their attention towards the factors concerned. Alternatively, collaboration expertise can be largely hidden from the participants, but used explicitly by the facilitator in the design of the overall process. These two approaches are not mutually exclusive, but in terms of the PCS model, they represent quite different focuses.

In the first case, collaboration is overtly considered to be part of the focus of the core group. The facilitator will be seen by the participants in the group as an **expert in collaboration** and expected to provide substantive expertise on how to collaborate. The use, by the consultant, of collaboration expertise in this way may thus be seen as a focus on S. The expertise may be used authoritatively – for example, 'you need to include all organizations with a stake in the issue' – or facilitatively – for example, 'what do you think would be the effect of not including that organization?' (though much of the literature is written in the former style).

In the second case, the use of collaboration expertise is used, not as S, but **to inform the design of the total intervention** – that is, the way in which **the combination of P, C and S** is interpreted. Though there may be some room for debate with the participants over the nature of the intervention, the key principles underlying it will represent the consultant's strongly held beliefs about appropriate processes for collaborative situations; these will be the basis of the distinctiveness of the particular consultant's approach. In the context of these key principles, collaboration expertise is being used authoritatively in the design of the intervention – the more so, the more it is hidden from the participants. As Schuman (Chapter 8) points out, there are moral issues associated with this.

In the economic development situation which provided the basis for the thinking in this chapter, collaboration expertise was used in the process design in both of these senses. In designing an overall intervention process for use with a core group (the second case, above), three principles – derived from the collaboration expertise perspective – were seen to be of particular importance. These then provided the rationale for the way in which other aspects of collaboration expertise could be introduced more directly to the group (the first case, above). The three principles will be considered in the next section. The implications of these for the design of a process which includes collaboration expertise will be discussed in the following section.

Key principles of collaboration

The three principles which underlie the design of the overall intervention have been discussed more fully in another article (Huxham, 1993c). Here, therefore, only a brief – perhaps rather over-assertive – overview is given.

Acknowledging collaborative processes

Many of the factors which affect success in collaboration tend naturally to act against it. For example, mismatches in collaborative capability, disparity of power, language and culture differences and differences in aims are inevitabilities in most circumstances (Huxham, 1996). This being the case, it would seem important that those involved are both aware of the forces acting against them, and able to **think explicitly and carefully** about how to manage the wider collaborative processes (that is, those beyond the immediate interaction of the core group) in the light of these negative forces. This means paying attention, not only to the processes of interaction between organizations, but also to the processes of dissemination and implementation of the collaborative intent within organizations.

Balancing tensions

Turning attention to the factors themselves, it is likely that there are generic factors – such as the nature of the membership, mutual trust, the role of the convenor, the political and social climate and so on – which will affect the success of any collaboration. What does not seem possible, however, is to specify, generically, the way in which such factors should be interpreted. Rather, this will usually be a matter of **balancing the tensions** surrounding each factor in the specific circumstance.

For example, it is generally accepted that having a social and political climate that is favourable both to collaboration *per se* and to the issue over which collaboration takes place is important (Mattessich and Monsey, 1992). However, in situations where the climate is unfavourable, collaboration could still be pursued if at least one of the organizations feels strongly enough that there would be value in doing so. In this circumstance, there would be one side of a tension in favour of not collaborating at all and another in favour of doing so. Balancing the tension would involve deciding not only *whether* to collaborate, but also, *what form* of collaboration would be appropriate. This would probably involve an exploration of *how*, if need be, the unfavourable environment could be managed.

It would therefore seem valuable to include in the process a way of highlighting what the important tensions are likely to be (based on collaboration expertise). However, it seems important to ensure that this is done facilitatively in a way which encourages debate about the relevance, nature and resolution of the tension **as seen by those involved, in their particular situation**.

Ignorance, resistance and gentleness

The second principle above suggests that consideration of collaboration issues (the first principle above) is likely to require a not-insignificant amount of time and commitment from those involved. In practice, however, despite the ever-increasing number of collaborations that both are conceived and fail, experience suggests that many of those involved appear to have little concept of the significance of the inter-organizational factors in their joint work. They thus tend to be unable to 'acknowledge their ignorance' (Nocon, 1989) about these factors and hence are often unwilling to regard consideration of them as anything other than trivial; not unnaturally, other priorities tend to dominate. Any suggestion that they should pay attention to the process of collaboration is likely to meet with resistance. This effect is likely to be compounded in situations where – as often happens – an organization is not highly committed to being part of the collaboration in the first place.

Unless one can be certain that such attitudes are not prevalent in any particular collaborative situation, it therefore seems appropriate that an intervention process should take a **gentle** (rather than dogmatic) approach to ensuring that attention is given to collaboration issues.

The essence of a process

To summarize, the three principles above together suggest an approach which:

1 encourages those involved to consider the process of collaboration;
2 as part of this, focuses attention on exploration of the key areas of collaborative tension; and
3 does this gently to ensure that it is seen as relevant and fully owned.

A fourth principle, which relies more on experience of GDS than on collaboration, is also key to the thinking. That is, that whereas it may be difficult to attract people's attention to collaboration, **there is likely to be little difficulty in engaging them in debate and discussion about the issue which is the subject of collaboration**. This suggests that the approach should:

4 acknowledge and use participants' commitment to the subject of collaboration.

GDS is designed to manage that very process of debate and discussion about an issue, and hence seems a good starting point for the design of a process. In adapting GDS ideas for use with groups involved in *inter-organizational* collaboration, however, one key concern is to include **parallel and interacting processes** for consideration of the issue over which collaboration takes place and for consideration of the nature of the collaborative processes themselves. A further concern is to ensure that **the overall process is led by consideration of the issue** rather than of the collaboration.

Thus, time must be designed into the process for both kinds of focus. However, as far as possible, the initial emphasis should be on the issue. The aim is to – as far as possible – **allow concerns about collaboration to fall out of discussion about the issue**. The process must then provide a forum in which they can be addressed explicitly and hence inform a self-made design for the collaborative practice of the group.

Central to GDS is, as was noted earlier, the use of models to form the focus for the discussions during workshops. In these parallel processes, the models must contain views of group members both about the issue *and* about the collaborative process. However, it is suggested that they should also include – and this makes them fundamentally different from models used in more common forms of GDS – some of the areas of tension in collaboration judged likely to be important *by the facilitator*, and not already included by the core group. In terms of the PCS model, this may be seen as a deliberate and predefined injection of S (in the form of collaboration expertise) into the process.

Whether or not it would be possible to do this with any GDS system is an interesting matter for discussion. The ideas expressed here are based in at least two key respects on the use of SODA in particular. First, the modelling method central to SODA is cognitive mapping which models the views people express around issues, as chains of argument (Eden, 1988). It is therefore equally well suited to modelling views about the issue and views about collaboration. Furthermore, it is possible to link the two sets of argument so that those concerned with collaboration can be directly linked with those about the issue and, hence, their relevance to the latter demonstrated. An example is shown in Figure 9.2.

The second respect in which the SODA approach is significant is in its emphasis on interviewing individual workshop participants in advance of the workshop. The rationale for this is that it allows individual perspectives to be captured in the absence of the team effects, such as groupthink (Janis, 1972), which are inevitable once the group is working together. A spin-off of this, however, is that an initial model is available at the start of the first workshop. This means that it is possible for the facilitator to add argumentation to the model about areas of tension he or she believes are crucial, prior to the workshop and without giving it any status different from that of the core group members' views.

It seems important to the philosophy of gentleness, as well as that of

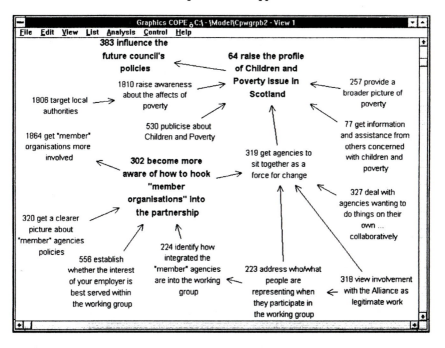

Note: in the above map, arrows may be read as 'leads to' and dots as 'rather than'. Concept numbers have no meaning and are simply labels. This map is extracted from a map containing hundreds of concepts which was produced from combining the views of participants involved in a series of workshops concerned with collaboration over child poverty issues. The map is stored, manipulated and analysed using the software Graphics COPE. In this extract, the concepts towards the top of the screen (for example, 383, 64, 1810) are concerned with the substantive issue over which the collaboration takes place. The concepts in the lower half of the screen (for example, 302, 223, 327) are concerned with the process of collaboration

Figure 9.2 *A cognitive map showing arguments both about the substantive issue and the process of collaboration*

facilitation, that as far as possible, the views on collaboration included in the model should be those of the team members. Thus the facilitator's collaboration expertise would only be included after the views from the initial interviews have been included and only where the facilitator judges there to be very important omissions. However, building them into the model increases the likelihood that these areas of tension will be brought into the debate and explored, alongside the exploration of the issue. Whether or not the group chooses to take on board those aspects injected by the facilitator when the model is subsequently used as the focus of a core group workshop will depend upon whether or not they see them as relevant; debate about them will only happen if there is a degree of consensus within the group that this is a valuable thing to do. The use of S in this way is thus intended to be strongly facilitative rather than authoritative.

Conclusion

This chapter has focused on issues in the design of a facilitated group process intended to help the core group of a collaboration not only to work together on the activities which are the reason for collaboration, but also to fashion for themselves ways of managing the collaborative process itself. The design rests on the ability to interlock the two activities – consideration of the collaborative purpose and of the collaborative process – in such a way that engagement with the collaborative process is integral to engagement with the collaborative purpose and in such a way that the facilitator's collaboration expertise can be introduced gently into the facilitative process.

It has not been the intention of this chapter to describe the proposed process in great detail, but simply to outline some of the thinking which underlies it. Conceptualization of this design rationale has drawn heavily on the PCS model of consultancy practice. In particular, it has focused on the role of 'S', in this case taken to be the consultant's expertise in (that is, understanding of) collaboration practice. It has been argued that collaboration expertise can play an important role within a GDS context at two levels. It can (indeed, will inevitably) be used first to inform the consultant's overall design of the process to be used with the core group and secondly to inform directly the participants' thinking about their wider collaborative practice.

This chapter began by focusing on the relevance of achieving collaborative advantage to addressing social issues. Most of the arguments put forward probably apply to many situations of collaboration, or indeed to other forms of inter-organizational relationships. The focus on collaborative advantage, however, serves to emphasize – when major social issues are at stake – the importance of finding processes which can make collaboration happen.

Acknowledgement

My thanks to David Macdonald, who was central to the design. What is written here, however, is entirely my own interpretation.

References

Ackermann, F. (1996) 'Participants' perceptions on the role of facilitators using group decision support systems', *Group Decision and Negotiation*, 5: 93–112.
Bryson, J. and Crosby, B. (1992) *Leadership for the Common Good: Tackling Public Problems in a Shared-Power World*. San Francisco: Jossey Bass.
Eden, C. (1988) 'Cognitive mapping', *European Journal of Operational Research*, 36: 1–13.
Eden, C. (1989) 'Using cognitive mapping for strategic options development and analysis (SODA)', in J. Rosenhead (ed.), *Rational Analysis in a Problematic World*. Chichester: Wiley. pp. 21–42.

Eden, C. (1990) 'The unfolding nature of group decision support: two dimensions of skill', in C. Eden and J. Radford (eds), *Tackling Strategic Problems: the Role of Group Decision Support*. London: Sage. pp. 48–52.

Eden, C. (1993) 'On evaluating the performance of "wide-band" GDSS's'. Department of Management Science, University of Strathclyde.

Eden, C. and Radford, J. (eds) (1990) *Tackling Strategic Problems: the Role of Group Decision Support*. London: Sage.

Friend, J. and Hickling, A. (1987) *Planning under Pressure*. Oxford: Pergamon.

Heron, J. (1990) *Helping the Client*. London: Sage.

Huxham, C. (1990) 'Categories of collaboration'. LEC Collaboration Project, research note 1. Department of Management Science, University of Strathclyde.

Huxham, C. (1993a) 'Collaborative capability: an intra-organizational perspective on collaborative advantage', *Public Money and Management*, 12 (July–Sept): 21–8.

Huxham, C. (1993b) 'Pursuing collaborative advantage', *Journal of the Operational Research Society*, 44 (6): 599–611.

Huxham, C. (1993c) 'Processes for collaborative advantage: a gentle exploration of tensions', in J. Pasquero and D. Collins (eds), *International Association for Business and Society, Proceedings*, pp. 90–5.

Huxham, C. (1996) 'Advantage or inertia? Making collaboration work', in R. Paton; G. Clark; G. Jones; J. Lewis and P. Quintas (eds), *The New Management Reader*. London: Routledge. pp. 238–54.

Huxham, C. and Cropper, S. (1994) 'From many to one and back: an exploration of the components of facilitation', *Omega*, 22 (1): 1–11.

Huxham, C. and Eden, C. (1992) 'The nature of interorganisational collaboration among community and public sector organizations'. Research Proposal, Department of Management Science, University of Strathclyde.

Huxham, C. with Macdonald, D. (1992) 'Introducing collaborative advantage: achieving inter-organizational effectiveness through meta-strategy', *Management Decision*, 30: 50–6.

Huxham, C. and Vangen, S. (1994) 'Naivety and maturity, inertia and fatigue: are working relationships between public organizations doomed to fail?' Working Paper 94/17, Department of Management Science, University of Strathclyde.

Janis, I. (1972) *Victims of Groupthink: a Psychological Study of Foreign Policy Decisions and Fiascos*. Boston, MA: Houghton Mifflin.

Mattessich, P. and Monsey, B. (1992) *Collaboration: What Makes It Work?* St Paul, MN: Amherst H. Wilder Foundation.

Nocon, A. (1989) 'Forms of ignorance and their role in the joint planning process', *Social Policy and Administration*, 23: 31–47.

Phillips, L. (1990) 'Decision analysis for group decision support', in C. Eden and J. Radford, (eds), *Tackling Strategic Problems: the Role of Group Decision Support*. London: Sage. pp. 142–50.

Phillips, L. and Phillips, M. (1993) 'Facilitated work groups: theory and practice', *Journal of the Operational Research Society*, 44 (6): 533–50.

Schein, E.H. (1969) *Process Consultation: Its Role in Organisational Development*. Reading, MA: Addison-Wesley.

Vangen, S., Huxham, C. and Eden, C. (1994) 'Understanding collaboration from the perspective of a goal system'. Paper presented to the International Workshop on Multi-Organisational Partnerships: Working Together Across Organizational Boundaries. EISAM, Brussels, September.

Webb, A. (1991) 'Co-ordination: a problem in public sector management', *Policy and Politics*, 19: 229–41.

Whyte, W. (ed.) (1991) *Participatory Action Research*. London: Sage.

10

Utilizing Stakeholder Strategies for Positive Collaborative Outcomes

Charles B. Finn

When groups and organizations begin to embrace collaborative processes to engage in intra- or inter-organizational strategic management and change, they are in essence, inventing a new type of organization. Yet these actors bring assumptions of decision-making, interpretation and ownership that are at the very least, unsuited to this process. In order to enhance the potentials for success in this type of transformational organization, participants must appreciate there are fundamental organizational differences in terms of structure and culture involved compared to traditional organizations. There are at least two basic assumptions of the 'firm' that do not apply to these processes and the organizations involved and/or created which lead to a very different interpretation of ownership. Managers and facilitators of collaborative processes must account for these differences in order to help ensure successful outcomes for their organizations or clients. In this context, this chapter introduces two strategic management techniques that may be implemented to address these differences.

As Himmelman and Eden (Chapters 2 and 3) and many other researchers have already pointed out (Gray, 1989; Huxham, 1993), the collaboration concept is a fundamentally new public policy approach to understanding and dealing with issues that are larger than the capacity of any one actor or organization is able – or perhaps willing – to comprehend or deal with. At the same time, the ability of any one organization or actor to undertake large problems through hegemonic leadership, partnership or some co-operative form has been significantly diminished. We now live in a world where 'no one is in charge' (Bryson and Crosby, 1992) and we must fundamentally re-think and challenge existing operations paradigms.

In this chapter, the theoretical differences between the construct of the 'firm' and a collaborative organization are discussed as are the reasons why new or modified approaches are required. Some techniques are then presented that take these differences into account. A case is presented in which these techniques were employed, and it is argued that the outcomes observed tend to support the above assertions. Finally, there is some reflection upon other potentials for the approach.

Theory of the firm

For this discussion collaborative change is defined as **processes that are utilized to allow new 'governance' structures to be developed and/or enabled.** These processes are required as existing operational structures and power relationships were not designed to appreciate or deal with new challenges because the nature of the solution to an identified problem is beyond the capacity of the traditional firm (Gray, 1989; Huxham with Macdonald, 1992)

Assumptions of stakeholder relationships and problem identification

To begin with, there are certain basic assumptions of the 'firm' or organiz-ation that hold whether issues involve either the private or public sector. The first assumption is these organizations are not altruistic, meaning they are motivated by profit or mandate. Secondly, they are competitive in the sense they are constrained by profit requirements or public monies. Third is the issue of 'comparative advantage' in that firms tend to be successful in (and therefore, dedicate their resources to) endeavours they have understanding and expertise to accomplish (Mintzberg, 1979, 1983). The combination of the three suggests the firm will be reluctant to take on a problem they do not recognize as 'theirs,' do not understand what they can do about, or will not be fairly compensated for. For these reasons, many rather obvious problems of perceived public domain are ignored. An example would be air and water pollution problems such as acid rain and deforestation. In this instance, it is the combined result of countless acts of pollution by individuals and industry which are too small by themselves to be addressed, yet result in millions of acres of deforested land.

Within a firm described by traditional intra- or inter-organizational management models, there exist assumptions of relationships between the members brought together to negotiate solutions. These assumptions are based upon hierarchical relationships that currently exist within the firm or negotiated agreements between firms who wish to enter a 'partnership' to achieve a solution (Trist, 1977). These agreements to marshal forces within, or partnerships negotiated without, are established to address solutions which are based upon the assumption that they have been able to identify the problem to the extent they are able to recruit the actors necessary to attain success. In other words, the 'domain' of the problem has usually been fairly well established, both in terms of what the problem is and why they must initiate a process towards solution.

In the case where collaborative solutions are needed, the common approach and procedures incorporated within the firm will not be able to respond to the needs of the situation. Typical answers generated in these situations are:

- It is not our problem.
- We are not equipped to handle this.

- There are so many people involved or responsible that we do not feel it is our responsibility to be the ones to deal with it.

Firms will seek to engage in collaborative processes only in situations where there is a perceived self-interest or an internal or external mandate. Firms sometimes deal with problems in 'grey' areas where the particulars of a given situation may not be clearly or completely understood. But as a rule the problem is well enough defined so that at least the most obvious reasons to invest in a solution are appreciated or the firm will act on one of the axioms listed above. Yet the problems that require collaborative solutions are often ones that are outside these regular working parameters. If a problem is too large – or complex – for this type of identification, it probably has, by this fact alone, defined itself for collaborative solution. Engagement of these actors in the collaborative solution requires definition of the problem to the extent they understand their involvement and understand they will be fairly compensated (whether compensation is paying or receiving is not important as long as it is understood).

To illustrate this situation, we will torture the Suni 'blind men and elephant' metaphor, which in this case, takes place at a zoo. The elephant has stepped on the feet of three blind men and will not get off. The men know they share a problem that requires solution (it hurts), but do not know what the problem is as, according to the metaphor, they do not understand what is on their feet. This problem is clearly larger than they can handle as no amount of co-operative pushing or pulling of whatever is hurting them will free their feet. What they need to do is to figure out how to collaborate in order to free themselves.

Who is at the table?

Within a problem that requires collaborative processes to attain solution, however, the act of defining of the problem becomes even more complex than the problem itself would suggest. This is because, within the context of this much uncertainty, it is probable that the problem is not well enough defined to ensure that all necessary actors are actually 'at the table'.

In the context of this chapter, these actors are classified as **internal stakeholders** as they share an interest or 'stake' in the outcome of the process and they have demonstrated an active, abiding interest in a solution. **External stakeholders**, by contrast, share a 'stake' but are not part of the process (Freeman, 1984). Barbara Gray (1989) points out that problems with potential for utilizing collaborative processes are defined as problems larger than any one collaborator. Indeed, the individual collaborators must recognize a certain 'equality' of power carried by other collaborators within the process as critical to a positive result. If a problem is so large or complex as to require collaborative action, how can one assume that identification of the relevant 'internal' stakeholders can be undertaken by sponsors who already appreciate they are not capable of dealing with the process?

One way of tackling this is through the implementation of a Group Support Systems (GSS) process that will encourage the initial members of the collaborative to define the problem and therefore, membership at the table. This can be accomplished through a procedure that allows the combined expertise of the members to be utilized. Such a procedure is consistent with the reason for collaboration in the first place; that is, with regarding the combined knowledge and power of the collaborative entity as essential to achieving success. In this respect, the process is similar to that described by Eden in Chapter 3; though both the rationale for doing the analysis and the perspective upon categorization of stakeholders are slightly different.

A second reason for initiating such a process is discussed by, for example, Bryson (1988) and Gray (1989). This is concerned with problems resulting from not including internal stakeholders in the formative processes. Collaborative processes that do not include these critical actors at an early stage risk having to begin all over again as new members insist on negotiating their understanding and inclusion within the problem definition and solution to the process. Collaborative initiatives, which already suffer from lack of adequate funding (Gray, 1989), risk complete failure as resources to begin again are even more problematic to garner.

To continue the metaphor: the blind men have concluded there are probably a few potential collaborators available. The first group probably encompasses the general public and emergency services who will try to help out as an act of citizenship (or to get them to stop screaming and upsetting their children). Another potential collaborator is another group who do share this problem, the zoo owners. Since the blind men are at the zoo, even though they do not know what the problem actually is they can intuit that the owners of the area they are in will bear some responsibility toward a solution. The solution to the problem is collaborative. The blind men summon the public, who are able to make an informed definition of the problem after exploring the issue (finding that the problem is an elephant standing on the blind men's feet); and through a rapid stakeholder analysis, determine who should also be involved; and seek involvement of the zoo and emergency services. The two firms – the public and the zoo owners – once they have been informed of the problem and are able to make a judgement as to their involvement and expertise, proceed to get a tractor and push the elephant off. The end of this story has to do with lawyers, which is not important to the metaphor, so will be left out.

Process: stakeholder influence mapping

Organizations in general and potential collaborative organizations in particular suffer the same problems of the metaphor above. Neither the problem itself nor the actors needed to work towards solution are necessarily self-evident at the onset. A first step toward a solution can be taken through use of a process of stakeholder identification. This process was developed by Bryson (1988) and modified by the author to ensure consideration of the problems of stakeholder inclusion. The modification is a variation of stakeholder identification first advocated by Freeman (1984).

This process requires stakeholders already at the table at the initiation of a collaborative venture to identify other potential stakeholders. In this context, a 'stakeholder' is defined as any person, organization, community or government that is affected or can affect the deliberations of and potential solution to the issue that requires the collaborative process. Members are asked to 'brainstorm' the stakeholder definition by listing individually all internal and external stakeholders involved in the problem. An 'ovals' or 'snowcard' process (Bryson et al., 1995) is then employed where members are broken into sub-groups, the stakeholders names are written on small oval cards (about 15 cm wide, 10 cm high) and placed upon a wall. Members then develop categories of stakeholders by grouping them on the wall. This begins to reveal the larger context of the issues they would be interested in. A descriptive sentence of the identified categories is then developed that further defines who and why identified stakeholders would be involved. Members are then asked to evaluate the problem from the perspective of each category of stakeholder, and then to list strategic options that:

1   would ensure continuation of activities which the stakeholder approves of;
2   will work toward solutions to problems the stakeholder perceives;
3   will tend to avoid potentially adverse consequences generated by the problem.

The entire group is re-convened and categories, evaluations and strategic options from each sub-group are presented and re-categorized into groups as a whole. The output from this process is recorded and a printout of these groupings and the strategic options becomes part of the record for the collaborative and possibly, the affected stakeholders. Insisting that the member group itself consider 'who' is involved and 'why,' allows for the utilization of the full collaborative potential of the organization to help define the issue and ensure the process does not fail due to lack of stakeholder inclusion. Collaborative members are required to articulate the perspective of their organizations, the composite perspective of the internal stakeholders that comprise the collaborative, and the perspective of the external stakeholders. This allows these statements of perspective to be investigated and elaborated or refuted if necessary.

A second step to the identification process, known as Stakeholder Influence Mapping, further develops stakeholder definition and also gives strategic direction to the evolving initiative. This procedure involves a process of 'targeting' stakeholders within the context of the collaborative group and problem. Members of sub-groups are asked to select a subset of

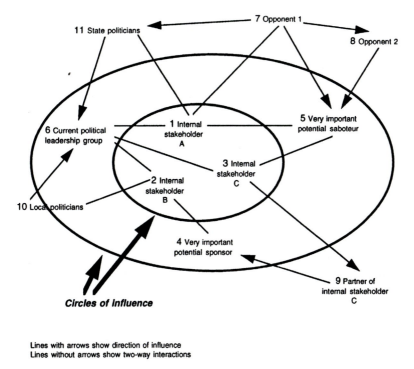

Figure 10.1 *Illustration of a force field map*

identified stakeholders that have some perceived level of relevance to the process (members are asked to select the top ten, or more, most important stakeholders from *their* perspective). The names of the key stakeholders are placed upon ovals located on a wall, using a defined central point as the place to position the most important stakeholders. By definition those identified near the centre are the internal stakeholders to the collaborative problem. The interest and power of the rest of the selected stakeholders, as evaluated by the group, is indicated by the distance they position them from the centre and the clusters of stakeholders they develop (see Figure 10.1). This focus on power and interest is similar to Eden's in Chapter 3.

The group is then asked to identify perceived cognitive relationships between stakeholder clusters, using arrows or lines to demonstrate relationships (Eden, 1989; Kelly, 1955). A final task is to draw 'circles of influence' that represent the interest/power relationships in groupings that allow associations of influence among groupings of stakeholders (Figure 10.1). Placing the stakeholders closer to – or within – the internal stakeholder circle represents their relative ability to affect the group's collaborative strategies. The circles do not necessarily need to be 'round'. The intent of this process is to help the organization group stakeholders by potential to influence the outcome. Again, members are asked: 'in the light of the relationships mapped, should any of the identified stakeholders be included in the collaborative process?'.

The two or more Stakeholder Influence Maps produced by this process are then presented, compared and discussed. Generally, each group will develop maps that are somewhat similar regarding placement of internal stakeholders and the lines of influence, but there seems to be quite a bit of variance regarding the clustering of external stakeholders. Differences in perspectives regarding internal stakeholders must be resolved as these should define the collaborative. Differences regarding the location and clustering of external stakeholders should be noted and stored as they reflect possible differences in the interpretation of the 'political landscape', which lend valuable information regarding definition and strategies for inclusion. As these are multi-dimensional constructs, a mapping program such as Graphics COPE (Cropper et al., 1990) is utilized to record the information and interactive dynamics represented by the maps.

The result of this exercise is to illustrate relationships graphically so the group can appreciate the larger collaborative picture necessary to gain a fuller understanding of the actors involved, and their relationships with each other; and therefore of the potential solution Another ancillary outcome of the exercise is the development of strategies to contact and include identified stakeholders in the process. The strategy not only tells the group who to contact or communicate with in terms of importance, but *how* and *who* should be responsible for that task. It therefore defines the relationships between stakeholders.

As a final process guideline, it is advised to restrict the initial meeting to the production of these products. The intent of the exercises is to give the group a more comprehensive understanding and definition of 'who' this new collaborative organization is, and which stakeholders should be at the table. Therefore it is advisable to delay the next meeting until any missing stakeholders can be invited so they can identify themselves with the collaborative organization.

Ownership of the problem/solution

Within a non-collaborative strategic management process where actors and problems are relatively easily delineated, members come to the process with some pre-formed cognizance of what the relationships within the process are and what will be expected of them. These processes take place outside the context of the problem and solution task and are not considered as a normal part of the initial agreement process. In other words, members know something about what they are getting into. Collaborative processes, however, are a relatively new experience (Gray, 1989; Huxham, 1993), which are not well understood by even the most knowledgeable actors. This point is elaborated by Huxham in Chapter 9. Also, the very nature of collaborative processes is the formulation of a new organization which requires an explicit definition of relationships, not only to set normative values for the group, but to promote 'ownership'. Generally, a primary question of members engaging in collaborative process is: 'how much of this solution will be "mine" and how much am I going to have to do?' One would posit that the answer to the first question will directly predict the second, in that members of the group will evaluate their allegiance to the collaborative organization and its outcomes by directly evaluating their input to it and the resultant effect upon themselves as representatives of their respective organization. Therefore, it is critical to successful collaboration to ensure that collaborative processes are designed to invoke the maximum possible 'ownership' of the organization by the stakeholders.

Process: stakeholder-owned options

The author, with colleague John Bryson, has developed a technique that generates a collaborative agenda for an organization by carrying out the stakeholder process delineated above and combining the options generated there with options generated through brainstorming issues within the collaborative. Through this process, an agenda of issues is generated and addressed that essentially defines the problems and suggests solutions from the perspectives of the members of the group itself. The problems and options are also reviewed from the perspective of the external stakeholders. Stakeholder Influence Mapping also gives further definition to the political landscape that defines the problem, solution and implementation.

$$P=S=I$$

From a strategic management perspective, problems should generate strategies for solution, which should then be implemented. The $P=S=I$ figure represents the proposition that Problem Definition should equal Strategies for Solution, which should equal Implementation. Indeed, in a pre-judicial sense, problem definitions are constrained by stakeholder perspectives dealing with mandates, beliefs, interests and resources. Successful endeavours in strategic planning and management occur as a result of careful attention to this formula.

This comprehensive agenda is more likely to be understood and adopted by the requisite organizations outside the collaborative organization as it was crafted by taking their perspectives explicitly into account. Therefore, this agenda will be more 'marketable' in the public policy arena.

The option generation requires the group, utilizing the same group procedure as in the earlier stage to brainstorm issues they feel are important from their perspective, cluster those issues by their sub-group and define the cluster with a descriptive sentence. The group then employs a SWOT

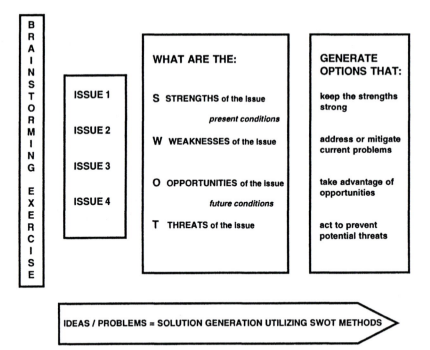

Figure 10.2 *Option generation process*

(strengths and weaknesses; opportunities and threats) analysis (Friend and Hickling, 1987; Nutt and Backoff, 1992) that will generate criteria they believe will determine a successful outcome from their perspective. A SWOT analysis encourages groups to consider a problem from the perspective that most issues have both positive and negative results initially (strengths and weaknesses) and also have future consequences that may be positive or negative (opportunities and threats). The SWOT analysis develops those perspectives, which allows for careful consideration of all consequences of the organization's actions. Finally, the group generates options that answer the criteria questions generated above in the SWOT analysis (Bryson and Finn, 1995).

This resultant list of options becomes the second set of strategies, developed from the perspective of the collaborative group. These options are then combined and put into categories that lend themselves towards strategic solutions that encompass a much larger set of interests than the collaborative organization itself (Figure 10.2). These categories identified are roughly equivalent to the 'strategic issues' developed from the SODA process (Eden, 1989) and become a good starting place for groups to employ that process toward *actions* and *goal* definition.

An illustration: the public teaching hospitals

I was asked to facilitate a series of workshops by a collection of public teaching hospitals in the US that had been working together as a 'trade association'. A trade association can be defined as a group of similarly interested parties that act as an 'information conduit' to keep the parties abreast of important issues in their respective fields. Generally, an organization of this type will not serve other collaborative type functions due to certain legal restrictions regarding 'restraint of trade' and monopolistic activities. This organization however was faced with a national crisis in the health care industries regarding provision and cost of medical care. The state where these hospitals exist has become one of the national leaders in medical systems reform. Indeed, much of the national legislation currently under consideration at the US national level is modelled after that state's legislation.

The effect of the new policies being developed at the national level may result in a radical change in the provision of health services that will include price controls, large medical network providers and doom for individual hospitals. These prospective changes will significantly impact upon high cost facilities including many of the public teaching hospitals which bear the additional cost of education, as well as a governmental mandate to serve certain low income and indigent populations. These hospitals were founded and to a certain extent, funded on the basis of provision of these additional medical services that serve the 'public good'. Yet, the new formulae for funding medical services do not account for these institutions which are the exception to the rule. While these institutions operate with budgets of hundreds of millions of dollars, they comprise a small percentage of their market area. Relatively small investments by large institutions in their markets could have devastating consequences to these institutions. With the future of medical care provision spelling almost imminent doom for the constituent hospitals, and agglomeration tendencies in the market putting them in increasing risk, they decided to explore the potentials of collaboration.

The process strategy employed for this potential collaborative organization involved first defining the problems these hospitals faced in an 'up close and personal' way. To accomplish this, the Chief Executive Officers (CEOs) of the four institutions were asked to prepare a presentation for the collaborative in terms of hopes and fears. They were to be as honest and explicit about their future planning as possible. Their assignments were discussed in detail with the CEOs before the meeting, which built up an expectation for realistic discussion. While these institutions 'compete' in that they all provide medical care services, their history within the organization allowed for a certain level of 'trust,' which translated into some almost shocking revelations regarding the pessimism of these units. They all knew they were in trouble and it was abundantly clear that their vision of survival encompassed collaboration with their peers. Yet, no unit was at all interested in mergers and was politically constrained from doing so.

The Stakeholder Influence Mapping process described above was employed to help the CEOs explore their relationships with the 'outside world'. They found that the group, as they had identified it previously (that is, the four CEOs), was not adequate. Indeed, they would not be viable without including the medical department heads, and another private hospital that had a significant teaching content as part of their portfolio. This process did not result in immediate recruitment of the other hospital. Indeed, negotiations began only after six months of consideration. In this case, it will increase the number of internal stakeholders from fourteen to nineteen.

An adaptation of the 'ovals' process was employed in this group. A day was set aside for identified stakeholders to meet and discuss their interests. The external stakeholders included legislators, CEOs of insurance companies, competitor hospital organizations, the professional association representing physicians and practising physicians who used the hospitals. These external stakeholders were encouraged to define their 'world' in the context of public teaching hospitals. In this mode, they identified several stakeholder groups and re-defined others. An example of such was the view of rural physicians, in which the concept of 'country doctor', who is a one-person health-delivery system, and their requisite needs was completely debunked as rural physicians strive for co-ordinated and supportive health care systems. Options were generated by the collaborative group and a position paper drafted.

The standardized issue generation technique described above was employed and provided the issues as interpreted by the current group. The options generated by both processes were then combined, resulting in a series of strategic issue areas which were then addressed. The relationships between these issues were explored by comparing and combining the two option sets generated. Each option category was carefully examined in terms of its relationship to the other categories. The identified stakeholder interests were taken into account by continually reflecting upon the criteria developed from the initial exercise. And finally, the strategy to act was designed with consideration of the cognitive relationships generated by the 'target diagram'.

The decision by the organization was to enact a strategy that would be implemented by state law. Essentially, the work of public teaching hospitals would be identified as a public good, which would be supported by a 'tax' on other hospitals and organizations that benefit from the product – licensed physicians – they provide. Allocation of the teaching 'mix' of physicians would be up to the state, but would be informed by a committee that had substantial (not a majority) representation by the teaching hospitals. The public teaching subsidy would be protected by requiring any hospital that wished to benefit to offer a whole range of teaching services, a position that would protect their niche. The public teaching hospitals would continue to treat the populations that were not particularly wanted by the other hospitals as an integral part of their services.

The newly construed organization is currently meeting with the Legislators to craft the new policies and at the time of writing, they are quite optimistic.

To sum up the case:

- The group, based upon a strategic assessment, re-construed their definition and membership to address the large environmental threat to their existence.
- Members of the new organization re-defined their approaches to key stakeholder groups, such as rural physicians and the legislature, based upon an options analysis and targeting exercise.
- The new organization is attempting to re-define the problem of medical services delivery in a manner that reflects their niche, based upon analysis of external stakeholder relations.
- The group has developed a common sense of ownership towards their problem, based upon a good understanding of the relationships between stakeholders and shared identification of the problem.
- To a certain extent, a 'social contract' has been created within the collaborative in that they have agreed upon expectations regarding their joint responsibilities and behaviour.

In other words, they have succeeded in the identification of the problem/ solution domain and have strategized on options based upon the larger context and stakeholder groups involved in the issue. This group transformed itself from an information-sharing group to a collaborative organization that is capable of recognizing options and opportunities within the context of large scale change . . . and acting upon them.

I would note that the experience was not as smooth as it reads here. As a facilitator of this experience, I was continually surprised by the options generated and opportunities that developed. In at least one meeting, I carefully planned the agenda, only to find the group had leaped completely past my thinking as the evolving sense of who they were opened new vistas of opportunity for them. In essence, I found that as an individual, I could not forecast in advance regarding the definition of the organization as I lacked the capacity the group developed by the exercise of 'collaborative advantage'.

Conclusions

There are inherent problems in terms of problem definition and group selection when approaching problems that require collaborative processes for solution. These processes presented address solutions regarding the initial stages of development and agreement in approaching collaborative change. Two particularly important problems have been identified regarding the formulation of successful collaborative process. Certainly, there are more to be discovered, with the requisite changes in strategic management techniques. Certainly, issues dealing with the representative function in terms of the internal stakeholders' perspective must be addressed also. We suggest, however, the successful adoption of collaborative processes as a preferred technique for complex problems is predicated upon the adoption of processes that explore the comprehensive potentials this technique promises. Only by identifying 'who' we are and 'what' the problem is in the context of the collaborative, is there hope of generating a successful solution (P=S=I).

References

Bryson, J.M., Ackermann, F., Eden, C. and Finn, C.B. (1995) 'Critical incidents and emergent issues in the management of large-scale change efforts', in D. Kettl and H. Brinton Milward (eds), *The State of Public Management*. Baltimore, MD: Johns Hopkins University Press.

Bryson, J. (1988) *Strategic Management in Public and Non-Profit Organizations*. San Francisco: Jossey Bass.

Bryson, J. and Crosby, B. (1992) *Leadership for the Common Good: Tackling Public Problems in a Shared Power World*. San Francisco: Jossey Bass.

Bryson, J. and Finn, C. (1995) 'Creating the future together: developing and using shared strategy maps', in A. Halachmi and B. Geer (eds), *The Enduring Challenges in Public Management*. San Francisco: Jossey Bass. pp. 247–80.

Cropper, S. Ackermann, F. and Eden, C. (1990) 'COPE-ing with complexity: computer based storage, analysis and retrieval of cognitive maps'. Working Paper 90/4, University of Strathclyde, Department of Management Science.

Eden, C. (1989) 'Using cognitive mapping for strategic options development and analysis (SODA)', in J. Rosenhead (ed.), *Rational Analysis in a Problematic World*. Chichester: Wiley. pp. 21–42.

Freeman, R.E. (1984) *Strategic Management: a Stakeholder Approach*. Marshfield, MA: Pitman Publishing.

Friend, J. and Hickling, A. (1987) *Planning under Pressure*. Oxford: Pergamon.

Gray, B. (1989) *Collaborating: Finding Common Ground for Multiparty Problems*. San Francisco: Jossey Bass.

Huxham, C. (1993) 'Pursuing collaborative advantage', *Journal of the Operational Research Society*, 44 (6): 599–611.

Huxham, C. with Macdonald, D. (1992) 'Introducing collaborative advantage: achieving inter-organisational effectiveness through meta-strategy', *Management Decision*, 30: 50–6.

Kelly, G.A. (1955) *A Theory of Personality*. New York: W.W. Norton and Company.

Mintzberg, H. (1979) *The Structure of Organizations*. Englewood Cliffs, NJ: Prentice Hall.

Mintzberg, H. (1983) *Power In and Around Organizations*. Englewood Cliffs, NJ: Prentice Hall.

Nutt, P.C. and Backoff, R.W. (1992) *Strategic Management of Public and Third Sector Organizations*. San Francisco: Jossey Bass.

Trist, E. (1977) 'A concept of organizational ecology', *Australian Journal of Management*, 2: 269–83.

11

Inter-Organizational Collaboration in the Policy Preparation Process

Arnold de Jong

A deep desire of the Dutch government is to involve, as much as possible, all important stakeholders in the judgement of new policies under development. Unfortunately, very often the results are disappointing. This chapter describes some possible ways in which the process of policy-making may be improved in order to achieve better results from involvement of participants.

The normal way in which involvement in policy design takes place is through the government developing a first design of the policy. The participation process is then enacted as a reaction of the 'public' to this first design. Most participants in the policy-making process (particularly at the strategic level) are, in practice, representatives of organizations. This 'reactive' process is much the same whether the policy be one of central or of local government.

In recent years there has been a rapid development in the use of network management in the policy development process. The aim is to turn the policy-making process into a form of inter-organizational collaboration. Such an approach requires a process which can address, in parallel, development of the technical design of policy and management of the socio-participation process. In this chapter some possible processes are described, as developed and used by the author and colleagues, which address these requirements and which have achieved improved results in involvement of participants.

The process is conceived of as a 'learning process' involving 'interactive working' through participation in interactive meetings. Modern philosophers (such as Arnold Cornelis, 1993) argue that a real learning process never goes from outside to inside but always from inside to outside. From this perspective, the value of the interactive way of working can be seen as addressing the need to start the policy development process from the inside.

The interactive processes to be described here have been used in the Netherlands since 1980. They are mostly based on the Strategic Choice approach (Friend and Hickling, 1987). A number of examples where this way of working has been used are discussed in this chapter in order to illustrate the variety of possibilities. Before this, however, we review first some key elements of inter-organizational collaboration in the context of the policy process and, secondly, the basic values which underlie the notion of 'interactive working' in the context of the methods described in this chapter.

The basis of inter-organizational collaboration in the policy process

The background of the switch to policy networks is that many western countries have abandoned the hierarchical model of policy-making. The basic assumption of the hierarchical model is that the government stands at the top of the policy-making process and has a one-way relationship with all the other actors. Under this model, the instruments of the government (such as the law) also lead to a one-way imposition of policy. In some countries – notably in the Netherlands, upon which this chapter is based – there has been a change to this attitude in recent years. The idea now is that the government should be seen to be in the 'middle' of all other actors with a two-way relationship occurring between the actors and government. Thus not only does the government try to influence the actors, but the actors also try to influence the government. Instruments which are appropriate to this model are agreements and treaties rather than law.

This new model thus sees the government as placed in the middle of a network. This network consists primarily of organizations; in principle any organization – public or private – that the government wishes to steer, and any organization that wishes to influence the government, with respect to the policy may be involved. The government tries to work together with the representatives of this network in a form of an inter-organizational collaboration. Crucial to success is that the government knows this network and understands the role the members of the network want to play in the policy-making process. Interactive working in a group process is thus one way of making collaboration in an inter-organizational network operational.

As has been argued by other authors in this book (see Eden, Chapter 3 and Finn, Chapter 10), it is very important to compose the group(s) in a careful way. Usually this is done by a so-called stakeholders-analysis (sometimes known as a network analysis or actor analysis).

A stakeholder analysis consists of:

- creating an 'inventory' of the stakeholders;
- analysis of the stakeholders in terms of their stake in the policy under development and their possible role in its development; and
- management of the stakeholders.

In principle it is a way of making the social network explicit and structuring it.

One of the most simple ways of carrying out a stakeholder analysis involves bringing together a small group of people who are involved in the project from the start. Every member of that group is given some 'system cards'. Each is asked to write the names of stakeholders he or she knows on a separate card. The cards are then sorted by the group by estimating the involvement of the stakeholder in the subject of the project. The cards are then pinned to flipcharts which are fixed onto the wall. A circle is drawn onto the flip chart; the cards representing stakeholders judged to be the most involved are placed in the middle of that circle, those representing stakeholders judged to be less involved are placed on the fringe. This process is similar to that described in more detail by Finn in the preceding chapter.

Another way of working is to develop a matrix on flipchart sheets with the group. The horizontal axis of the matrix represents the phases of the policy process: recognition of the need for policy; problem analysis; policy development; policy decision-making; and implementation. The vertical axis represents the organizations who might have an interest in the policy (the stakeholders). The group discusses what role each organization might play at each stage of the process. Typical roles are: none; being kept informed; advising; co-ordinating; and doing. These roles are written into the cells of the matrix.

In both cases (either with the cards or with the matrix) the information obtained is the basis for the way the stakeholder will participate in the policy process. This can be as a direct participant in the group policy-making process or as part of a 'reference' or 'platform' group consisting of those not to be directly involved in making policy but who are the subject of that policy.

The basic concepts of interactive working

As has been mentioned above, until recently most policy-making by the Dutch government has used the reactive process; the government gives a start with a proposal and the participants react to that proposal. Under such a process, it may be expected that the perception of each of the participants over the developed policy will be quite different. This can be particularly significant in situations in which there are many actors involved. The reactive process thus often degenerates to an attack on the policy from participants and a defence of the policy from the government. Disappointing results thus often arise from this kind of participation process because:

- the attack and defend atmosphere is not ideal for the generation of consensus; and
- the mental ownership of the developed policy stays only with the government and is not taken on board by the other participants.

These two notions – **achieving consensus** and **establishing the mental ownership** of the policy under development by the participants – are the most important ideas behind interactive working.

The differences between the two processes are clear. In the reactive process the real policy development takes place by the (one or two) individuals who developed the first draft of the policy. In subsequent meetings this first draft is simply commented upon. In the interactive process the real development takes place *during* the group meeting. Documentation of the policy takes place in between the meetings.

Elements of the interactive approach

The structure for the interactive group meeting is based upon the principles of the **Strategic Choice** approach. The Strategic Choice approach has been described in detail elsewhere (Friend and Hickling, 1987); in this section, therefore, we simply provide an overview of the approach by focusing on some of the key elements which make it a practical method for working with a network. These basic elements are:

(a) Interactive working.
(b) Cyclic learning.
(c) Synergy.
(d) Commitment.
(e) Shared knowledge.
(f) Mutual understanding.

(a) Interactive working As has already been stated, policy preparation is done through an interactive group process guided by a process expert, 'the facilitator'. The facilitator must be seen to be disinterested in the content of the policy to avoid being regarded as a manipulator rather than facilitator. The result of the process is that the group members gain mental ownership of the developed policy. The composition of the group is largely determined by the result of a stakeholders analysis as described above. The basic 'working rules' for the group are discussed and approved by the group. These often include an obligation for group members to keep their 'constituency' informed of debates and progress.

(b) Cyclic learning Policy preparation is seen as a learning process. In the beginning nobody knows exactly what is going on in the policy that has to be developed. During the preparation the learning begins. 'Looping backwards' to revisit earlier phases in the process means that the learning can be used to improve the policy. Attention has to be paid to ensuring that all important participants are involved in the learning. Too often the decision-takers (for example, city councillors) or civilians are neglected because of the differences in their knowledge.

(c) Synergy Policy preparation is always a combination of elements that are 'hard', such as knowledge and certainty, and elements that are 'soft', such as intuition, feelings and uncertainty. Hard elements are sometimes referred to as 'boxes' while soft ones are referred to as 'bubbles' (Hurst,

1984). Both elements need a balanced place in the policy preparation process but the combination of both elements – 'boxes plus bubbles' – needs to be more than the sum of parts. The elements must combine synergistically. It is the role of the facilitator in an interactive process to be focused on the 'plus'.

(d) Commitment In practice there is often a gap between policy preparation and policy implementation. In the interactive approach commitment to policy implementation is generated through ensuring the mental ownership of the policy by involving those who will have to implement it in its preparation. Commitment, the mental ownership of the policy, comes through consensus and conversely, consensus generates commitment.

(e) Shared knowledge In interactive group processes people are facilitated to get the knowledge they have out their heads and shared with the other participants. This is particularly important when the group consists of experts (a civil engineer, a lawyer and so on) who each hold only one part of the total knowledge necessary. In general it is not sensible to start by making an inventory of facts; it is the *process of sharing* which provides understanding, and hence value to the group. One 'invisible product' of interdisciplinary working in interactive mode is thus shared knowledge.

(f) Mutual understanding The perceptions of the participants over the policy under development will generally be different at the outset of the process. The interactive group process is thus used as a structure for communication. The 'boxes plus bubbles' concept is used to help participants express themselves and understand each other. Mutual understanding is thus the vehicle for co-operation. Mutual understanding is also regarded as an 'invisible product' of the process.

The Dutch examples

It is not the purpose of this chapter to give a detailed report of cases of interactive policy-making in the Netherlands. Instead four examples, in which the author has been involved as facilitator, have been selected of cases from different government levels (national, regional and local) and with different focuses, to demonstrate the wide variety of application. In each of the examples the focus is on a single element of the interactive process that was of particular importance in the particular case.

The first Dutch national environmental policy plan

This first example relates to national level government. The first Dutch national environmental policy plan came out in 1989. In this account, the main attention will be given to the starting phase of the policy development project.

Early in 1988, a series of one-day interactive group meetings was planned, one for each 'target group' identified through a stakeholder analysis. The purpose of the days was to enable each of the target groups to develop together a shared policy perspective. In preparing this plan, the aim was to reach mutual agreement with several target groups. At the start 18 target groups were mentioned, examples being: the target group 'agriculture', the target group 'traffic', the target group 'chemical industry', the target group 'construction companies', and so on.

The stakeholder analysis provided a clear focus for the target groups' meetings. The target groups were to generate 'chapter 5' of the draft policy plan, the policy itself. When the target groups first met, drafts had already been prepared of chapters 1 to 4, concerning the general starting points for the national environmental policy.

Thus, in this process the early part of each target group's work involved discussion of the first four chapters. It was therefore, in principle, a reactive process task. In order to make this more interactive, however, the first task of the target groups in their initial meetings was to carry out in four sub-groups a 'SWOT analysis' based on the drafts of the first four chapters. Each group was asked to consider the strengths, weaknesses, opportunities and threats of the proposed policy. This can be seen as an interactive way of dealing with written documents. It is a process which is likely to generate much more interest than a page by page discussion. In this case, the SWOT analysis turned out to be an effective way of handling, in an interactive way, a process that had started on a reactive basis.

The SWOT analysis provided the basis for the second and most central task of the groups which was to identify issues to be considered in the environmental policy. This issue-analysis was to form the basis of the chapter about the policy for the specific target group. This was tackled through a facilitated group discussion in which the issues were structured in the usual Strategic Choice manner in terms of:

- decisions that must be taken;
- criteria for choosing between alternative directions;
- uncertainties;
- boundary conditions (factors which are not changeable by the group); and
- assumptions.

The policy plan for the Amsterdam–Rhine canal

This second example is concerned with regional level policy. The Amsterdam–Rhine canal was dug in approximately 1950 to give the main port of Amsterdam a better connection with the densely populated and industrial areas of Germany. The main function of the canal was commercial shipping. Over the past few years, however, the local situation has changed. New functions of the canal such as recreational shipping and water management along with ecological considerations have had to be taken into account. It was therefore necessary for the central government to develop a new policy plan for the future of this canal.

Creation of the policy plan for the Amsterdam–Rhine canal was conceived as a two-phase approach. The first phase was undertaken with a limited group of the stakeholders – only the involved civil servants – so was more on an inter-departmental, rather than inter-organizational, basis. With this first group a first draft policy plan was prepared using an extension of the original Strategic Choice techniques.

In this example the focus of the following description is on the part of the process concerned with the option-generating activity. That is, the activity in which the alternatives are developed. The normal Strategic Choice approach for this activity would be the AIDA (Analysis of Interconnected Decision Areas) method. This method is based upon the presumption that decisions are often interconnected so that a decision taken in one 'decision area' will decrease the options available in a connected one (Friend and Hickling, 1987; de Jong and Hickling, 1990). AIDA provides a structure for managing participants' views about the nature of related decision areas in the context of a particular piece of policy development. The output is a set of feasible alternatives with 'impossible' combinations of options left out.

AIDA proved unsuitable for the comparison of options in this situation, however, because many combinations of options were not seen as technologically or politically possible or impossible, but simply as more or less feasible. For example increasing the commercial shipping does not make recreational shipping impossible, just more difficult. For this reason the so-called 'triangular matrix' shown in Figure 11.1 was used. This allows combinations of options to be identified either as 'impossible', or as 'very strong', 'strong', 'weak' and 'very weak' possibilities.

The second phase of the approach was to present this plan to the other stakeholders. The stakeholder groups consisted of those with interests in commercial shipping, recreational shipping, water management, ecology and the group of organizations (such as municipalities and farmers) who suffer from the physical barrier that the canal represents (that is, those who have interests on both sides of the canal). The aim was to give each group the opportunity to comment on the plan. An approach known as the 'carousel' was used. Each group was located in a corner of the available room, with its own colour of pen and was asked to write its comments about the policy plan on flip chart sheets. When this activity was completed, the groups rotated; group one moved to group two's corner, group two went to group three's corner and so on, while the flip chart comments remained in their original location. Each group was then asked to comment on the former group's comments using their own colour of pen. The procedure was repeated twice more so that each group had the opportunity to comment on the work of every other group. Each group then returned to its original corner and was asked to review their original opinions on the basis of the comments of the other groups. Later a plenary discussion was held.

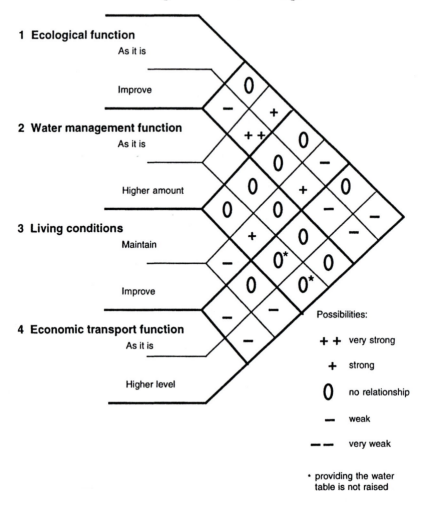

1 **Ecological function**
  As it is
  Improve

2 **Water management function**
  As it is
  Higher amount

3 **Living conditions**
  Maintain
  Improve

4 **Economic transport function**
  As it is
  Higher level

Possibilities:

+ +   very strong

+   strong

0   no relationship

—   weak

— —   very weak

* providing the water table is not raised

Figure 11.1 *'Triangular matrix' for option structuring*

As in the first example, this process was a successful way of creating interactive working on a process – reviewing a document – that is essentially reactive. People become much more involved than they would in an ordinary reactive meeting, where they might, for example, review the document on a page-by-page basis.

The cultural plan from the municipalities Enschede and Hengelo

The third example is concerned with municipality level policy. Enschede (146,000 inhabitants) and Hengelo (76,000 inhabitants) are towns in the eastern part of the Netherlands, close to the German border. The two municipalities decided to start a process of closer collaboration, to form a counterweight to the four big cities in the western part of the country (Amsterdam, Rotterdam, The Hague and Utrecht). There is a possibility that both towns, Enschede and Hengelo, will merge together as one municipality. It can be imagined that such an aim of closer collaboration means embarking on a unique and difficult process. As with the first example, the focus of discussion here will be on the early stages of the project.

As a starting point for more concrete developments, it was decided that both municipalities should, amongst other priorities, develop a mutually agreed cultural policy plan. The whole process of development of this plan involved six days of interactive working. The first session lasted one day, and was followed by two sessions each of two days with a closing session of one day.

The start of the process was especially interesting. The first meeting of the group started with a so-called 'issues analysis'. This was not, however, the normal process in which everyone is asked to bring forward issues in plenary sessions. As was expected at the start of the day the members from Hengelo were sitting together at one side of the room and the representatives from Enschede were sitting on the other side. The aim was to encourage them to merge and to make informal contacts.

In order to achieve this, a process was devised which involved them working in couples. The two aldermen, the two directors of the cultural departments and so on were coupled together. Each couple was given a set of cards on which they were asked to write mutually agreed issues. When this exercise had been completed, the couples remained sitting together. Informal contact had hence been initiated.

Such an analysis of issues can be an effective way to start a process of real interactive working. The following parts of the process involved discussions in which the issues were structured, as in the first case, in terms of:

- Decisions that must be taken
- Criteria for choosing between alternative directions
- Uncertainties
- Boundary conditions
- Assumptions

The 'couples' process thus led into the decision-focused way of working which is characteristic of the Strategic Choice approach.

The (operational) policy for a day nursery in a ward from Amsterdam

The final example focuses on policy development within a ward of city government.

In the Netherlands, the central government is concerned to provide more opportunities for day nurseries, so that mothers can go out to work. In

1989 it announced its intention to provide an extra 130 million Dutch Guilders (Dfl) in order to extend the number of day nurseries for children up to four years old. The money could only be used to create new places – not for the take-up of existing places. In principle a place for one child costs Dfl 13,000. The central government grant is Dfl. 5,000 and the average payment of the parents is Dfl. 3,000. The rest has to be provided by the municipality or others such as businesses.

In the quarter known as Amsterdam-South, which is a formal ward of the city of Amsterdam with its own council, an interactive session was arranged in order to develop a new policy for day nurseries. In this account, attention will mainly be focused on the selection of important decision areas.

The composition of the group for the interactive process included the alderman, civil servants, managers of day nurseries and nursery leaders. In this case, the process started with a 'normal' analysis of issues. The issues were written onto flipchart, structured in the way described in the previous case.

Quite a large number of decision areas were identified – about 20 in all. In order to manage them effectively, the group assessed them in terms of relative urgency and impact and prioritized them accordingly so that a selection could be made. The use of sticky-backed coloured dots for priority ranking offered a quick and easy way of working, in order to arrive at an agreed focus. In this technique, every group member is given four dots and asked to stick these by the decision areas that they regard as of highest priority. Any number of dots (up to the four) may be placed against any one decision area. When all participants have finished placing their dots, a joint dot-count is made. Those decision areas with high joint dot-counts are generally taken to be those that need high priority attention, though further discussion may lead to a review of this. In this kind of process, it can be useful to give different groups 'dots' of different colours, so that information about the particular priority suggestions of each of the interest groups participating in the process may be obtained.

Summary and concluding remarks

In the short space available for this introductory review, four projects have been discussed, each of a different government level and focus, and each illustrating a different aspect of the interactive approach.

- *Central government level: the development of a national environmental policy plan.* Special attention was given to a way of starting the process which can turn a reactive process into one which is as interactive as possible.
- *Regional level: a policy for the Amsterdam–Rhine canal.* Here additional techniques were used, the 'triangular matrix' to facilitate the option generation process and the 'carousel' as an alternative

way of facilitating an interactive response to a previously prepared document.

- *A (combined) municipality level: the preparation of a cultural policy plan.* Here again the attention was with the start of the process where coupling of people with similar roles was used to initiate informal contacts.
- *A city ward level: the development of a day nursery policy.* In this case the focus was on the assignment of priorities to decision areas.

Overall, experience in these and other situations suggests that the interactive approach has many advantages, especially for consensus-building in policy preparation. The approach can be used at any level of government and for any kind of policy content.

The biggest problem in promoting wider use of such processes is the availability of enough well-trained and experienced facilitators. Special training courses have been started up in the Netherlands for this purpose. However, real knowledge and experience can only be built up by following the precept of 'learning by doing'. Only if a junior facilitator works at least four or five times a year in a genuine interactive process can he or she build up the kind of knowledge and experience required.

References

Cornelis, A. (1993) *Logica van het Gevoel: de Stabiliteitslagen van de Cultuur als Nesteling der emoties.* Amsterdam: Stichting Essence.

Friend J. and Hickling, A. (1987) *Planning under Pressure.* Oxford: Pergamon.

Hurst, D. (1984) 'Of boxes, bubbles and effective management', *Harvard Business Review*, May–June: 78–88.

de Jong, A. and Hickling, A. (1990) *Mens en Beleid.* Leiden/Antwerpen: Stenfert Kroese.

PART FIVE

CLOSURE

12

The Search for Collaborative Advantage

Chris Huxham

Some conceptual handles

This book opened with a view that collaboration is difficult but valuable if done successfully. The book has aimed to contribute to an understanding of how to manage the difficulties in order to maximize the value – the **collaborative advantage** – to be gained from collaboration.

One way of viewing the way in which this book has contributed to such an understanding is at two levels. First, many of the chapters make an important contribution to a picture of collaboration in practice through highlighting considerations which can affect its success and value. Such conceptual insights can inform the actions of future collaborators or of those facilitating collaborative groups. Secondly, many of the chapters describe processes which can directly be used to assist those involved in collaboration. Thus Eden (Chapter 3), Huxham (Chapter 9), Finn (Chapter 10) and de Jong (Chapter 11) all provide suggestions for facilitation of collaborative groups, while Himmelman (Chapter 2) provides a 'do-it-yourself' guide to collaboration.

The value of the conceptual insights is to provide handles for debate about collaborative practice – both 'theoretical' debate which can move the field forward and 'practical' debate which can move actual collaborations forward. It is not easy to summarize the variety of experience and insight in the earlier chapters but it may be helpful simply to list some of the most prominent concepts developed there.

1   Concepts relating to the nature and purpose of collaboration:
    Collaborative advantage – provides a language for legitimizing collaboration and a focus on the distinctive value of collaboration.
    Sustainability and consequential and constitutive value – focuses on

keeping collaboration alive over the longer term and recognizes that the character of collaborative efforts is as important as the products.

Invisible products – emphasizes the value of 'spin-off' improvements in relationships between individuals and organizations – such as shared knowledge and mutual understanding – which can follow from collaboration.

Collaborative inertia and hazards – contributes to acceptance that collaboration is not straightforward and needs special attention and resources.

Framework of collaborative rationales – highlights the variety of purposes that collaboration can serve.

Collaborative betterment and empowerment – directs attention to the practical possibility of collaboration as a way of empowering the disadvantaged in society.

Community involvement – directs attention to the practical need to involve community members in community-based collaborations.

Convener modes – highlights the importance of demonstrating that a convenor must be seen to have a legitimacy or credibility in the role.

Internal and external stakeholders – focuses attention both on who should be invited to be part of the collaboration and on managing those who will not be invited.

Power and interest – provides a tool for considering the way in which other parties may view the collaborative purpose.

2   Concepts relating to facilitation of collaborative groups:

Morality and gentleness – emphasizes that facilitators must make a choice about the extent to which they direct the collaborative group.

Facilitator roles, process and content – provides a means of describing, and hence debating, the way in which facilitators direct the collaborative group.

Collaboration expertise – focuses attention on the use of insights about collaboration in the facilitative process.

Interactive process – directs attention to the value of interactive processes in achieving consensus in and ownership of collaborative agreements.

Taken together these concepts begin to provide a language through which collaboration and processes to facilitate it may be discussed.

Who is involved?

The diversity of the concepts above reflects the deliberately diverse range of backgrounds of the authors. This diversity is also reflected in the range of examples, theories and approaches described in the previous chapters. Despite this variety, however, some common threads do emerge. In particular, one theme recurs time and again, and therefore seems worthy of some discussion. This is concerned with who should be involved in a collaboration and how.

It is not really surprising that this issue should be so prominent; its importance has frequently been noted by others. For example, a literature review on factors affecting success in collaboration argues 'having an appropriate cross-section of members' as the most frequently cited success factor (Mattessich and Monsey, 1992). Nevertheless, the perspectives on 'who's involved' in this book are varied and probably rather unusual.

Coming from a perspective of group facilitation for strategy development and implementation, Eden (Chapter 3), Finn (Chapter 10) and de Jong (Chapter 11) all appear to view their initial contact in the collaboration as being, in a sense, at the 'heart' of the collaboration. Each then suggests a form of stakeholder analysis for deciding who else to involve.

Finn argues the keenest case for doing this with his suggestion that it is impossible for those initially involved in a collaboration to know straightforwardly which other parties should be involved. He also argues that the nature of the collaborative purpose and the nature of the parties involved are intricately interlinked issues; the problem that the collaboration is convened to address cannot be identified until the collaborative group can identify it – and hence own it – together.

The three approaches to stakeholder analysis advocated by the above authors are interestingly different from one another. Finn makes an important distinction (not often recognized in the collaboration literature) between 'internal' and 'external' stakeholders. Internal stakeholders are those who are subsequently invited by those initially involved to become a part of the collaboration. External stakeholders are those that have an interest in the collaboration, but for one reason or another are not invited to be a part of it. External stakeholders have to be managed by the collaboration.

De Jong's 'matrix' approach to stakeholder analysis involves a similar notion to the internal–external distinction except that de Jong suggests that it may be appropriate to involve some stakeholders in the collaboration at certain stages in the process and not at others. This rather unusual approach derives perhaps from a perspective on collaboration as a consultation process rather than as a long-term joint activity.

Finn suggests that the criteria by which an initial group may decide whether a stakeholder should be internal or external are, first, its level of power and interest relative to the proposed collaborative purpose, and secondly, the perceived cognitive relationships between one stakeholder and another. In this sense, Finn's approach is similar to Eden's power-interest matrix analysis. Clearly Eden's categorization of stakeholders by their level of interest in the issue of concern and their level of power to act with respect to it is a means of deciding which are to become internal and which external. However, Eden emphasizes the value of considering whether it is possible – for example, through coalition-forming – to increase the power of those initially categorized as low power. By implication it would also be valuable to consider ways of raising the interest level of players with high power. It might also be worth considering ways of reducing the power or interest of certain parties.

All three versions of the stakeholder approach are in contrast to the focuses on who should be involved implicit in other authors' commentary. Himmelman (Chapter 2), Sink (Chapter 6) and Barr and Huxham (Chapter 7) each argue for the value of involving specific kinds of organizations or groups in the collaboration in a generic fashion.

In his 'design step 3', Himmelman suggests collaborators should ask the general question, 'Who else should be involved?' but supports this with a follow-up, 'How could community organizing become a central method of ensuring the participation of those traditionally excluded from decision-making?' He is effectively arguing for the involvement of community organizations in collaborations which affect them. The same plea for the involvement of the community in collaborative social development projects also comes from the collaborative groups in the Barr and Huxham study. In Himmelman's case, however, the call for community involvement is driven by an ideological stance; in Barr and Huxham's groups the call is mostly a pragmatic recognition that involving the community will promote achievement of the collaborative aims. Sink, while implicitly arguing for community involvement for ideological reasons also argues for involvement of public officials on purely pragmatic grounds.

Each of the above approaches addresses the issue of who – which organizations – should be involved in a collaboration. From an entirely different perspective, Gray implies the question, 'how can those deemed to be important internal stakeholders be persuaded to participate?' Her focus is on the relevance of alternative modes of convening collaborations. In particular, she makes a distinction between whether a convener is in some way requested by other stakeholders to convene a collaboration or whether the convening organization takes it upon itself to initiate the collaboration.

Taken together, these approaches suggest that:

1 Consideration of stakeholders is an important activity in collaboration *per se*.
2 It is important to recognize that the distinction between internal and external stakeholders is a deliberate choice of those who are already internal to the collaboration at any point in time. However much effort is put into ensuring as full a level of participation as possible, there will always be some stakeholders that remain external to the collaboration.
3 The distinction between internal and external stakeholders does not have to be clear-cut – a stakeholder can be a part of a collaboration for certain of its activities and not for others.
4 Power and interest can be important determinants of who should be external and who should be internal.
5 The power and interest of organizations and groups is not fixed but can be manipulated.
6 For some kinds of collaboration an argument can be made that some groups should, generically, always be internal stakeholders – for example, in community-based collaborations, groups representing the

community may be essential either for pragmatic or for ideological reasons.
7   The perceived legitimacy of the convener of a collaboration to be the convener will affect whether and how stakeholders are willing to become 'internal' (that is, to join the collaboration).

The search for collaborative advantage

Consideration of stakeholders would thus appear to be centrally important in collaboration. What else is important in being successful is a second theme which runs through much of the book. For example, there are references to collaborative inertia (Chapter 1), to hazards (Chapter 6) and to ignorance (Chapter 9), all of which mitigate against success, and which thus need to be carefully managed. On the other hand, there are also references to factors which influence the manner in which a collaboration can be successful (Chapter 4) and to the bases of collaborative value and hence sustainability of collaboration (Chapter 5). None of these perspectives on success or failure provides tight guidance for good collaborative practice; neither do any of the other concepts listed in the first section of this chapter. Given the variety of collaborative settings and the complexity of the difficulties inherent in it, it would be naive to suppose that precise recipes could exist. The search for collaborative advantage is simply not that simple. The various insights in the book do, however, provide frameworks through which, in any particular situation, consideration may be given to many of the factors involved.

References

Mattessich, P. and Monsey, B. (1992) *Collaboration: What Makes It Work?* St Paul, MN: Amherst H. Wilder Foundation.

Index

Ruck, N., 94
Rutqvist, H., 93

samenwerken, 1
Schein, Edgar, 128, 143
Schnelle, E., 52
Schon, D.A., 53
Schorr, Lisbeth B., 26
security, 83, 84, 86–7, 90
self-determination, 25, 29, 30
self-interest, 2, 3–4, 9, 12, 15, 154
Selznick, P., 89, 90–1, 95
Senge, Peter M., 33
shared knowledge, 15, 169
shared resources, 22, 28
shared vision, 11, 12, 13, 15, 20, 57, 61, 66
Sharfman, M.K., 69, 70
Sheats, Paul, 128
Shields, Katrina, 33
Sink, David, 29, 31, 103
Smith, B.L.R., 77
Smith, Gerald, 128
social change, 31
social contract, 163
Social Democrats (Sweden), 24
social issues, 16–17, 23, 26, 141, 150
social justice, 19–40
social learning, 135, 138
social process, 129, 130, 134–5, 137
social services, 19–40
SODA, 44, 142, 148, 160
SRC, 111
stakeholder/collaborator strategy workshop, 44–55
stakeholder-owned options, 159–60
stakeholder influence mapping, 155–8, 159, 162
stakeholder strategies, 152–64
stakeholders, 168, 170
  analysis, 45–50, 166
  as collaborators, 51–5
  cross-sectoral partners, 57–77
  power/interest matrix, 46–50, 177, 178, 179
Stanford Research Institute, 45
Steele, James B., 23
Stefanini, A., 94
Steiner, Ivan, 129
Stone, C.N., 103
strategic alliance, 2
Strategic Choice, 142, 165, 168, 170–1
strategic intent, 46, 55
strategic management techniques, 152, 164
Strategic Options Development and Analysis (SODA), 44, 142, 148, 160
strategy development, 44–55

Strathclyde Poverty Alliance, 123, 124
Strathclyde Regional Council, 111
Straus, David, 34
Strauss, A., 89
structural form, 8, 82
subjects (stakeholder analysis), 48–50, 53, 55
substantive change, 12
success criteria (judging), 65–6
  cross-case analysis, 75–7
  illustrations (four cases), 67–74
success factors (theoretical overview), 58–65
sunk costs, 86
supply chain management, 2, 87
Susskind, L., 57
sustainability, 3, 66, 176
  collaborative working and, 80–98
Sweezy, Paul, 23
SWOT analysis, 159–60, 170
symbiotic interdependence, 84–5
synergy, 14, 86, 141, 168–9
'system cards', 166–7
Systems/Operational Research, 45

target group, 170
targeting, 156–7
task-based change, 11, 12, 15
teamwork, 24
technical assistance provider, 36
tendering, compulsory competitive, 2, 85
terminology (alternatives), 7–8
theoretical perspective, 17
Thompson, G., 86
time factor (logistics of collaboration), 6
timeliness (facilitation role), 135–6
Tolman, Edward, 129
total quality management (TQM), 131
trade associations, 161
transactional relations, 86
transformation (betterment to empowerment), 105–6
transformational collaboration (in social services), 19–40
triangular matrix, 171–2, 174
'triggers', 52–3
Trist, E.L., 58, 74, 85, 93, 94, 153
trust, 65–6, 68–9, 86–7, 95–7, 161
turbulence/turbulent conditions, 58, 59
Tyler, T.R., 97

urban regimes, 103

value, consequential (bases), 84–97
Van de Ven, A.H., 89, 94, 95, 96
Vangen, S., 4, 52, 55, 110, 111, 121, 141, 144